New Mexic

Off the Beaten ~~Path~~WITHDRAWN®

Help Us Keep This Guide Up to Date

Every effort has been made by the author and editors to make this guide as accurate and useful as possible. However, many things can change after a guide is published—establishments close, phone numbers change, and facilities come under new management, etc.

We would love to hear from you concerning your experiences with this guide and how you feel it could be improved and kept up to date. While we may not be able to respond to all comments and suggestions, we'll take them to heart and we'll also make certain to share them with the author. Please send your comments and suggestions to the following address:

The Globe Pequot Press
Reader Response/Editorial Department
P.O. Box 480
Guilford, CT 06437

Or you may e-mail us at:
editorial@globe-pequot.com

Thanks for your input, and happy travels!

OFF THE BEATEN PATH® SERIES

New Mexico

FOURTH EDITION

by Todd Staats

The
Globe
Pequot
Press

Guilford, Connecticut

Cover and text design by Laura Augustine
Cover photo by DigitalVision
Maps created by Equator Graphics © The Globe Pequot Press
Art on page 59 by Daisy dePothod; all other art by Carole Drong

Library of Congress Cataloging-in-Publication Data

Staats, Todd.
    New Mexico : off the beaten path / Todd Staats. —4th ed.
        p. cm. —(Off the beaten path series)
    Includes index.
    ISBN 0-7627-0533-7
    1. New Mexico Guidebooks. I. Title. II. Series.
    F794.3.S73   1999
    917.8904'53—dc21   99-44247
                                                  CIP

Manufactured in the United States of America
Fourth Edition/First Printing

For my parents and Shawna,
for Catherine,
and for Joseph

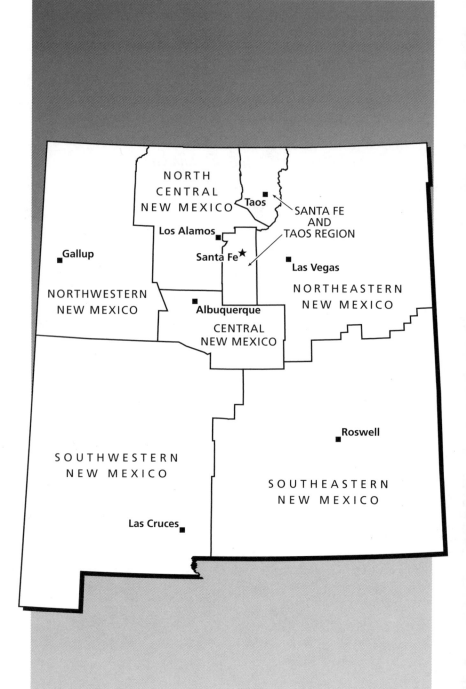

Contents

Acknowledgments

Though I couldn't incorporate all their suggestions, this book benefited from the input of several members of the Tourism Association of New Mexico as well as the advice from members of the Old West Country organization. Also, many of the state's chambers of commerce, convention and visitor bureaus, and the New Mexico Department of Tourism provided key leads. In addition, *New Mexico Magazine, Southern New Mexico Magazine,* the *Albuquerque Journal, Albuquerque Tribune, Crosswinds,* and *Weekly Alibi* proved invaluable as research tools. Also, for revisions to the third and fourth editions, the Internet emerged as the most efficient information-gathering tool, second only to the telephone and my car. Thanks also go to Renée James. I'd like specifically to thank Jo Kaestner for her keen eye and deep knowledge of New Mexico's special spots. But mostly I'd like to thank Catherine Lemmon and Joseph Aguirre for providing support and patience during this ongoing project and for giving up months of weekends to go "on the road" in The Land of Enchantment.

Introduction

Renowned New Mexico artist Georgia O'Keeffe once said, "If you ever go to New Mexico, it will itch you for the rest of your life." Millions of folks from all over the world have come to know exactly what she meant. The people, the culture, the landscape, the climate—New Mexico just gets under your skin and takes hold. Whatever form it takes, the New Mexico mystique is a powerful force to reckon with. It may hit you when you're hiking among the ruins of an ancient civilization, strolling along the narrow streets of Santa Fe, or just silently soaking up the smells and sounds of the forest. Frequently, visitors become so seduced by The Land of Enchantment that they're compelled to make it their home. When asked why, they can't always explain it. But on a broad scale it has a lot to do with space and freedom and pure light. The ever-present blue skies and spectacular sunsets are also addicting.

Tucked into the southwestern United States, New Mexico itself is essentially off the beaten path. Our state is often confused with Arizona on maps and is even mistaken for the country of Mexico. But most residents cherish this anonymity and obscurity about the place they call home. New Mexico's wide-open spaces, unique history, rich cultural diversity, and endless natural wonders combine to create an ideal atmosphere in which to escape and explore—or even get lost, if that's what you're after.

This is by no means a comprehensive guidebook to New Mexico; there are plenty of good ones around. Rather, it's a selective guide to the state's out-of-the-way treasures—some well known, some not—all of which are unique and offer something special to the adventurous traveler. Geographic diversity and vastness are paramount in New Mexico's 121,330 square miles. The state will delight you with its hidden charms as you explore its ghost towns, quaint bed-and-breakfast inns, quirky cafes, ancient Indian ruins and present-day Indian pueblos, isolated museums, and all the breathtaking scenery you can bear.

While satiating your wanderlust in our expansive state, remember that although New Mexico is the fifth-largest state (after Alaska, Texas, California, and Montana), it ranks thirty-seventh in population—a scant 1.6 million people, of whom approximately a third reside in the Albuquerque metropolitan area. The point: lots of space, few people. Because everything is so spread out, plan some time to get around and always carry a detailed, current map. (Call the New Mexico Department of Tourism, 505–827–0291 or 800–545–2040, for a free one.)

As one of the youngest states in the continental United States (it didn't achieve statehood until 1912, though it boasts the oldest capital in the nation, Santa Fe), New Mexico is a land of ancient civilizations. The Anasazi Indians, ancestors of the state's present-day Pueblo Indians, first occupied parts of New Mexico more than 1,000 years ago, and the state is still very much a home to Native Americans. There are nineteen autonomous pueblos (communities on the Indian reservations) inhabited by the different tribes of New Mexico's Pueblo Indians, and part of the Navajo Nation—the largest Indian reservation in the United States—lies in northwestern New Mexico. Native Americans and their rich culture remain a vital part of life in most of our state.

Though several pueblos are included as entries in this book, many are not. It's important to realize that the pueblos and other Native American lands do not exist for tourists. However, many pueblos welcome visitors and even host such events as Feast Days, arts and crafts shows, and ceremonial dances that are open to the public. Keep in mind that the reservations are sovereign nations with their own laws and policies (and languages, though most Native Americans now speak English), and so call ahead before you venture out. A list of the Indian tribes of New Mexico begins on page 193.

A strong Hispanic heritage also exists in New Mexico. The Spanish first came to New Mexico with Coronado's expedition in 1540, and the first Spanish colony was established near San Juan Pueblo in 1598. Later, additional Spanish settlers came north on El Camino Real ("The Royal Road" connecting Mexico City to Santa Fe). The Spanish influence took hold, and Hispanic traditions and culture are very much inherent in New Mexico. This heritage is responsible for New Mexico's designation as the oldest wine-growing region in the United States, starting with the missionaries' vineyards in the 1600s. Though a few of the state's many modern wineries are included in this book's narrative, refer to page 195 for a complete list.

New Mexico is also a land of newcomers. Anglo settlers didn't begin arriving until the opening of the Santa Fe Trail in 1821. Later, the railroad connected New Mexico to the population centers of the East. During the early part of this century, Anglo settlers from the East, seeking a remedy for tuberculosis and other ailments, headed to New Mexico's dry climate on their doctors' advice. Many of these latter-day pioneers subsequently made their fortunes here.

New Mexico has held an allure for artists since the turn of the century. The northern New Mexico community of Taos is a picturesque arts enclave; Santa Fe is firmly established as an art capital of international prominence; and, more recently, Albuquerque too has become known as a major art center. Despite the concentration of galleries in these three cities, small towns throughout the state also offer quality museums and galleries just waiting to be explored.

People often travel the world over without visiting places that have a lasting effect on them, but after your first visit to New Mexico, expect to feel the urge to come back. It was Georgia O'Keeffe's itch, and soon it will be yours as well.

Introduction to the Fourth Edition

Much has changed in New Mexico since this book was first published in 1991, though, of course, more has remained the same, which is fortunate for those of us who like our state pretty much the way it is. Revised editions, such as this book, not only allow information to be updated, but also permit the addition of new attractions not included in any previous edition. The third edition of *New Mexico: Off the Beaten Path* marked the advent of a new source of additional New Mexico travel data: an Internet site that includes links to attractions found in this book—a site that's proving valuable to readers with Internet access. You'll find it at www.toddstaats.com/nmotbp.htm. But the best way to begin experiencing New Mexico from cyberspace is with a visit to the official website of the New Mexico Department of Tourism at http://www.newmexico.org. Come on, surf the high desert of the American Southwest, where the vibes are cool and the sun always shines.

Climate Overview

A clue to New Mexico's climate: Before "Land of Enchantment" became the state slogan, New Mexico went by the nickname "The Sunshine State," based on the fact that every part of New Mexico receives at least 70 percent sunshine year-round. However, as with most states, New Mexico's weather depends on the region and season.

Autumn weather is the most pleasant and predictable, usually sunny and mild. Early spring, while often quite warm, usually brings strong, dusty winds. June is the hottest month, often reaching the upper 90s, with late July through August bringing the state's cooler monsoon season, when brief afternoon thunderstorms are common. Keep in mind that even during summer it can get quite cool during the evenings, often requiring a sweater or jacket, especially in communities at higher elevations, which tend to be cooler throughout the year. Winter is a mixed bag because while it is usually sunny and relatively mild, the state does receive snowfall, which ranges from less than 2 inches annually in the lower Rio Grande Valley to as much as 300 inches in the mountains of north-central New Mexico.

Key to restaurant prices:

Inexpensive: Under $8

Moderate: $8–$14

Expensive: $15–$20

Very expensive: More than $20

Fast Facts about New Mexico

New Mexico Tourism:

New Mexico Department of Tourism, 491 Old Santa Fe Trail, Santa Fe, NM 87501, (800) SEE–NEWMEX (800–733–6396), www.newmexico.org

Useful Web sites:

Author's Web site for this book, www.toddstaats.com/nmotbp.htm

State of New Mexico, www.state.nm.us

New Mexico State Parks, www.emnrd.state.nm.us/nmparks/

New Mexico's National Parks and Monuments, www.nps. gov/parklists/nm. html

Ski New Mexico, www.skinewmexico.com/

New Mexico museums and other cultural offerings, www.nmculture.org/

(Note: other useful Web sites are scattered throughout this edition.)

Major Newspapers:

Albuquerque Journal, P.O. Drawer J, Albuquerque, NM 87103, (505) 823–7777, www.abqjournal.com

Albuquerque Tribune, P.O. Drawer T, Albuquerque, NM 87103, (505) 823–4444, www.abqtrib.com

Santa Fe New Mexican, 202 East Marcy Street, Santa Fe, NM 87501, (505) 983–3303, www.sfnewmexican.com

Las Cruces Sun–News, 256 West Las Cruces Avenue, Las Cruces, NM 88005, (505) 541–5400

Farmington Daily Times, P.O. Box 450, Farmington, NM 87499 (505) 325–4545, www.daily-times.com

Gallup Independent, 500 North 3rd Street, Gallup, NM 87301 (505) 863–6811, www.cia-g.com/~gallpind/

Roswell Daily Record, 2301 North Main Street, Roswell, NM 88201, (505) 622–7710, www.roswell-record.com

Public Transportation:

Amtrak, 214 1st Street SW, Albuquerque, NM 87102, (505) 842–9650/ (800) USA–RAIL, www.amtrak.com

Albuquerque International Airport, Albuquerque, NM 87106, (505) 842–4366

Greyhound, 300 2nd St. SW, Albuquerque, NM 87102, (800) 231–2222, www.greyhound.com

Fast Facts about the Land of Enchantment

- **Area (land):** 121,336 square miles; rank: 5
- **Capital:** Santa Fe
- **Largest city:** Albuquerque, population ~500,000
- **Number of counties:** 33
- **Highest elevation:** 13,161 feet, Wheeler Peak
- **Lowest elevation:** 2,840 feet, Red Bluff Lake, along the Texas border south of Carlsbad
- **Population:** 1,736,931 million (1997); rank: 36
- **Statehood:** January 6, 1912; the 47th state
- **Nickname:** Land of Enchantment
- **State Song:** "O, Fair New Mexico"
- **State Motto:** Crescit Eundo ("It grows as it goes")

- **State Flower:** Yucca
- **State Tree:** Piñon
- **State Grass:** Blue Grama
- **State Bird:** Roadrunner
- **State Fish:** New Mexico Cutthroat Trout
- **State Animal:** Black Bear
- **State Vegetables:** Chile and Beans
- **State Fossil:** Coelophysis dinosaur
- **State Insect:** Tarantula Hawk Wasp
- **State Gem:** Turquoise
- **State Cookie:** Biscochito (or bizcochito)
- **State Poem:** "Asi es Nuevo Mexico" by Luis Tafoya
- **State Ballad:** "The Land of Enchantment" by Michael Martin Murphy

Famous New Mexicans:

- **Buffalo Bill Cody,** showman famous for his Wild West Show
- **Black Jack Ketchum,** notorious train robber
- **Gen. John (Blackjack) Pershing,** served as cavalry officer in the 1880s
- **Gen. Douglas MacArthur,** World War II hero
- **Ralph Bunche,** Nobel Peace Prize winner
- **Manuel Lujan, Jr.,** Secretary of Interior during Bush administration
- **Miguel Trujillo,** Isleta Pueblo activist who campaigned to win Indians right to vote
- **Ezequiel C' de Baca,** nation's first Hispanic Governor
- **Ernie Pyle,** renowned World War II correspondent
- **Conrad Hilton,** founder of the Hilton Hotel chain
- **Ernest Thompson Seton,** author, naturalist, artist, cofounder of the Boy Scouts

- **Harrison J. Schmitt,** astronaut, moonwalker, former U.S. Senator
- **Clyde Tombaugh,** astronomer who discovered Pluto
- **J. Robert Oppenheimer,** head of Manhattan Project, which developed atomic bomb
- **Robert H. Goddard,** developed world's first liquid–fuel rocket
- **Edgar D. Michell,** Apollo 13 astronaut
- **Nancy Lopez,** Golf Hall of Fame with LPGA
- **Al, Al, Jr., and Bobby Unser,** famous race car driving family
- **Don Meredith,** former Dallas Cowboy
- **Trent Dimas,** Olympic Gold Medal winning gymnast

La Comida de Nuevo México
The Cuisine of New Mexico

Some of the most enjoyable moments during any vacation are meal times, especially when you find yourself someplace with a unique cuisine. New Mexico is one such place. The traditional food of New Mexico—la comida de Nuevo México—is centered around the crops that American Indians were growing in this area when Spanish explorers arrived in the late 1500s: corn, beans, squash, and chile (always spelled with an "e" on the end in New Mexico).

New Mexico cuisine is very different from the Tex–Mex cuisine of our neighbor to the east, where chile is spelled "chili," and rather than denoting a vegetable (the chile pepper), it connotes a spicy bean-and-beef concoction. New Mexican cuisine can be as basic as a plate of red or green chile enchiladas, which can be found anywhere in the state, or as elaborate and experimental as an entree of piñon-laced corn crepes filled with chipotle chiles and topped with squash blossoms, which can only be found in a trendy Santa Fe bistro.

While dishes such as enchiladas or posole (a chile-infused hominy stew) are omnipresent in New Mexico restaurants, they can be time-consuming to prepare at home. Therefore, scattered throughout this edition are several simple recipes for some of my other favorite traditional (and adapted) New Mexico dishes and accompaniments—everything from green chile stew to a classic margarita. I hope you enjoy this little taste of the Southwest!

Southwestern New Mexico

This rugged region of the state is often referred to as Old West Country. Its wild-and-woolly past echoes in the remains of ghost towns, museums, and the memories of many old-timers. Mining and ranching have traditionally dominated the landscape and have given residents their fiercely independent nature.

This is also the only region in New Mexico that borders a foreign country—our state's namesake to the south, Mexico. In southwestern New Mexico you'll find the nation's first designated wilderness area, the Gila National Wilderness, as well as our state's largest lake, Elephant Butte. And on a more somber note, this region was the site of the world's first nuclear bomb explosion.

Socorro County

As you approach the **Very Large Array** (VLA, for short) from the east, you'll start to see a pattern of massive white dishlike objects interrupting the grassy plains of the horizon. As you get closer, the picture focuses a bit—"Looks like rows of huge sci-fi ray guns aimed at distant otherworldly enemies," you muse. But at this point, little do you know that the Plains (of San Agustin) are alive with the sounds of outer space.

You can't get more basic or accurate in the naming business than whoever came up with the name of this oft-photographed, high-tech haven: The Very Large Array is a very big deal. Really. The VLA is an astronomical observatory used to study not only our solar system but also distant galaxies at the edge of the universe. Consisting of twenty-seven dish-shaped antennas (each 82 feet in diameter) that are connected to form a single radio telescope, the VLA is the most powerful of its kind in the world. And visiting astronomers from all over the world come here to study the universe. (The acclaimed sci-fi blockbuster *Contact*, starring Jodie Foster, was filmed here.)

Southwestern New Mexico

N

0 ——————— 40 mi
0 ——————— 40 km

(36)

(60)

CATRON
CO.

(60)

(60) **Socorro**

(25)

(12)

(180)

SOCORRO
CO.

(380)

■ **Reserve**

Rio Grande

*Whitewater
Baldy*
+

*Elephant
Butte Res.*

(78)

SIERRA
CO.

Gila R.

GRANT
CO.

(152)

**Truth or
Consequences**

■ **Silver City**

(180)

DOÑA
ANA
CO.

(70)

(90)

(25)

(26)

(185)

(70)

■ **Lordsburg**

(70)

Las Cruces ■

(80)

(10)

(70)   (10)

■ **Deming**

(180)

Rio Grande

LUNA
CO.

(11)

(10)

N. MEX.

TEXAS

HIDALGO
CO.

NEW MEXICO

CHIHUAHUA

UNITED STATES

MEXICO

ARIZONA

NEW MEXICO

Very Large Array

In the unstaffed visitor center, a fifteen-minute slide show orients you to the history of the VLA, after which you can check out displays in the museum dedicated to radio astronomy. Next, take the walking-tour trails on the grounds of the VLA. One of the first stops is the "Whisper Gallery," where two dishlike structures face each other about 50 feet apart. Have a friend stand at one while you stand at the other. By whispering into a small ball attached to the dish by a string, the two of you can communicate clearly. On a minute and simplified scale, the structure illustrates how the VLA works.

To get to the VLA, drive about 20 miles west of Magdalena via U.S. Highway 60, turn south on Highway 52, and then take a right onto Highway 166 to the visitor center; (505) 835–7000. It's open daily, 8:30 A.M. to sunset, and there's no admission charge.

Clear on the other side of Socorro County, in the small community of San Antonio, you'll find the Owl Bar Cafe & Steak House, commonly known as the *Owl Cafe.* Serving customers since 1945, the Owl Cafe is a watering hole with a reputation—for its green chile cheeseburgers, that is. (Keep in mind that green chile and red chile refer to the peppers that are used extensively in New Mexican cooking. "Chile" with an "e" should never be confused with the bean or meat concoction, "chili.") New Mexicans traveling in these parts make a point to pass through San Antonio around lunchtime just to get their daily chile fix at the cafe.

Choose one of the many booths to get a good view of the old wooden bar that runs the length of the dining area, or, better yet, prop yourself on a bar stool as a vantage point from which to count up all the "wise ones" that constitute the cafe's owl-deco motif. The bar was saved from a fire that destroyed the town's A. H. Hilton Mercantile Store in the early 1940s. It was in Hilton's San Antonio hotel that his son Conrad began as a baggage carrier, only to end up starting one of the world's largest luxury hotel chains years later.

The Owl Cafe is just off Interstate 25 on U.S. Highway 380, about 10 miles south of Socorro; (505) 835–9946. It's open daily except Sunday from 8:00 A.M. to 9:30 P.M. (or 10:00 P.M., if they're busy).

Though you won't find many owls at the 57,191-acre **Bosque del Apache** ("Woods of the Apache") **National Wildlife Refuge,** if you time your visit for late fall or winter you're sure to spot lots of migratory birds in this sanctuary along the Rio Grande. Bring plenty of film—and a telephoto lens if you have one–to join the ranks of international photographers who are drawn by the beauty of the *bosque* and its birds.

New Mexico Trivia

Created in July 1850, Socorro County is New Mexico's oldest county.

Established in 1939 as a "refuge and breeding grounds for migratory birds and other wildlife," the refuge also provided winter habitat for greater sandhill cranes. In 1941, only 17 cranes visited the refuge, whereas their number is now as high as 17,000.

There's a visitor center that can fill you in on what to expect on the driving or walking tours. The migratory patterns of different bird species are highlighted, and you can put your back against the wall, spread-eagle, in the "How Big Is Your Wingspan?" display to see how you measure up to the feathered ones. Then there's the Birdcall Game, in which you listen to a recorded call and try to match it to a list of birds.

The self-guided, 15-mile Auto Tour Loop takes you through the birds' habitat in the *bosque.* Here's where you get a close view of snow geese, sandhill cranes, peregrine falcons, bald eagles, and the rare whooping cranes, along with 290 other bird species. Don't forget to pack your binoculars—the visitor center doesn't sell or loan them.

Each year during the third weekend in November the refuge hosts the Bosque Fall Festival. It celebrates the wildlife of the Middle Rio Grande Valley and the return of the snow geese and cranes. The festival includes bird-related demonstrations as well as wildlife arts exhibits and area tours.

Bosque del Apache is 8 miles south of Highway 380 (at the Owl Cafe) on Highway 1; (505) 835–1828. There's no admission fee at the visitor center, but there's a $3.00-per-car charge for the auto tour. Visitor center hours are 8:30 A.M.–4:30 P.M. weekdays and 8:00 A.M.–5:30 P.M. weekends. The Auto Tour Loop opens daily from one hour before sunrise to one hour after sunset.

SOUTHWESTERN NEW MEXICO

And if you're a serious birder who just can't get his fill on only a day trip to the *bosque*, book a room at the **Casa Blanca Bed and Breakfast Guesthouse** in San Antonio. Less than 10 miles from Bosque del Apache, the 1880s Victorian country farmhouse is owned by innkeeper Phoebe Wood. Whether you're into birds or not, a stay at Casa Blanca is a relaxing experience away from the noise of the city.

During fall and winter, guests enjoy the warmth of a wood-burning stove in one of three guest rooms—all with private baths—and, in warmer times, avail themselves of the rural serenity of Casa Blanca's large veranda surrounding the front of the home. In addition, the bed and breakfast has two sitting areas, one with a piano, and a large selection of books and board games.

Casa Blanca is a couple of blocks from the Owl Cafe, at 13 Montoya Street in San Antonio; (505) 835–3027. Rates range from $60 to $80. The inn closes during the summer.

One of the least accessible and most eerie places in New Mexico is open to the public only twice a year. The **Trinity Site,** ground zero to the world's first nuclear explosion, is located in a remote part of the usually off-limits White Sands Missile Range deep in southeastern Socorro County. Following more than two years of research and development in Los Alamos (see Los Alamos County entry on page 69), the Manhattan Project culminated in the detonation of the bomb at 5:29.45 A.M. on July 16, 1945. The blast was seen across a radius of 160 miles, which included Albuquerque and Santa Fe, and windows were shattered in Silver City, 120 miles from the site.

Most signs of the blast have been removed; even the 1,200-foot-diameter, 8-foot-deep crater resulting from the blast has been filled in, though part of the blast area at ground zero has been left intact for display purposes. A fence encloses much of the ground-zero area. Small pieces of Trinitite, the fused silica rock formed by the extreme heat of the blast, still litters the site, and folks say it's radioactive enough to fog

FAVORITE ATTRACTIONS/EVENTS IN SOUTHWESTERN NEW MEXICO

Very Large Array, *Socorro County, (505) 772–4208*

Bosque del Apache National Wildlife Refuge, *Socorro County, (505) 835–1828*

Mogollon Catwalk, *near Glenwood, No phone*

Gila Cliff Dwellings National Monument, *north of Silver City, (505) 536–9344*

Los Olmos Guest Ranch, *Catron County, (505) 539–2311*

Whole Enchilada Festival, *October, Las Cruces, (505) 524–7824*

Great American Duck Race, *August, Deming, (888) 345–1125*

Hatch Chile Festival, *Labor Day weekend, Hatch, (505) 267–4468*

Hillsboro Apple Festival, *September, Hillsboro, (505) 895–5686*

Festival of the Cranes, *November, Bosque del Apache National Wildlife Refuge, (505) 835–0424*

Gila Bird and Nature Festival, *May, Silver City, (505) 538–9700*

photoraphic film. A black lava monument erected in 1965 and a National Historic Landmark plaque dedicated by the National Park Service in 1975 are about all that remain.

The two guided tours are held on the first Saturday of April and October. For information on the Trinity Site tours, call the Alamogordo Chamber of Commerce (800–545–4021; in New Mexico, 800–826–0294).

Catron County

n the nation's most lightning-struck region sits *The Lightning Field* by American sculptor Walter de Maria. You can't just drop by for the show, though: All visits are overnight affairs and require reservations. The Lightning Field is large-scale environmental art created by de Maria and completed in 1977. The work, which was commissioned and is maintained by the New York-based Dia Center for the Arts, is composed of four hundred 15- to 20-foot shiny steel poles placed in a grid measuring 1 mile by 3,330 feet. The tips of the poles form an exactly even plane, like a bed of nails for some evil giant. During thunderstorms the poles act as lightning rods, creating a dazzling light show.

The adventure starts in the town of Quemado, where, after meeting with the caretaker early in the afternoon, you're taken for a forty-five-minute ride on dirt roads to a visitor cabin. You, along with any other visitors, are then left until late the next morning. During the day, take the two-hour hike to the field to get a closer look at the rods and wander among them; as long as there's no lightning, you're safe. Otherwise, you can safely view the lightning strikes as long as you stay outside the perimeter of the field.

Because late summer is prime time for thunderstorms, a visit in late July or August gives you the best chance for a spectacular show. The field is also attractive during other times of the year, however, because the shiny rods provide shows of another sort with the help of sunshine or, on a clear night, moonlight.

Visiting season is May 1–October 31. For more information and to make reservations, call (505) 773–4560 or (505) 898–3335. For comprehensive information and to make reservations online, visit the Dia Center's Web site at www.diacenter.org and click on "Long-term Installations." A one-night stay costs $85 (minimum) per person, which includes meals and transportation to and from Quemado. (Note: During July and August, rates go up to $110, which still does not cover the center's actual cost of operations; therefore, additional contributions are appreciated.)

Despite the high adventure of viewing the lightning field, keep in mind that it is fine art on a grand scale; no photographs are permitted.

As New Mexico's most sparsely populated but geographically largest county, Catron County contains the bulk of the three-million-acre Gila National Forest. In this region you'll find *Mogollon,* set in a narrow valley flanked by canyon walls along Silver Creek. For about sixty years after its great gold strike of 1878, Mogollon earned a reputation for lawlessness as the Mogollon Mountains continued to give up millions of dollars' worth of gold, silver, and copper. Perhaps because of its inaccessibility, neither territorial troops nor the Apache warriors Victorio and Geronimo could tame this onetime headquarters of Butch Cassidy and his crew.

Today Mogollon is only semighostly: A handful of residents live here, and the old buildings are only slightly marred by the presence of facades built for the 1973 Western *My Name Is Nobody,* starring Henry Fonda. Mogollon is, however, still one of New Mexico's best-preserved ghost towns. During the summer, a couple of residents open shops for the trickle of visitors who venture into these parts.

Mogollon is located about 9 miles east of U.S. Highway 180 (about 37 miles south of Reserve) on Highway 159—a very narrow, cliff-hugging road with many hairpin turns. (It is paved, though.) If you're feeling adventurous and you have the time, keep going past the town and into the Gila National Forest and Mogollon Mountains for exquisite backcountry hiking and camping.

New Mexico Trivia

The state of New Mexico shares 175 miles of border with the country of Mexico in Hidalgo, Luna, and Doña Ana Counties.

Roads and trails are generally well marked, but take a U.S. Forest Service map, available at the general store in Glenwood, for more precise exploring expeditions.

About 3¹/₂ miles farther south on U.S. Highway 180, you'll come across the tiny village of Glenwood. Here you can explore one of the truly awesome sites in New Mexico: the *Mogollon Catwalk.* Plan this outing in late fall or early winter, during the week if possible, to avoid seeing another soul. You can't find a better site for a picnic.

Set in the beautiful Whitewater Canyon just outside Glenwood, the Catwalk trailhead is covered with stately old sycamores and cottonwoods. The perfectly clear Whitewater Creek rushes alongside the trail, completing the pristine setting. The canyon was a favorite hideout for Apaches and desperados, including Butch Cassidy, in the 1880s.

The initial rocky trail soon turns into the Catwalk, a narrow metal walkway (with a sturdy rail) that hugs the sheer-rock wall of the gorge as it winds along the creek up the canyon for about 1 mile past the gorge. Though the gorge is 100 feet deep (and the canyon walls rise 1,400 feet), the Catwalk stays about 20 feet above the river. The point is that a walk on the Catwalk is exciting and visually stimulating, but it's not scary. The Catwalk is well maintained for safety.

The Catwalk got its start as the result of pipelines that were laid through the canyon in 1893 to provide water for a mill that serviced nearby gold and silver claims. Because the lines needed continual maintenance, the workers who had to walk along the suspended pipes referred to them as the catwalk. Today you can even see parts of the old pipelines.

The Mogollon Catwalk is located about 5 miles from U.S. Highway 180 in Glenwood (40 miles south of Reserve), at the end of Highway 174 (well marked with signs), also known as Catwalk Road. There are no set hours, admission charges, or phones.

The best place to stay in Catron County is **Los Olmos Guest Ranch** in Glenwood. A stay in one of the fourteen roomy, well-appointed rock cabins runs from $60–$150, which includes a hearty breakfast in the sunny dining room located in the main house. Besides the cabins, available to guests are a pool and hot tub in a beautifully landscaped gated patio, a saloon with pool table, and fishing. Los Olmos now offers

Solamente En Nuevo México . . . The Mystery of Victorio Peak

*T*hough inaccessible to the public for more than forty years, the lure and legend of Victorio Peak remains strong. Thousands of gold bars are rumored to be stashed in a crevice of the domed mountain, located on the federal government's White Sands Missile Range in Doña Ana County.

Milton "Doc" Noss, a foot doctor and well-known treasure hunter, was killed in 1949, allegedly by a disgruntled business partner, over ownership issues regarding the gold. Noss's widow, Ova "Babe" Noss, along with a crew of treasure hunters, tried unsuccessfully for

years to locate the gold—even after she was forced to leave the site when the military boundary was extended in the 1950s. After she died in 1979, her grandson Terry Delonas inherited the family's gold fever. It literally took an act of Congress in 1990 to allow Delonas prolonged access to the range to explore. After years without success, the latest expedition was evicted in the mid-1990s by the military over a dispute regarding fees paid for access. And so, the legend lives on, and future treasure-hunting dramas will no doubt play out, as Victorio Peak remains victorious when it comes to giving up her gold.

guided two-hour horseback rides, with 24-hour advance reservations; cost is $30 per person. A fish hatchery offering daily self-guided tours, practically next door, is also an interesting diversion. Los Olmos is located near the intersection of U.S. Highway 180 and Highway 174; (505) 539–2311. Dinner is not generally available for guests from December through March, except by special arrangement. Call ahead.

Another dining option within walking distance is the *Blue Front Bar and Cafe* (505–539–2561). The food is great—especially the hearty breakfasts and smoked barbecue on weekends—and reasonably priced.

Grant County

ilver City is the largest community in Grant County and home of Western New Mexico University. As its name implies, mining played a key role in the town's history. Billy the Kid also figures into Silver City's past—he spent part of his childhood here before moving on to establish his notoriously lawless career.

Unlike most of New Mexico's old mining towns, Silver City survived the boom-bust pattern of the industry to become Grant County's trade center and county seat. At the turn of the century, the town capitalized on its dry climate to become a haven for people with tuberculosis. This delightful climate, with its four distinct seasons, continues to attract new residents, particularly retirees.

Take a stroll down Bullard Street (around Broadway Street) near the city's center to check out its historic downtown district. You'll find an eclectic mix of shops and cafes housed in architecturally significant, late-1800s buildings. Like Las Vegas, New Mexico, up north (see San Miguel County entry on page 149), Silver City's inner core is enhanced by a choice selection of Victorian homes. During the past few years, Silver City has become somewhat of a budding artists' colony, and, as such, there are now contemporary art galleries and even an espresso bar.

One of the city's finest examples of Victorian architecture is now the home of the *Silver City Museum.* But this unusual brick structure was originally the home of mining magnate Harry Ailman, who had it built in 1881. Later it served as the city hall and as a fire station before becoming a museum in 1967. This is the place to start investigating Silver City's rich history, from the prehistoric Mogollon Indians who inhabited the area, through the mining days, to the present. The museum sponsors special, long-running exhibits, such as "More Than Civilizers: Women of Silver City, 1870–1910." Visitors can even climb to the top in the museum's cupola, built for ventilation, and get a 360-degree view of the town.

The Silver City Museum is located at 312 West Broadway; (505) 538–5921. It's open Tuesday through Friday from 9:00 A.M. to 4:30 P.M. and weekends from 10:00 A.M. to 4:00 P.M. There's no admission charge.

Experience the delights of Silver City's past with a stay at *The Carter House,* a bed-and-breakfast inn on the edge of the town's historic district. Silver City got its start in 1870 with the founding of the Legal Tender silver mine, located behind the present-day Grant County Courthouse, which is next door to the inn. The stately Carter House was built in 1906 by copper baron and architect Theodore Carter, who made his fortune as owner of the nearby Burro Mountain Copper Mine. Today, innkeeper Maura Gonsior pampers her guests in five guest rooms, each with a private bath, in her fully renovated oak-trimmed home. For your relaxation, the inn offers several sitting rooms, a library, and a large front porch with a view of downtown Silver City and the Gila Mountains in the distance. A full breakfast is served each morning, and tea and homemade cookies are available for guests at any time.

The Carter House also offers a dormitory-style American Youth Hostel with fully equipped kitchen and laundry facilities. You'll find the Carter House at 101 North Cooper Street; (505) 388–5485. Rates for the inn range from $57 to $75; for the hostel, $12.50 for AYH members and $15.50 for nonmembers.

Just north of Silver City, on the edge of the Gila National Forest, the village of *Pinos Altos* ("Tall Pines") is a prime spot for any off-the-beaten-pather. Though Pinos Altos's mining history dates from 1803, it was a later gold discovery by three Forty-Niners from California in 1860 that led to the establishment of Pinos Altos as a mining camp. Roy Bean operated a general store here with his brother before moving to Texas to become "the law west of the Pecos." During the past few years, several of the town's old stores have been replaced by modern shops.

Pinos Altos's points of interest include the *Hearst Church,* the Buckhorn Saloon, and the Pinos Altos Museum. The near-century-old Hearst Church was built with money donated by Phoebe Hearst, whose late husband, George (father of William Randolph Hearst), had left her mining interests in Pinos Altos. The small adobe church, originally called the Gold Avenue Methodist Episcopal Church, now houses the Grant County

SOUTHWESTERN NEW MEXICO

Art Guild. It also contains the hearse that carried the body of Pat Garrett (killer of Billy the Kid), along with other horse-drawn vehicles. Unfortunately, the church is not kept open regular hours.

With its faded whitewashed facade, the **Buckhorn Saloon** is one of the West's finest old bars, distinguished by 18-inch-thick adobe walls and rustic timbers. Stepping through the old watering hole's doors at dusk is like stepping back a hundred years. The saloon glows with soft lighting and smiling people clustered around the bar and small tables. The Buckhorn now also has a fine restaurant, serving burgers, steaks, seafood as well as vegetarian dishes.

On closer inspection, two perennial bar patrons aren't even real–they're realistic-looking mannequins. Indian Joe keeps his seat at one end of the bar; though occasionally a newcomer offers to buy him a drink, he has yet to acknowledge the offer. Debbie DeCamp, the other mannequin, keeps an eye on the saloon entrance from a balcony; she's based on a young woman who lived in Pinos Altos at the turn of the century and met an untimely death during a brawl. A friend, the story goes, wrote the following "memorial" over the door to Debbie's room:

> *Shed a tear for Debbie DeCamp,*
> *Born a virgin and died a tramp.*
> *For 17 years she retained her virginity.*
> *(A real good record for this vicinity.)*

The Buckhorn is open daily except Sunday. Bar opens at 3:00 P.M. and dinner is served from 6:00–10:00 P.M. It's located on Main Street in Pinos Altos; (505) 538–9911.

The Pinos Altos Museum, just across the road from the Buckhorn, details the village's history. The tin-roofed log cabin was the county's first private schoolhouse, built around 1866.

Pinos Altos is located about 6 miles north of Silver City, just off Highway 15. Be aware that in Pinos Altos most of the roads are dirt but are in good condition unless there's been a lot of rain.

Deep within the Gila National Forest but less than 40 miles farther on Highway 15, you'll find the rather hidden **Gila Cliff Dwellings National Monument** (505-536-9344). It's dedicated to preserving and celebrating the ancient Pueblo Indians of the Mogollon culture who inhabited the area for about a hundred years starting around 1280. These cliff dwellers were approximate contemporaries of the Anasazi Indians who lived in New Mexico's northwestern region. Similar to the Anasazi, the Mogollon Indians mysteriously disappeared, and archaeologists have been puzzled ever since the dwellings were discovered. Drought, disease, and tribal wars top the list of theories.

A visit to the park involves a healthy mile's hike along a trail that ascends some 200 feet up the canyon walls to the cliff dwellings. The dwellings themselves are tucked into caves in the cliff and are made of adobe and timber. Most visitors are extremely quiet when walking among the rooms of the dwellings, partly because the caves' acoustics amplify voices but also because they're showing respect for the people who lived here so long ago. On the edge of the Gila National Wilderness, the monument is a peaceful and beautiful place for a hike.

The Gila Cliff Dwellings are open daily 8:00 A.M.–6:00 P.M. (visitor center, 8:00 A.M.–5:00 P.M.) Memorial Day through Labor Day and

A Glimpse of Southwestern New Mexico: *Impresiones de la Gila*

*W*ith its abundance of forests, mountains, and wilderness—and its absence of people—southwestern New Mexico has long provided nourishment for my soul. My affinity for the area began many years ago during a late spring excursion to the Mogollon Catwalk (see page 7). I had strongly felt the need to get away from Albuquerque for quite some time, and I imagined that the distance and remoteness provided by "the Gila" would be exactly what I needed.

Driving south on Interstate 25 from Albuquerque, past Truth or Consequences, I envisioned my road trip as a long, leisurely loop that would take me south and west through the Black Range of the Gila National Forest and on to Silver City, and then north to Glenwood and into the Mogollon Mountains. After a few days, I would

complete the loop by heading northeast to Datil, east to Magdalena—passing by the Very Large Array—and then rejoining Interstate 25 in Socorro.

Though there were serendipitous discoveries along the way, I often reminded myself that my destination had been the Catwalk, the old metal structure that would provide me intimate, cliff-hugging access to one of the most beautiful canyon valleys in the state. But even before I started walking toward the trailhead, I was spellbound. Before me was Whitewater Creek, tumbling freely over boulders and gurgling from abundant snowmelt. Its image, along with the splendor of a stand of towering sycamores being played by a spring breeze, was enough to provide the transcendence I'd been searching for.

9:00 A.M.–4:00 P.M. (visitor center, 8:00 A.M.–4:30 P.M.) the rest of the year. There's no admission charge. (*Note:* The park is actually in Catron County but is accessible only through Grant County.)

One of the more relaxing lodging experiences in the Silver City area can be had at *The Cottages at Piñon Canyon Hideaway* (505– 388–3000/800– 938–3001). Tucked away just northeast of the city limits, at 2037 Cottage San Road, The Cottages are nestled among eighty acres in the secluded foothills of the Gila National Forest. The estate, which includes a main house and cottages, was built in 1939 by the wealthy Burnside family. It was later sold and became the boyhood home of Harrison (Jack) Schmitt, New Mexico's most famous astronaut who not only has a moon walk to his credit, but later went on to become a U.S. Senator from New Mexico. Each cottage is situated in its own private setting and comes complete with a fireplace, hot mineral bath, TV/VCR, and fully equipped kitchen, perfect for extended stays. Rates range from $89 to $199, double occupancy, with $25 for each additional person.

> ### New Mexico Trivia
>
> *Noted astronomer and professor Dr. Clyde Tombaugh, who discovered the planet Pluto in 1930, helped found the astronomy department at New Mexico State University in Las Cruces, where he died in 1997, two weeks and four days before his 91st birthday.*

Heading southeast of Silver City toward Deming you'll find *City of Rocks State Park.* This relatively flat park is filled with vertical rock formations, some as high as 50 feet, resembling the monoliths at Stonehenge. The rocks are the result of erosion on the remains of volcanic eruptions that occurred millions of years ago. Because you can climb on the rocks, as well as hide behind them, this park is a natural playground for kids of all ages. Picnic and camping facilities are available. The park is located 31 miles southeast of Silver City via U.S. Highway 180 and Highway 61; (505) 536–2800. It's open daily, from 7:00 A.M. to 9:00 P.M. Admission is $4.00 per vehicle. Camping is available for $8.00 per night.

In the eastern Grant County village of San Lorenzo, you'll find one of the finest places to eat in southwestern New Mexico—an elegantly simple restaurant called *Sisters.* The village of San Lorenzo was first inhabited by Spanish settlers in the 1700s, and later by Mexican farmers who were drawn to the fertile valley. The building occupied by the restaurant is relatively new, circa 1930, compared with the hundred-year-old adobes in the neighborhood. It started out as a general merchandise store and a saloon. Ben Lilly, the famous mountain man, is reported to have frequented the place. Restaurateurs and sisters Nancy and Rita Schubert bought the house at a yard sale—yes, a yard sale—in 1991. They believe it was fate that brought them to it. Sisters is the type of restaurant you hope to find when traveling through remote areas, one that offers quality food, generous portions, reasonable prices, and a pleasant down-home atmosphere. Rita and Nancy do all of the cooking themselves and prepare all meals from scratch, including their well-known breads and pies. You'll find Sisters at 137 Galaz Street in San Lorenzo. It's open from 11:00 A.M. to 2:30 P.M., Wednesday through Friday; 11:00 A.M. to 8:00 P.M., Saturday; and from noon to 4:00 P.M. on Sunday; (505) 536–9888.

Hidalgo County

Texas and Oklahoma may have their panhandles, but New Mexico's got its boot heel and Hidalgo County is it. Closer to Tucson, Arizona, than to Albuquerque, most of this area is desolate, although cattle ranching and, more recently, vineyards have made their imprint on the land.

The largest town is Lordsburg, but perhaps the most unique place is **Shakespeare,** a ghost town 2¹/₂ miles southwest of Lordsburg.

Originally settled in the 1850s as Mexican Springs, a stage stop on the Butterfield Overland Trail, Shakespeare was named in 1879 by mine promoters to honor the bard and perhaps improve the town's fortunes. The town was the site of a couple of mining hoaxes including the Diamond Swindle of 1870—when the area was seeded with diamonds to attract investors—before a real silver boom hit in 1879, only to fizzle some fifteen years later. Shakespeare's last hurrah came with a second silver strike in 1907. The silver played out in the 1930s.

New Mexico Trivia

Hidalgo County was named for the town of Guadalupe Hidalgo in Mexico, where the Treaty of Guadalupe Hidalgo was signed to bring the New Mexico Territory into the United States.

Because the town has been privately owned since 1935, it has been protected from weekend ghost-town looters, and the admission charge goes toward further preservation and restoration. It's accessible to the public only through guided tours that include the interiors of several buildings. One of these structures, the Stratford Hotel, is said to have briefly employed Billy the Kid as a dishwasher.

To get to Shakespeare, take the Main Street exit off Interstate 10 in Lordsburg, turn south, and follow the signs. Tours are held at 10:00 A.M. and 2:00 P.M. on the second Sunday and preceding Saturday of the month; on the fourth weekend of April, June, August and, October, historical reenactments are staged. Call (505) 542–9034 to verify the current year's dates. The admission charge is $3.00 for adults and $2.00 for children six to twelve ($1.00 higher for reenactments).

Luna County

una County's primary community is Deming, known for its pure air and fast ducks. Yes, ducks. Deming is home of the world-famous Great American Duck Race (800–848–4955), held annually the fourth weekend in August. Thought up more than fifteen years ago in a bar as a way to create more interest in the area, the duck races have captured international media coverage for Deming. More than just a duck race, the "fowl event" includes a parade, a golf tournament, a chili cookoff, a hot-air-balloon rally, several sporting tournaments, and even a "Duck Queen" contest. It has also become one of New Mexico's most well-attended events.

Deming's more than ducks, though. The city's also home to the impressive **Deming Luna Mimbres Museum.** Located in the three-story, 1916 red-brick National Guard Armory building, the museum has about 25,000 square feet of exhibition space. There's a bit of everything here, as evidenced by the many "theme rooms," including the Military Room, the Quilt Room, the Doll Room, and the Tack Room. The museum also depicts life in the Southwest, focusing on ranching, railroading, and mining. The Mimbres Room showcases examples of centuries-old Mimbres Indian pottery. The pottery's distinctive, black-on-white geometric designs are known for the way they mismatch animal body parts.

The museum is at 301 South Silver in Deming; (505) 546–2382. It's open Monday through Saturday from 9:00 A.M. to 4:00 P.M., and Sunday from 1:30 to 4:00 P.M. There's no set admission charge, but nominal contributions are expected. Across the street the museum has renovated an old "customshouse" into another space that showcases the area's border-town past.

Most parks make a big deal about leaving everything as you found it and strictly forbid visitors to take anything with them when they leave. But at **Rockhound State Park,** located on the west side of the Little Florida Mountains, "taking a little of the park" is encouraged. That's right—visitors may each take up to fifteen pounds of rocks with them per visit. You'll find all kinds and colors here, including varieties of quartz crystals, agates, and opals. Even after years of rock hounds carrying away

> **New Mexico Trivia**
>
> *The grave of Billy the Kid's mother, Kathrine Antrim, is located in Silver City.*

mementos of their visit, old-timers say it's hard to tell that the place is any different than it was years ago. Plan to spend a lot of time staring at the ground here, and while you're on the lookout for your personal gems, watch out as well for loose rock and inconspicuous drop-offs.

Rockhound State Park is off Palomas Road via Highway 11, southeast of Deming; (505) 546–6182. It's open daily, from 7:30 A.M. to sunset. There's a $4.00-per-vehicle admission charge.

Sierra County

Sierra County is home to New Mexico's largest body of water, *Elephant Butte Lake*. It's named for a huge gray rock formation, or butte, that rises from the water and resembles an elephant. Near the lake you'll come across the city of *Truth or Consequences.* The city changed its name from Hot Springs to Truth or Consequences in 1951, following an open challenge over the airwaves from the popular radio show of the same name to honor its tenth anniversary. As a reward for the name change, the show pledged the city an annual festival during which the show would be broadcast. The show, along with its later television incarnation, has long since ended, but the annual Truth or Consequences Fiesta is still going strong. And Ralph Edwards, former host of the show, hasn't missed one yet.

Truth or Consequences (often "T or C," for short) is popular for its many therapeutic hot springs (from which the community got its first name). In fact, there's a contingent of folks who'd like to change the town's

State Parks in Southwestern New Mexico

Caballo Lake/Percha Dam State Park, 18 miles south of Truth or Consequences, (505) 743–3942

City of Rocks State Park, 28 miles northeast of Deming, (505) 536–2800

Elephant Butte Lake State Park, 7 miles north of Truth or Consequences, (505) 744–5421

Leasburg Dam State Park, 15 miles north of Las Cruces, (505) 524–4068

Pancho Villa State Park, in Columbus, (505) 531–2711

Rockhound State Park, 14 miles southeast of Deming, (505) 546–6182

Web site: www.emnrd.state.nm.us/nmparks/

name back to Hot Springs (some old-timers and newcomers alike use "T or C–Hotsprings" as part of their return address), but after several ballot defeats through the years, the name Truth or Consequences seems destined to endure for this funky community, which continues to attract retirees and "snowbirds"—those seniors who like to winter where its warm.

The ancient Mimbres Indians of southern New Mexico—who, like the Anasazi of northern New Mexico, are the ancestors of present–day Pueblo Indians—sought out the area's natural hot springs more than one thousand years ago for the water's sacred, healing powers. And though much has changed through the centuries, the healing waters remain—but now they come with scientific mineral analysis. There are currently eight bathhouses in Truth or Consequences that offer soaks for as little as $3.00 or $4.00, which is quite a bargain when compared to the pricier hot springs options in northern New Mexico. One such bathhouse is the historic and evolving **Marshall Hot Springs**.

Originally established in the late 1920s, "the Marshall," as it's locally known, was recently rescued after years of deferred maintenance and lack of vision. Gerald Liebovitz and Jane Ehrenreich, who formerly ran a popular vegetarian restaurant in Guatemala for eleven years, bought the place in 1998 and began renovations to transform the Marshall into their vision of a healing center, complete with massage therapy, reflexology and acupuncture.

Boasting natural flowing pools, as opposed to "pump and drain" tubs like many of the local hot springs establishments, the Marshall exudes unpretentious New Age New Mexico at its laid–back best. A private soak in one of their tubs is quite a treat, especially with the knotted rope dangling above the center of the square cement pool, playfully perfect for stretching tired muscles. A dimmer switch and peaceful Native American flute music playing low in the background complete the truly sensory experience. During my visit, lodging was limited to an upstairs guesthouse ($55) or a funky 1964 Airstream trailer ($30) across the street. However, plans call for at least three more guest rooms as Gerald and Jane renovate the wings of the old on-site motel, which were once the cabins used by workers during the construction of nearby Elephant Butte Dam.

You'll find the Marshall, along with the other free–flowing hot springs near downtown T or C, at 311 Mar Street (near Pershing); (505) 894–9286; www.marshallhotsprings.com.

Another nearby choice is **Riverbend Hot Springs,** the only outdoor soaking option in T or C. On the banks of the Rio Grande, Riverbend offers a variety of lodging accommodations—private suites, semi-private rooms, dormitory style rooms, and campsites—and is also an American Youth Hostel. The communal tubs, which are filled twice per day, morning and evening, for Riverbend guests, have a nice view of Turtleback Mountain. If you're not staying at Riverbend, you may still book a private day-soak there ($5.00 for one hour).

Riverbend Hot Springs is at 100 Austin Street near the city park; (505) 894–6183; www.riolink.com/~rivrbnd. Lodging ranges from $13 for camping and dorm rooms to $40 for a private room.

Near the town's center, you'll find **Geronimo Springs Museum,** named after a spring frequented by Geronimo, the famous Apache war chief. The spring has been "modernized" with the addition of a circular enclosure and a roof, but you can still see and hear it bubbling around the rocks.

The museum is one of those community types for which residents have donated a broad assortment of artifacts from the area's past. The museum is laid out according to four categories: the Historical Past, Natural Resources, Ralph Edwards and the Fiesta, and the Cultural Heritage Room. This last space really takes visitors by surprise, with its floor-to-ceiling murals of famous locals painted by noted muralist Delmas Howe, who was born in Truth or Consequences. The room also contains four bronze statues of other famous New Mexicans, each sculpted by Hivana Leyendecker, an accomplished native New Mexican artist.

The museum is located at 211 Main Street across from the post office; (505) 894–6600. It's open Monday through Saturday, 9:00 A.M.–5:00 P.M. Admission charges are $2.00 for adults and $1.00 for children over five.

Truth or Consequence's newest museum is worth a stop for old-car enthusiasts. **Callahan's Auto Museum** was founded in 1992 by Bill Callahan, who relocated to Truth or Consequences with the idea of opening New Mexico's only automobile museum. He even passed up a position as curator of an automobile museum in California to move to New Mexico in the mid-1980s.

The museum, housed in a former grocery store, contains about twenty vehicles, most on indefinite loan from members of the Truth or Consequences Auto Club. You'll find several 1926 models, a 1936 DeSoto Airflow III (models of which were aerodynamically tested in a wind tunnel that belonged to the Wright Brothers); a 1951 Chrysler convertible once owned by the late actor Steve McQueen; and a 1950 Chrysler limousine, official vehicle of a former governor of New Mexico.

To complement the auto showroom, the museum has displays of other car-related items such as old highway maps, owner manuals, spark plugs, and oil cans. The museum's policy is look all you want, but please don't touch. As one of several hands-off signs proclaims: A CAR IS LIKE A WIFE: IF SHE AIN'T YOURS, KEEP YOUR HANDS OFF!

Callahan's Auto Museum is at 410 Cedar Street; (505) 894–6900. It's open Monday to Saturday 10:00 A.M.–4:30 P.M. The admission charge is $3.00 or two for $5.00, but children under twelve are admitted free.

If you're a gardener in practice or in spirit, don't miss **Buffalo Bill's Exotic Cactus Ranch** in T or C. What initially looks like a translucent warehouse is actually a huge greenhouse, where all forms, colors, sizes, and textures of prickly plants transform the indoor space into a cacti wonderland of sorts. Co–owner Dave Lamb confirms that most visitors' first reactions are ones of awe and wonder as they gaze at the magnificent displays of exotic plants from the world over, including Africa, Central America, Mexico, South America, and Australia.

With names such as Living Stones, Fairy Castle, Sticks on Fire, and Monkey Tails, these cacti are sure to delight kids and adults alike. If you visit, take note of the globular Blue Myrtle cacti—my favorite—which look as if bluish green molten lava flowed out of the tops of the plants and formed into beautiful, knotted sculptures. If you're on the move but

---

Solamente en Nuevo México . . .
Ted Turner: Buffalo Rancher, Environmentalist

*J*ust as miners and conquistadores did in past centuries, entrepreneur and media-mogul Ted Turner recently staked his claim in the Land of Enchantment when he acquired another famous New Mexico ranch. His latest acquisition, the 580,000-acre Vermejo Ranch in Colfax County in northeastern New Mexico, officially makes him the second largest private landowner in the state. (Only Henry Singleton of Beverly Hills, California, owns more).

In addition to Vermejo, Turner's holdings include the 360,000-acre Armendaris Ranch in southwestern New Mexico and the 155,000-acre Ladder Ranch near Truth or Consequences. Turner primarily raises buffalo on the ranches; however, the Vermejo Park Ranch also includes a grand old hunting and fishing lodge.

Turner's certainly no modern-day miner or conquerer, however. In fact, he's quite the opposite: He's a generous, active environmentalist. Along with his famous wife, Jane Fonda, Turner donates millions of dollars each year to organizations supporting green, or environmental, issues.

find a specimen you like, Ranch employees will package it for both car or air travel, and shipping is also available.

While the ranch predominantly features exotic cacti for indoor use as houseplants, in the spring and summer, the ranch also stocks plants for desert landscaping. A demonstration garden between the greenhouse and the gift shop provides ideas for the home gardener. The gift shop features a variety of unique terra cotta pots and other items for garden decor.

You'll find Buffalo Bill's Exotic Cactus Ranch at 1600 South Broadway in Truth or Consequences; (505) 894–0790. It's open daily, 9:00 A.M. to 5:00 P.M., except Tuesday.

Southwest of Truth or Consequences, the village of **Hillsboro** is the quintessential one-horse town. Established in 1877 as the result of a gold discovery in the hills surrounding Percha Creek, Hillsboro is perfect for just pulling off the main street and strolling around town. You'll find several antiques shops, a couple of galleries, a general store, an old saloon, and the **Black Range Museum.** Hillsboro is the kind of place where all the townspeople and merchants know one another and where a few well-cared-for "community" dogs take naps in the middle of Main Street. Steeped in mining history, the town is an enchanting, slow-paced marvel that has lured more than its share of artists and writers to become residents.

Speaking of enchanting, the **Enchanted Villa Bed & Breakfast** (505–895–5686) has a home along Hillsboro's main street. Run by innkeeper Maree Westland, this large, bright, whitewashed home was designed by Maree's great-aunt in 1941 as a romantic retreat for English nobleman Sir Victor Sassoon. The two-story inn's five large guest rooms all have lots of well-positioned windows for maximum light, and there are antiques and oak floors throughout. All rooms feature king-size beds and private bathrooms. Rates range from $40 to $70.

The **Hillsboro General Store** deserves more than a casual mention. This is the real thing. Continuously open since 1879, the store has survived boom and bust while serving as a post office, stage stop, telegraph office, soda fountain, and phone company. Though it still stocks most things the rural household needs at a moment's notice, these days most folks visit the store when they're hungry. A large part of the store is now the Country Cafe and serves up hearty breakfasts and lunches featuring soups, sandwiches, burgers, and a few New Mexican selections.

If you're lucky enough to be traveling through Hillsboro on a weekend,

Hillsboro General Store

make sure to stop into **Hillsboro Woodworks** (505–895–5331), the shop of master clockmaker Gregory A. Gaylord. Located in the old Pole Barn next to the Black Range Museum, Gaylord's shop features his handcrafted fine clocks in addition to antique timepieces he's restored. Because Gaylord's clocks are particularly popular with high–end buyers—including celebrities, whose identities Gaylord prefers not to publicize—his work often takes him to Santa Fe and Tucson during weekdays, which means his shop is only open Saturday and Sunday, 9:00 A.M. to 4:00 P.M.

Hillsboro is 30 miles from Truth or Consequences: 12 miles south on Interstate 25 and then 18 miles west on Highway 152.

Nine miles farther west on Highway 152, you'll enter the Black Range of the Mimbres Mountains in **Kingston,** a blink-and-you'll-miss-it community—so check your odometer and don't blink. Kingston, population thirty, is pretty much deserted now, though a tiny museum is housed in the old Percha Valley Bank building and the original schoolhouse is used as the meeting place for the Spit and Whittle Club. Kingston's history mirrors Hillsboro's; it saw more prosperous days during the silver boom of the 1880s, when the population soared to 7,000.

The three-story, ivy-covered **Black Range Lodge** stands as testimony to those earlier days. Run by Hollywood escapee and filmmaker/innkeeper Catherine Wanek and her husband, Pete Fust, the lodge is now a bed and breakfast with the feel of an Old West boardinghouse. It's one of the few bed and breakfasts that welcome pets—a great relief when the kennel fills up at the last minute and Rover needs a weekend getaway just as much as you do.

The innkeepers' background in the entertainment business is evident in the large common area of the lodge's second floor. Those who need more stimulation will find a pool table, a cassette deck, a satellite-television-and-VCR system complete with videotape library, and video games. For those who appreciate the tranquility of the lodge's natural setting, however, hunting for crystals along the rocky trails near the inn is a relaxing pastime—sort of like hunting for seashells on the beach.

If you find Kingston, you'll find the Black Range Lodge—trust me; (505) 895–5652. Rates range from $49 to $59 with an extra $15 charge for each additional person in a suite. Discounts are available for multi-night stays.

Doña Ana County

D oña Ana County is home to New Mexico's second-largest city, **Las Cruces** ("The Crosses"), which in turn is home to New Mexico's second-largest college, New Mexico State University. Located in the fertile Mesilla Valley between the Organ Mountains and the Rio Grande, Las Cruces hosts the Whole Enchilada Festival each October, culminating in the cooking of the world's largest enchilada.

Fine art and hospitality meet at **Lundeen Inn of the Arts,** the most distinctive place to stay in the Las Cruces area, only five minutes from Old Mesilla (see page 23). Run by Linda and Jerry Lundeen, this bed and breakfast adjoins Linda's gallery and Jerry's architectural office, but it's hard to tell where one begins and the other ends. Works by southwestern artists are everywhere, including the guest rooms. And since most of it's for sale, if you enjoy your stay in a particular room, you can arrange to take a piece of it home. If you've always wondered what's entailed in making adobe bricks, Jerry might just give you a lesson, time permitting. Once you find out the process, you'll understand why real adobe homes are so expensive in comparison with stucco-covered-concrete homes passed off as adobe.

The inn was formed by joining two historic adobe homes by a great room that has a soaring ceiling. In addition to being the place where breakfast is served, this naturally lighted common area is the focal point for much of the inn's art. Each of the twenty oversize guest rooms is unique in both configuration and decor and is named after an American artist, such as Georgia O'Keeffe and R. C. Gorman. All rooms have queen-size beds and private baths, and some even have fireplaces and limited kitchen facilities. Another one-hundred-year-old adobe on the grounds has been renovated, providing two additional suites, with kitchens and kiva fireplaces, perfect for extended stays; and most recently, a pair of two-bedroom condos have been added.

Arts classes, including silversmithing and pottery making, are offered through the inn, which is located at 618 South Alameda; (505) 526–3326. Rates range from $68 to $150; weekly and monthly rates are available.

Although a separate community, **Mesilla** (alternately La Mesilla or Old Mesilla) connects to the southwest side of Las Cruces. This rural "part" of Las Cruces played an important role in the history of New Mexico. The Gadsden Purchase—which annexed Mesilla to the United States from Mexico and established the current international borders of New Mexico and Arizona—was signed here in 1854. Mesilla is also the place where Billy the Kid was convicted of murder, sentenced to hang, and jailed for a short time in 1881. The village was even briefly declared the Confederate capital of a territory extending all the way to California. The tree-lined Old Mesilla Plaza is anchored by the San Albino Church and is surrounded by uncluttered shops and restaurants; it's a great place to visit on an autumn Saturday afternoon. Just across Highway 28 from Old Mesilla Plaza on Calle del Parian, you'll find the **Gadsden Museum,** which displays Indian, Civil War, and Old West artifacts.

If you've got a few hours after your visit to the museum and would like to savor the flavors of the countryside, consider heading south from Mesilla on the scenic **Oñate Trail** (Highway 28). Named for Spanish explorer Don Juan de Oñate, often cited as the founder of New Mexico, the roadway traces part of the route that Oñate took into New Mexico more than 400 years ago. Roughly parallel to both the Rio Grande and Interstate 25, this more leisurely route connects the many rural communites southwest of Las Cruces, which are home to several interesting places to stop and shop.

Six miles south of Mesilla, near the village of San Miguel, you'll arive at **Stahmann's Farms** (800–654–6887). Originally started in the 1930's as an innovative move to supplant the one-time cotton farm with the then-foreign pecan crop, Stahmann's now boasts 180,000 pecan trees on 4,000 acres, making it one of the world's largest pecan groves. Besides the beautiful canopy of trees, which produce up to 10 million pounds of pecans annually, Stahmann's has a country store filled with pecan confections, specialty foods, gift baskets, and, luckily, samples of their delectible pecans.

About 11½ miles farther south, check out the **Pepper Tree Farm** (505–233–3699) in the community of Chamberino. Basically a chile-themed gift shop—featuring everything from gourmet foods and chile ristras (decorative strings of red chile peppers) to kitchen gadgets, jewelry, and clothing—the Pepper Tree Farm is open daily.

A half mile farther south, you'll come across **La Viña Winery** (505–882–7362), New Mexico's oldest winery, down a dirt road west of the highway. It's only open on Saturday and Sunday from noon to 5:00 P.M. La Viña has a tasting room, which features its Zinfandels and Chardonnays, as well as a wine and gift shop. In addition, the winery also hosts wine festivals each April and October.

Heading north on Interstate 25 out of Las Cruces, you'll come across **Fort Selden State Monument.** The now-abandoned adobe military fort that contributed to the growth of Las Cruces was one of many forts built in the mid-1800s to protect settlers and travelers from Apache Indian attacks. It was the boyhood home of General Douglas MacArthur from 1884 to 1886, when his father was the post commander; moreover, the acclaimed Buffalo Soldiers, a regiment of black soldiers honored for their success in subduing the Plains Indians, were also stationed here.

Famous New Mexican Entertainers and Artists

Greer Garson, actress	*Val Kilmer, actor*
William Hanna, cartoonist	*Roger Miller, musician*
Eliot Porter, nature photographer	*Gene Hackman, actor*
Kathy Baker, actress	*Bo Diddley, singer and songwriter*
Demi Moore, actress	*Vivian Vance, actress*
Burl Ives, musician	*Bill Daily, actor*
Jim Morrison, lead singer of The Doors	*Ali McGraw, actress*
Georgia O'Keeffe, artist	*R.C. Gorman, Navajo artist*
Buddy Holly, musician	*Ottmar Liebert, musician*

Martha's Black Dog
Coffeehouse,
110 West Manzanares,
Socorro,
(505) 838–0311.,
Inexpensive. Fare:
Sandwiches, pasta, soup
and salads, including
vegetarian entrees.

CATRON COUNTY
Blue Front Cafe and Bar,
Highway 180,
Glenwood;,
(505) 539–2561.,
Inexpensive. Fare:
Traditional family dining,
excellent breakfasts;
smoked barbecue on
weekends.

The Red Hen Cafe,
Highway 180,
Alma;,
(505) 539–2610.,
Inexpensive. Fare:
Small-town American.

Grandma T's Restaurant,
Highway 12, Reserve,
(505) 533–6234

GRANT COUNTY
Sisters,
137 Galaz Street,
San Lorenzo;
(505) 536–9888.
Inexpensive to moderate.
Fare: Homestyle favorites;
known for fresh pies.

Buckhorn Saloon,
Main Street,
Pinos Altos;
(505) 538–9911.
Inexpensive. Fare: steaks,
burgers, chicken, seafood,
vegetarian.

Jalisco Cafe,
100 South Bullard Street,
Silver City,
(505) 388–2060. Inexpen
sive to moderate. Fare:
Traditional Mexican and
eclectic Southwestern.

Selected Chambers of Commerce/Visitors Bureaus in Southwestern New Mexico:

Deming Chamber of Commerce,
P.O. Box 8, 800 East Pine,
Deming, 88031, 505–546–2674,
Web site: www.zianet.com/deming/

Hatch Chamber of Commerce,
P.O. Box 38, Hatch, 87937,
505–267–5050

Las Cruces Convention and Visitors Bureau,
211 North Water Street, Las Cruces, 88001,
505–541–2444/800–FIESTAS,
Web site: www.lascruces.org

Lordsburg Chamber of Commerce,
208 East Motel Drive, P.O. Box 699,
Lordsburg, 88045,
505–542–9864

Magdalena Chamber of Commerce,
P.O. Box 281, Magdalena, 87825,
505–854–2261

Reserve Chamber of Commerce,
P.O. Box 415, Reserve, NM 87830,
505–533–6116

Silver City/Grant County Chamber of Commerce,
1103 North Hudson Street, Silver City, 88061,
505–538–3785/800–548–9378,
Web site: www.silvercity.org/

Socorro County Chamber of Commerce,
P.O. Box 743, Socorro, 87801,
505–835–0424

Truth or Consequences/Sierra County
Chamber of Commerce,
P.O. Box 31, Truth or Consequences, 87901,
505–894–3536/800–831–9487
Web site: www.globaldrum. com/
sierra_newmexico/torc.htm

Last Ditch Cafe,
700 North Bullard Street,
Silver City,
(505) 388-5850.
Inexpensive to moderate.
Fare: Eclectic,
modern American.

Cucina Rustica,
3420 East Highway 180,
Silver City,
(505) 538-3711. Moderate
to expensive. Fare: Italian
and Continental.

The Red Barn,
708 Silver Heights
Boulevard,
Silver City,
(505) 538-5666.
Inexpensive to moderate.
Fare: Steaks and seafood.

HIDALGO COUNTY
Nightmare Cafe,
Intersection of Highways 9
and 338,
Animas (southwest of
Lordsburg). (No phone
listing). Inexpensive. Fare:
Green chile burgers and
more.

El Charro,
209 South P Boulevard,
Lordsburg,
(505) 542-3400. Inexpen-
sive to moderate. Fare: New
Mexican and American.

Kranberry's Restaurant,
1405 South Main,
Lordsburg,
(505) 542-9400.

Our Place Cafe,
608 West Motel Drive,
Lordsburg,
(505) 542-9472.

LUNA COUNTY
El Camino Real,
900 West Pine,
Deming,
(505) 546-7421. Inexpen-
sive to moderate. Fare: New
Mexican and American.

La Fonda Restaurant,
601 East Pine,
Deming,
(505) 546-0465. Inexpen-
sive to moderate. Fare: New
Mexican and American.

Primo's Restaurant,
123 South Silver Avenue,
Deming,
(505) 546-0800. Inexpen-
sive to moderate.

SIERRA COUNTY
Hilltop Cafe,
1301 North Date Street,
Truth or Consequences,
(505) 894-3407. Inexpen-
sive to moderate. Fare:
American.

Hot Springs Bakery,
313 Broadway,
Truth or Consequences,
(505) 894-5555. Inexpen-
sive. Fare: sandwiches, pizza.

La Bella Milan,
404 Main Street,
Truth or Consequences,
(505) 894-6787.
Inexpensive to moderate.
Fare: Fine Italian food and
fantastic desserts.

La Cocina,
280 North Date Street,
Truth or Consequences,
(505) 894-6499. Inexpen-
sive to moderate. Fare: New
Mexican and American.

Los Arcos Restaurant,
1400 North Date Street,
Truth or Consequences,
(505) 894-9797. Inexpen-
sive to moderate. Fare: New
Mexican and American.

DOÑA ANA COUNTY
The Double Eagle,
On the Plaza,
Old Mesilla,
(505) 523-6700. Moderate
to expensive. Fare: Eclectic,
featuring steaks and New
Mexican food.

La Posta,
On the Plaza,
Old Mesilla,
(505) 524-3524. Inexpen-
sive to moderate. Fare: New
Mexican cuisine.

Mesón de Mesilla,
1803 Avenida de Mesilla,
Old Mesilla,
(505) 525-9212. Moderate
to expensive. Fare: Continental.

Nopalito's,
310 South Mesquite,
Las Cruces,
(505) 524-0003. Inexpen-
sive to moderate. Fare: New
Mexican.

Northwestern New Mexico

Because of its large population of Native Americans, northwestern New Mexico proudly bears the name Indian Country. Part of the Navajo Nation—the largest Indian reservation in the United States—is located in this region, as are the Zuni, Acoma, Ramah Navajo, and Laguna reservations. The vast juniper-dotted mesas and multihued rock formations will leave you in awe, especially if you're an urban dweller. It's a great place to just wander for a few hours or even a few days.

The three counties composing this region are huge, so notable attractions are often widely scattered in this sparsely populated region. Look closely at the mileage scale on your trusty map and come along to discover some of the special spots in northwestern New Mexico.

McKinley County

Named after David L. Gallup, a paymaster for the Atlantic and Pacific Railroad, the city of *Gallup* was founded in 1881. Situated near the Arizona border along old Route 66, Gallup thrives in the heart of Indian Country. The Navajo and Zuni Indians swell this small town's population to more than 100,000 on weekends, when they come to town to trade.

Almost everything in Gallup is located along its main street (alternately Highway 118 and East or West 66 Avenue), a healthy stretch of old *Route 66,* "America's Mother Road," which was stripped of its legendary identity when Interstate 40 homogenized its path in the 1960s. For an overview of Gallup's past, check out the Gallup Historical Society's Rex Museum (505–863–1363) at 300 East 66 Avenue.

Gallup's downtown main strip is lined with its own brand of distinctive pawnshops. Whereas in most cities pawnshops are seen as seedy places of last resort for desperate borrowers, in Gallup this image couldn't be farther from reality. In addition to providing ready markets for Indian wares, Gallup's pawnshops act as financial institutions for many Native Americans. An advanced system of barter and credit has evolved over the years.

Northwestern New Mexico

COLORADO
NEW MEXICO

ARIZONA
NEW MEXICO

Shiprock

San Juan R.

Farmington

Aztec

COLORADO
PLATEAU

SAN JUAN
CO.

MCKINLEY
CO.

Gallup

Grants

+ *Mount
Taylor*

Zuni Pueblo

CIBOLA
CO.

+ *Cebolleta
Peak*

N

0   30 mi

0   30 km

NORTHWESTERN NEW MEXICO

FAVORITE ATTRACTIONS/EVENTS IN NORTHWESTERN NEW MEXICO

El Morro National Monument, near Ramah
(505) 783–4226

La Ventana Natural Arch,
El Malpais National Monument
(505) 240–0300

Zuni–Acoma Trail, Cibola and McKinley Counties
No phone

El Rancho Hotel, Gallup
(505) 863–9311

Mission Church,
Zuni Pueblo
(505) 782–4481

Acoma Pueblo,
Cibola County
(505) 470–4967/
(800) 747–0181

Chaco Canyon, San Juan County *(505) 786–7014*

Shiprock, San Juan County
No phone

Four Corners Monument,
New Mexico, Arizona, Colorado, Utah *No phone*

Inter–Tribal Ceremonial,
August, Gallup
(505) 863–3896

Crownpoint Rug Weavers Auction, third Friday of the month, Crownpoint
(505) 786–5302

The pawnshops are veritable museums of Indian jewelry and other artifacts. Display cases and vaults gleam with turquoise and silver. If you want a good deal on authentic Indian arts and crafts, including jewelry, here's the place to buy. Retailers come from all over to Gallup to buy Indian wares, which they then sell elsewhere—at a sizable markup. A favorite of Native Americans and others since 1918, **Richardson's Trading Post** is perhaps the best place to view the trade, as well as to get a great price from a reputable dealer with a wide selection. Located at 222 West 66 Avenue (505–722–4762), Richardson's is open Monday through Saturday, 9:00 A.M.–6:00 P.M.

East of downtown, the notable **El Rancho Hotel** commands attention from passing motorists. In 1987 the well-known Indian trader Armand Ortega bought the historic property, as it was threatened with demolition. After extensive renovations, the hotel reopened in May 1988.

Originally built in 1937 by the brother of movie mogul D. W. Griffith, the El Rancho became known as a Hollywood hideaway in the 1940s and 1950s. Scores of actors were drawn to Gallup by the many films (mostly Westerns) made in the area. Spencer Tracy, Katharine Hepburn, Humphrey Bogart, Rita Hayworth, and Ronald Reagan all stayed at the hotel. Restored to its former rustic glamour, the hotel's two-story lobby is lined with autographed photos of Hollywood's brightest stars of the era who stayed at the El Rancho.

The El Rancho is located at 1000 East 66 Avenue, (505) 863–9311. Room rates range from $35 for a single in the motel section to $79 for a two-bedroom suite in the original hotel.

Red Rock State Park, minutes from the center of town, is a wonderful place to explore. Red Rock Museum, located in the park, showcases area artifacts from the Ice Age to the present, and rare Indian arts and crafts are also on display. The museum's garden areas identify the plants native to the high mesa region. The park itself, with its exquisite crimson cliffs, is one of New Mexico's top nonforest spots for camping. If you want solitude, however, visit during the week. For good weather without the crowds, plan your stay during early spring or late fall.

Red Rock State Park is off Highway 566 via Highway 118 or Interstate 40, about 10 miles east of Gallup; (505) 722–3839. The museum is open daily from 8:00 A.M. to 6:00 P.M. Memorial Day through Labor Day and Monday through Saturday from 8:00 A.M. to 4:30 P.M. the remainder of the year. Suggested donations are $1.00 for adults and 50 cents for children.

The park hosts the annual *Inter-Tribal Ceremonial* (ITC), held each year since 1922. The ITC includes an all-Indian rodeo, an arts and crafts show, and the ceremonial dances of many tribes throughout the West, from Canada to Mexico. The four-day ITC begins the second Thursday in August and is known as the largest Indian gathering of its kind in the world. The ITC Association can be reached at (505) 863–3896.

Between Gallup and the city of Grants along Interstate 40, you'll find the small community of Thoreau located near the Continental Divide, the demarcation separating streams that flow to opposite sides of North America. (Though possibly named after writer Henry David Thoreau, the name of the town is pronounced "through.") It's south of Thoreau, perched above Bluewater Lake in the foothills of the Zuni Mountains, that you'll find some of the most comfortable accommodations in the region at *Zuni Mountain Lodge.*

Run by innkeepers Dick Morrow and Bob McCuen, Zuni Mountain Lodge offers guests all the natural beauty of a stay in the mountains with all the comforts of home. The lodge's ten large guest rooms, each with its own private bath, are modern and thoughtfully appointed. (There's even a filled candy dish on the dresser!) Two of the guest rooms are located in what's called the "Tree House," a detached building so named because of the piñon trees growing in a corner (and up through the roof!) of each room. In addition, there are communal areas

State Parks in Northwestern New Mexico

Bluewater Lake State Park, 28 miles west of Grants, (505) 876–2391

Navajo Lake State Park, 25 miles east of Bloomfield, (505) 632–2278

On the web at: www.emnrd.state.nm.us/nmparks/

for guests to enjoy, including the Kiva, a comfortably furnished, spacious room complete with cable television and VCR, a video and book library, and various games.

The three-story lodge has magnificent views of Bluewater Lake from the glassed-in wraparound veranda on the upper floors, and the grounds, which include a small orchard and lawn area with a gazebo, are nicely landscaped and also provide views of the lake. Dick and Bob are very knowledgeable about the area's natural environment and history and also welcome the opportunity to direct guests to the scenic hiking and mountain biking trails nearby. As wildlife is abundant, these forest trails are perfect for wilderness enthusiasts and birders alike.

With reservations, and for an additional fee, Zuni Mountain Lodge also provides guided day tours, as well as its popular Western Heritage Tour, a 7-day all-inclusive tour package with day trips to Chaco Canyon, Zuni and Acoma Pueblos, and Arizona's Canyon de Chelly, among other sites.

To get to the lodge, take Exit 53 off of I–40 at Thoreau; turn south onto Highway 612 and go about 13 miles until you come to a ZML sign at Perch Drive. Take a right, and the lodge is about one-fourth mile up the hill at 40 Perch Drive; (505) 862–7616; www.cia-g.com/~zuniml/. Rates range from $55 to $85, which includes a hearty breakfast and, incredibly enough, a delicious dinner to boot.

For those interested in authentic, hand-loomed Navajo rugs, plan your stay at Zuni Mountain Lodge to coincide with an internationally acclaimed local event—the monthly *Crownpoint Rug Weavers Auction*, held the third Friday of every month in the Navajo Nation community of Crownpoint, 25 miles north of Thoreau via Highway 371. Attracting Navajo weavers from around the region and individual and commercial buyers internationally, the auction is more than just a market event—it's also like a small town fair with arts and crafts and Navajo food vendors. Because you're purchasing direct from the source during the auction, most of the rugs sell for less than comparable ones found in local trading posts. Depending on quality and size, rugs may go for as little as $20 or as much as several thousand dollars. Auctions are held in the local elementary school cafeteria; preview starts at 3:00 P.M., with the auction beginning at 7:00 P.M.; (505) 786–5302.

About 38 miles south of Gallup you'll come across *Zuni Pueblo,* New Mexico's largest Indian pueblo, with a population of about 9,000. Zuni's isolation from New Mexico's Rio Grande–situated pueblos makes its history, culture, and language unique.

The Zuni people have occupied the area of the reservation for more than 1,700 years. Their ancestors played an important role in the early recorded history of the Southwest. In search of the Seven Cities of Cibola–the fabled cities of gold–Spanish explorers first discovered Zuni in 1539. Encouraged by persistent rumors (as well as Indian fabrications to persuade the Spaniards to go elsewhere in search of the gold), more explorers, including Coronado, followed but failed to find riches.

The pueblo has several shops where you can purchase Zuni-made arts including stone- and shell-carved fetishes (birds and other animals used since prehistoric times for luck in hunting and fertility in crops) and the turquoise petit point and needlepoint jewelry for which the pueblo is famous. Zuni is located on Highway 53, via Highway 602, about 38 miles south of Gallup.

Tips for Visiting New Mexico's Indian Lands

While visiting New Mexico's pueblo or nonpueblo Indian reservations, keep in mind that they're all sovereign, self-governing nations with their own laws. While almost all pueblos welcome visitors, visitors are expected to observe local rules and etiquette. Here are a few commonsense tips.

If there's a pueblo visitors center, stop there first and register. Many such centers screen films or have museums, which are great ways to orient yourself before visiting pueblo sites. Some pueblos, like Acoma, offer guided tours for a fee.

Photography should always respect people and place. Most pueblos allow photography only by permit, for which a fee must usually be paid. Never photograph dances or ceremonies. These events are traditional, and often religious, ceremonies rather than entertainment. Applause is not appropriate.

Never photograph a person or group without asking first. If permission is given, you may be asked to pay a small fee for the privilege.

Sketching or painting on the pueblos may also be restricted. Check with the pueblo governor's office or visitors center.

Observe quiet and orderly conduct when watching pueblo dances and ceremonies. It's good form to stand toward the back of the crowd, so as not to block the ceremony from pueblo residents or participants.

Never enter a pueblo home, kiva, or building without being invited to do so. However, most pueblo churches are open to visitors without special request.

Never take alcohol onto Indian lands.

Do not hike, bike, or four-wheel across open Indian lands without permission. Contact local authorities for permits and information.

The first place to stop during a visit to Zuni is the temporary location of the *A:shiwi A:wan Museum and Heritage Center*. The center's unusual name comes from the name for the Zuni people in their native language. (Note: Early Spanish explorer in the New Mexico territory gave Spanish names to all of New Mexico's pueblo Indians, which are the common names used today; however, each pueblo has its own unique name in its own language.) While the center's location is deemed temporary, as a larger facility will eventually be built, its present facility and exhibits are certainly impressive. Using an ecomuseum approach—because this approach was determined the most compatible with the Zunis' reverent beliefs toward nature—the center contains historic photographs along with contemporary exhibits to bring alive the history and culture of the Zuni people.

The museum is located adjacent to the Pueblo of Zuni Arts and Crafts Gallery on Highway 53 in Zuni; (505) 782–4403. It's open Monday through Friday, 9:00 A.M. to 5:30 P.M. Call for summer hours, which may include Saturday hours.

In 1629 the Spanish established *Mission Church of Nuestra Señora de Guadalupe* (also known as Our Lady of Guadalupe and the Old Mission) at Zuni. The church was restored in 1970, and internationally known Zuni artist and muralist Alex Seowtewa began painting his colorful murals on the interior of the church walls. Seowtewa's work has drawn some famous admirers to Zuni, among them Jackie Onassis and Mother Teresa. In fact, Ms. Onassis had never visited the American Southwest until the mid-1980s, but she is reported to have been affected deeply by its beauty. She was given a personal tour by former Secretary of the Interior and author Stewart Udall and noted photographer Jerry Jacka. The two were collaborating on a book called *Majestic Journey: Coronado's Inland Empire,* the latest edition of which is dedicated, in memory, to Ms. Onassis. Seowtewa continues work on the murals with the assistance of his son Kenneth and a grant from the National Endowment for the Arts. The church is generally open daily from 9:00 A.M. to 4:00 P.M. during the summer and from 10:00 A.M. to 4:00 P.M. the remainder of the year. Call the tribal offices at (505) 782–4481 for more information or for group tours.

The Inn at Halona offers guests a rare bed-and-breakfast experience, as it's located in the heart of Zuni Pueblo on the south side of the Zuni River at the prehistoric pueblo site of Halona. Operating under special license by the Zuni Tribe, the Inn at Halona is the only such establishment in the pueblo and, as far as I know, in any Indian pueblo. Run by innkeepers Roger Thomas, a native of Chambéry, France, and his wife

Elaine Dodson Thomas, the pueblo–style inn was completely remodeled in 1998. Elaine is the granddaughter of Andrew and Effa Vander Wagen, Dutch immigrants and missionaries who first arrived in Zuni in 1897 and later opened a trading post near Halona Plaza, which is currently also run by the Thomases.

The inn boasts five unique guest rooms on three levels, some with private baths, which are decorated with Zuni and other southwestern art. Each room contains an ongoing "Room Diary," and guests are encouraged to record their thoughts and impressions during their stay. Several comfortable common areas are available for lounging, including a private flagstone patio, which is lit by lamp posts in the evening. Unlike many bed and breakfast inns, guests may select their breakfast from a diverse menu, which includes a European-style continental offering, a traditional, full American breakfast, and such chef specialties as *huevos rancheros* or breakfast burritos.

The Inn at Halona is located three blocks south from Highway 53, at 23B Pia Mesa Road; (505) 782–4547/800–752–3278. Rates range from $79 to $99, and may vary depending on the season and length of stay. Group rates are also available.

Solamente en Nuevo México . . . Zuni Pueblo's Shalako

*A*ll of New Mexico's Indian pueblos conduct annual ceremonials and feast days—some open to the public and some not—to honor or celebrate certain events or deities. One of the more dramatic is the Shalako Ceremonial at Zuni Pueblo, which is held in late November or early December. As one of the most important events in the Zuni religious calendar, Shalako celebrates the end of the current year and the beginning of the new.

During the ceremony six men impersonate Shalakos, or divine beings, by wearing wood-framed, 10-foot-tall costumes covered with colorfully designed fabrics and topped with masks of Shalakos. The ceremony, which begins with the ritual crossing of the Zuni River, winds through the pueblo's streets as the Shalako performers dance throughout the night and bless the houses that were built during the year. A ritual footrace is conducted the next day, during which participants plant offering sticks in the ground to bring health and fertility to the pueblo.

Because of past instances of disrespect shown by outsiders during Shalako, the event is not necessarily open to the public every year. (Call 505–782–4481 or 505–782–4403 for current Shalako information.) For a dramatic, fictionalized Shalako scene, read Tony Hillerman's Dance Hall of the Dead, a murder mystery set on and around the Zuni Reservation.

Though there have been controversial reintroduction efforts of the endangered Mexican wolf, or *lobo*—limited numbers of which live only in captivity—into the wilderness areas of southeastern Arizona and southwestern New Mexico, most have not survived. The efforts are applauded by environmentalists as loudly as they're cursed by area ranchers. Politics nothwithstanding, the best way to begin to experience the untamed majesty of wolves is with a visit to **Candy Kitchen Rescue Ranch**, south of Ramah.

Founded in 1991 by artist Jacque Evans, Candy Kitchen Rescue Ranch is a nonprofit organization providing sanctuary to abused and abandoned captive-bred wolves and wolf dogs. Its unlikely name comes from the fact that the refuge is located at an old ranch headquarters of the same name. Some of the ranch buildings served as headquarters for the Candy Kitchen Ranch, where piñon nut candy was made during the 1920s and 1930s. During prohibition, it's rumored that liquor was distilled here, with the piñon candy serving as a front for the large amounts of sugar used to make the illegal moonshine.

Visitors may take advantage of guided tours of the ranch and visit its noble residents, which by necessity are kept in pens; however, to the extent possible, the animals are kept in compatible pairs or small groups. With a focus on education, ecology, and the responsible ownership of wolf dogs, the ranch currently cares for sixty-four wolves and wolf-dogs, with the hope that rescue organizations will someday no longer be needed.

To get to Candy Kitchen, turn south on Highway 125 off Highway 53 (2½ miles west of El Morro National Monument or about 8 miles east of Ramah). Go 8 miles (about halfway, you'll pass through Mountain View); then turn west on Highway 120 and go 4 miles; (505) 775-3304. Visiting hours are Tuesday through Sunday, 11:00 A.M. to 5:00 P.M. in the summer and 11:00 A.M. to 4:00 P.M. the remainder of the year. Tours are given at 11:00 A.M., 1:00 and 3:00 P.M.

Back in the small community of Ramah, check out the **Ramah Museum**, located just off Highway 53 in downtown Ramah. Housed in the Joseph A. B. Bond House, circa 1905, the museum focuses on pioneer Americana and the history of the village, from its earliest days as a Mormon settlement. Hours vary, but you're more likely to find it open during the summer months; no phone.

Across Highway 53, you'll find the **Stagecoach Café** (505–783–4288), just about the only place to eat in the area. Serving New Mexican and American favorites, the Stagecoach is open Monday through Saturday, 8:00 A.M. to 9:00 P.M.

Enchanted Mesa

Cibola County

coma Pueblo, or "Sky City," as it's sometimes called, is the oldest continuously inhabited community in the United States; archaeologists have traced the pueblo's occupation to 1150. But it wasn't until 1540 that the Spanish explorer Coronado became the first non-Indian to enter Acoma, and outsiders have been fascinated with Sky City ever since.

The pueblo, located on a 367-foot mesa on the Acoma Indian Reservation outside Grants, operates a visitor center that includes a museum and gift shops at the base of the mesa. Guided tours of Acoma—the only way outsiders can view the pueblo—are offered hourly from the visitor center every day, with the exception of three private ceremonial periods. Small buses provide transportation to the top of the mesa, and from there an Acoma guide will point out the various elements of the pueblo while filling you in on Acoma's long and colorful history. The mesa-top pueblo provides stunning views of the surrounding area, including the spectacular 400-foot-tall *Enchanted Mesa,* said to be the home of the ancestral Acomas.

The singularly most impressive structure in the pueblo is Mission San Esteban Del Rey, a church completed in 1640 after eleven years of intense labor by Acoma residents. The massive roof beams were carried from the forests of Mount Taylor 40 miles away—without ever touching the logs to the ground, according to Acoma legend. The church, whose adobe walls are 7 to 9 feet thick, has no windows, because it was used as a fortress.

Even though the pueblo has no electricity or running water, about twelve families live here; most Acoma Pueblo Indians, however, live in communities nearby. Some of the pueblo residents sell their world-famous, intricately designed pottery during tours, and often you can purchase bread baked in the beehive-shaped *hornos,* or adobe ovens, that dot the pueblo. The tour guide will also point out and explain the use of kivas, or sacred ceremonial chambers; note, though, that entrance to kivas is strictly prohibited for visitors.

To get to the visitor center from Grants, head east on Interstate 40, take exit 96, and follow the signs to the visitor center; (505) 470–4967/(800) 747–0181. From Albuquerque, head west on Interstate 40 (about 55 miles), take exit 108, and do the same. Tours are held as follows: fall and winter, 8:00 A.M.–4:00 P.M.; spring, 8:00 A.M.–6:00 P.M.; and summer, 8:00 A.M.–7:00 P.M. Each year tours cease during Easter weekend (it varies, call ahead), June 24 and 29, July 10–13, July 25, and either the first or second weekend in October (it varies). (*Note:* The pueblo may be closed to the public during other times of the year without much

Ladders at Acoma Pueblo

advance notice, so call ahead before you venture out.) Tour admission is $8.00 for adults, $7.00 for senior citizens, and $6.00 for children over the age of five. Camera and sketching fees apply, and there are photographic restrictions. There's no admission fee for the visitor center and museum, however.

The *Shrine of Los Portales* lies in a hidden grotto near the old Spanish land-grant village of Syboyeta (sometimes spelled Cebolleta on maps), north of Laguna Pueblo and east of the city of Grants. A statue of St. Bernadette of Lourdes is the focal point of the beautiful, mysterious shrine.

Brought from Spain, the original statue for the shrine, *Our Lady of Sorrows,* is now protected in the mission church of the same name in Syboyeta. The legend goes that during one of the last Navajo raids in the 1800s, the women and children took refuge in the natural fortress while the men were away. The women vowed that if their husbands and sons returned safely, the women would build a shrine to the Virgin Mary at which to hold an annual mass.

The shallow cave or overhang of the rounded cliff that forms the large semicircular enclave is perfect for meditation or prayer, as evidenced by the many melted candles that can be seen at the shrine. Weather-worn wooden pews face the shrine at an angle. Spring water, considered holy, seeps from the cliff and collects in several small pools. Because of the abundance of moisture, this protected area is unusually green and forms a small oasis that contrasts with the barren land of the surrounding region.

Syboyeta is on Highway 279, off Highway 124, which connects to Interstate 40 near Laguna Pueblo. To get to the shrine, proceed on the main road to Our Lady of Sorrows church at the center of town. Continue winding around the church as the paved road turns to dirt. After 1–10 mile, turn left and continue for 1 mile until you see a very large tree with exposed roots around its base; the approximately 100-yard trail to the shrine begins here. (*Note:* If there's been a lot of rain, do not attempt this trek unless you have a four-wheel-drive vehicle.)

Heading west on Interstate 40 you'll soon be in Grants, the largest town and county seat of Cibola County. Grants's past as a classic Route 66 town is preserved with 1950s-era motels, shops, and cafes along the main strip, now called Santa Fe Avenue. Just off Santa Fe Avenue you'll find the *New Mexico Museum of Mining* at 100 Iron Street (505–287–4802)—though it was uranium, not iron, that put Grants on the map. The first floor of the museum traces the history of uranium mining in the area from 1950, the year Paddy Martinez, an Indian laborer and occasional prospector, discovered a mother lode of the dusty yellow rock.

The best part of the museum is the underground portion called Section 26, an eerily accurate reproduction of a working uranium mine. You start by taking an elevator down the mine "shaft." Although you don't travel very far, it feels as though you're hundreds of feet below the earth's surface. The tour uses hand-held listening devices that explain the exhibits at scheduled stops. Adding to the realism are artifacts from working mines that fill the space—right down to the tool company "girlie calendar" in the miners' lunchroom.

From May 1 through September 30, the New Mexico Museum of Mining is open Monday through Saturday, 9:00 A.M.–5:00 P.M., and Sunday, 9:00 A.M. to 4:00 P.M. The remainder of the year hours are Monday through Saturday, 9:00 A.M.–5:00 P.M. Admission is $3.00, seniors and children 7–18 $2.00, and children under seven free.

Highway 53, which connects Grants with Zuni Pueblo (see McKinley County entry on page 29), is the most scenic drive in northwestern New Mexico—and you'll find a few interesting stops along the way.

The recently designated *El Malpais National Monument and Conservation Area* encompasses more than 590 square miles of lava flows and caves, volcanos, sandstone canyons, and forests centered between Highway 53 and Highway 117 south of Grants. Although some of the natural sites are accessible to passenger cars traveling along the two highways, El Malpais (roughly "The Badlands" in Spanish) is heaven to hikers and backpackers.

After several years with only minimal development, the monument and conservation area now have two remote sites where visitors may get information and maps. You'll find a U.S. Park Service visitor center (505–783–4774) about 23 miles south of Grants on Highway 53, as well as a U.S. Bureau of Land Management ranger station (505–240–0300) on Highway 117. In addition, you may still visit the U.S. Park Service office in Grants at 201 Roosevelt (505–285–4641) for information on El Malpais.

Among the sites accessible along Highway 117 are the Sandstone Bluffs Overlook (10 miles from Interstate 40), *La Ventana Natural Arch* (17 miles south of Interstate 40), and The Narrows (1 mile farther south), where the highway passes through a narrow corridor created when lava flowed near the base of huge sandstone cliffs. You'll see intriguing lava formations in this area. If you were farsighted enough to pack a picnic, you'll find great spots for lunch at the south end of The Narrows, as well as underneath La Ventana.

One of the more accessible hiking adventures in El Malpais can be had in *Junction Cave* in the El Calderón Area of the monument, 20 miles south of Grants on Highway 53. A well-marked trail from the parking area leads to the cave entrance. Though not really a cave, but rather a 3,000-foot-long lava tube, Junction Cave provides hikers with a relatively safe and easy spelunking experience. Plan on bringing good shoes with gripping soles, long pants to protect your legs against the sharp lava if you stumble, and more than one quality flashlight. At times, you may notice bats clinging to the cave's wall; however, don't disturb them, as they're harmless. Another trail from the El Calderón parking lot leads you past interesting sinkholes to Bat Cave, which is closed off to humans; however, it's a great area from which to enjoy a dramatic New Mexico sunset and watch the bats emerge at dusk.

Negotiating with private property owners for the sale of parts of El Malpais has been quite a process, and some agreements have yet to be finalized. As a result, two of the most interesting and accessible features of El Malpais are still privately owned, but you can visit them.

The *Candelaria Ice Cave and Bandera Crater* are located in a parklike setting covered with ponderosa pine, spruce, and piñon trees. You start your trek at the trading post on the property, which was once a summer resort complete with cabins. After paying the fee, you hike $1/2$ mile alongside lava flows until you reach a wooden stairway. The steps lead to Candelaria Ice Cave (named for the present owners of the property), located in part of a collapsed lava tube where the temperature never rises above thirty-one degrees. Though walking into the cave is prohibited (liability, you know), and this is slightly disappointing, you can get a good view of the greenish ice from the viewing platform.

To see Bandera Crater, brace yourself for a longer and steeper hike—about $1^1/2$ miles. The 1,000-foot-deep crater was formed during a volcanic eruption 5,000 years ago. Nature has since transformed the crater into a beautiful spot flecked with hardy ponderosa pines. The breezy coolness of the 8,000-foot altitude makes the ridge of the crater a nice place to relax on a hot summer day.

The entrance to the Candelaria Ice Cave and Bandera Crater is located a little less than 26 miles south of Grants on Highway 53; (505) 783–4303 or (888) ICE-CAVE; www.icecaves.com. Hours are 8:00 A.M. to about an hour before sunset, and admission is $7.00 for adults and teenagers and $3.50 for children with those under five admitted free. But remember, both the ice cave and the crater are slated to become part of El Malpais and thus will be administered by the National Park Service (though this has been dragging out for years, so don't hold your breath); accordingly, check at the El Malpais Information Center in Grants before planning a trip.

El Morro National Monument is the nation's oldest national monument. Also known as Inscription Rock, the monument is an oasis in the middle of nowhere; nevertheless, travelers have been stopping here for centuries to drink from the pool of water at the base of the cliff—and to leave behind a little graffiti. A sporadic account of southwestern history from 1605 through the nineteenth century is recorded on what Spanish conquistadores named El Morro, meaning "The Bluff." The inscriptions etched into the vertical stone surface provide a permanent record of the different cultures that influenced the area over the past 400 years. Fifteen years before the Pilgrims landed at Plymouth Rock, the first Spanish inscription was made by explorer Don Juan de Oñate on April 16, 1605, extolling his discovery of the "Sea of the South," now known as the Gulf of California.

Touching the inscriptions or defacing any surface is strictly forbidden. For those who just can't resist the urge to write in stone after viewing El Morro, however, the visitor center provides a rock near the parking area on which travelers may etch a word or two.

Much earlier visitors to El Morro left their own graffiti in the form of petroglyphs, or ancient rock drawings. You'll find ruins of ancient pueblos here as well. Dating from the thirteenth century, these have been traced to certain Anasazi peoples (the ancestors of the Zuni Indians) and can be found, largely unexcavated, on the top of El Morro.

You can stay here if you wish, at the monument's nine-site, primitive campground.

El Morro is located just off Highway 53, 43 miles from Grants; (505) 783-4226. Admission is $2.00 per person, with a maximum charge of $4.00 per carload; children under seventeen and seniors are admitted free. Use of the campground is free, except during summer, and is on a first-come, first-served basis; water is available May through October. Daily hours are 9:00 A.M.–7:00 P.M. from Memorial Day through Labor Day and 9:00 A.M.–5:00 P.M. the remainder of the year. (Times are for visitor center; trails close one hour earlier.)

San Juan County

Similar to Gallup's role in McKinley County, Farmington serves as the major trading center in San Juan County for the Navajo Nation just west of the city. Though Farmington is near the center of the vast, dry Four Corners (more about this later) region, the city is a virtual oasis and a fisherman's paradise with its three rivers flowing around town—the San Juan, the Animas, and the La Plata. San Juan County is also a great place to get in touch with New Mexico's past by visiting its three significant Anasazi ruins sites.

Chaco Culture National Historical Park (Chaco Canyon, for short) contains the finest example of Anasazi pueblo ruins in New Mexico. It may be the singularly most remote tourist attraction in the state, yet people from all over the world find it every year.

Chaco Canyon emerged as the center of Anasazi life in the early tenth century. (The Navajo word *Anasazi,* meaning "enemies of our ancestors," is the name scientists gave to prehistoric farming peoples of the Four Corners region. They are the ancestors of the present-day Pueblo Indians of New Mexico.) Partly because primitive roads connected Chaco Canyon with outlying Anasazi communities, archaeologists believe Chaco was the "capital" of the Anasazi world. In many ways—in their architecture, community life, and social organization—the Anasazi of Chaco Canyon were far more advanced than any other of the Anasazi peoples of the region.

New Mexico Trivia:

Four Corners Monument is the only place in the United States where you can be in four states at once: New Mexico, Arizona, Colorado, and Utah.

Though Chaco Canyon has been intensely studied for more than a hundred years and scholars theorize about the people who once lived here, many mysteries remain. One of the most intriguing aspects of Chacoan life is the possible connection with the great civilizations of Mexico, such as the ancient Toltecs. Feathers of macaws and other parrots, copper bells, and seashells, all unknown in this area but common in parts of Mexico, have been found in Chaco Canyon. There are also fascinating connections between architecture and astronomy in the remains of the pueblos in the canyon.

The Anasazi's belief that Chaco Canyon was the center of the earth is a powerful one, and the fact that as many as 5,000 people once lived here in a highly civilized society and then mysteriously disappeared is centermost to the lure of the canyon and its ruins. Although rainfall was adequate during the time the Anasazi inhabited Chaco Canyon, persistent droughts are thought to be the reason they finally abandoned the canyon between 1130 and 1180.

To fully experience the park, set aside an entire day for your visit. Otherwise, a stop at the visitor center and a hike around Pueblo Bonito, the largest and most impressive ruin in the canyon, will provide a good overview of the Chaco mystique. Well-marked trails (keyed in a trail guide to selected stops) lead through the maze of chambers.

The park's visitor center has a fine museum and many books on Chaco culture. It's also the only place in the park with water available. The canyon consists of extremely barren, arid land—especially in the summer—so it's smart to bring your own water supply.

Although there are two main routes to Chaco Canyon—neither paved—the best approach is to turn off Highway 44 onto San Juan County Road 7800 at the outpost community of Nageezi, proceed 11

A Glimpse of Northwestern New Mexico: *Impresiones de la Frontera . . .*

For some, it's the austerity of southeastern New Mexico that gets their blood flowing; for others, it's the preserved historic and natural beauty of Santa Fe and Taos; and for still others, it's the timeless grasslands of the northeastern plains. But for me, it's the Zuni Mountains of northwestern New Mexico. The grandeur of the area's natural landscape initially captured my heart when I was researching the first edition of this book back in 1989. But it was the region's lack of populace and overt mainstream culture that has since captured my soul. The stark redrock formations and the endless vistas always provide me a sense of wonder, and the peaceful beauty of the gentle mountains and the solitude that comes with isolation continue to entrance me. It remains my place of dreams.

The Western frontier has always beckoned pioneers, and living most of the time in Albuquerque—as one-third of the state's population does—I often feel its pull at sunset. Along with the sun's luminescent rays, the West spills away from Albuquerque behind a flat mesa dotted with five dormant volcanoes and high-desert scrub. If you head out of town at this time, the highway will climb that mesa for about 10 miles, following the sun, until finally the city disappears behind you. As you chase the sun, watching its rich colors fade into the night-blue sky, a feeling of freedom and exhilaration intoxicates you. There is nothing in your way. You are leaving the gateway and treading onto New Mexico's frontera, where solitude and adventure are at once always possible.

miles to Highway 57, and continue on Highway 57 for 15 miles to the visitor center. These are 26 miles of washboard-type dirt and gravel roads. Though passenger cars are usually adequate, the roads can be impassable during or after substantial rainfall; accordingly, call ahead to check road conditions. Once you get to the federally maintained park, however, the roads are perfectly paved; (505) 786–7014. Admission is $8.00 per vehicle or $4.00 per person for groups and singles. The park is open daily Memorial Day–Labor Day, 8:00 A.M.–6:00 P.M. The remainder of the year it's open 8:00 A.M.–5:00 P.M.

For those who are intrigued by Anasazi ruins but aren't up to a trek to Chaco Canyon, two other sites are closer to Farmington: Aztec Ruins National Monument and Salmon Ruin. Both are easily accessible on paved roads.

The first thing you'll notice about **Aztec Ruins National Monument**— especially if you visited Chaco Canyon first—is the abundance of trees and a nearby river. Despite the name, these ruins had nothing to do with the Aztec Indians of central Mexico. In fact, the Aztecs lived hundreds of years after this Anasazi pueblo was abandoned. Early Anglo settlers named the site Aztec because they mistakenly believed the Mexican Indians had built the pueblos.

The monument's amazing number of ruins concentrated in a small area make things convenient for visitors. The site of these ruins contains the only fully restored Great Kiva, an especially sacred ceremonial chamber, in North America. A walk through the kiva is definitely the highlight of the visit.

The visitor center of Aztec Ruins is northwest of the city of Aztec (northeast of Farmington), near the junction of U.S. Highway 550 and Highway 44; (505) 334–6174. The monument is open daily from 8:00 A.M. to 6:00 P.M. Memorial Day through Labor Day and from 8:00 A.M. to 5:00 P.M. the remainder of the year. Admission is $4.00 per person, with those under seventeen admitted free.

Salmon Ruin, a Chacoan pueblo village once connected to Chaco Canyon by a prehistoric road, is the other major Anasazi ruin area in San Juan County. Though unique itself and the site of the San Juan Archaeological Research Center and Library, this smaller site, if you're "ruined out," may be the one to skip.

Salmon Ruin is on U.S. Highway 64, 2 miles west of the community of Bloomfield; (505) 632–2013. Hours are 9:00 A.M.–5:00 P.M. daily, (winter hours, December–March, on Sunday are 12 noon–5 P.M.), and admission is $3.00 for adults, $1.00 for children ages six to sixteen, $2.00 for seniors, and free for children under six.

Each summer the city of Farmington hosts the historical drama *Black River Traders* at the Lions Wilderness Park Amphitheater. Although times and dates change from year to year, performances usually run from about late June to mid-August. Call the Farmington Convention & Visitors Bureau (505–326–7602 or 800– 448–1240) for details.

For an otherworldly experience in northwestern New Mexico, plan a visit to the **Bisti Wilderness,** commonly known as the Bisti Badlands, south of Farmington. The almost 4,000-acre wilderness is a barren landscape of steeply eroded badlands topography, featuring unusual rock spires called "hoodoos." The area's desolate present belies its ancient past as a lush swamplands roamed by dinosaurs and other life forms millions of years ago. Time and the natural elements have etched

---

La Comida de Nuevo México

*G*reen Chile Stew

Green chile stew is New Mexico's wintertime equivalent to chicken soup for the rest of the country—good for what ails you. Flavorful and satisfying, this dish is made in most homes and available in most restaurants serving New Mexican food. In my home, we prepare it without meat, and add fresh corn— muy sabroso!

2 pounds pork or beef, cubed

1 small can tomatoes

3 medium potatoes, peeled and cubed

¼ cup flour

6 cups water

2 tablespoons shortening or corn oil

3 cloves garlic, minced

2 medium onions, chopped

2 cups chopped green chile (more or less, according to taste)

2 teaspoons salt

1 teaspoon ground cumin

Makes 6–8 servings

1. Dredge the meat in flour. Place the shortening in a heavy skillet and brown meat at medium heat. Place meat in a large stewing pot.

2. Sauté the onions and garlic in the remaining shortening and add to stewing pot.

3. Add all remaining ingredients to stewing pot and simmer at low heat for 1 hour. Serve hot with plenty of warm flour tortillas.

out a fantasy world moonscape of strange rock formations and fossils, creating an ever-changing environment.

An easy way to experience the Bisti is to take a leisurely day hike by following the Gateway Wash from the undeveloped parking lot into the heart of the badlands. Because there are no developed trails or signs inhibiting your wilderness experience, take extra care to avoid getting lost. Because this is a primitive wilderness area, there are no services, so plan accordingly and bring lots of drinking water, as this area can get quite hot during summer. The Bisti is a great place not only for hiking, but also for photography and primitive camping, especially on full-moon nights.

Besides the natural landscape, you may also find the fossilized remains (isolated teeth and bones) of the various life-forms that once lived here: fish, turtles, lizards, mammals, and dinosaurs. However, federal law prohibits the collection of vertebrate fossils and petrified wood. Any collection interferes with scientific research and eliminates the opportunity for others to view and to photograph these unusual wilderness features. Also, climbing on rock formations is dangerous, and prohibited, as it accelerates erosion and destroys the scenic value of the area.

To get to the Bisti Wilderness from Farmington, head south on Highway 371 for about 30 miles and then exit left for 6 miles on a gravel road that will take you past the old Bisti Trading Post to an undeveloped parking area and access to the wilderness. The area can also be approached from Crownpoint, by traveling north on Highway 371 for about 46 miles and following the same gravel road described above. Travel on the gravel road is good during dry conditions but the road can get slippery and rutted during the rainy season, normally in spring and late summer. There's no phone, but for more information, you may contact the U.S. Bureau of Land Management in Farmington at (505) 327–5344, or the Farmington Convention and Visitors Bureau at (505) 316–7602/ 800–448–1240.

If you've been inspired by the ancient Anasazi cliff dwellings at nearby Mesa Verde National Monument in southwestern Colorado, are in excellent physical condition, and are looking for adventure, then look no further than *Kokopelli's Cave Bed & Breakfast* north of Farmington—the only such establishment I know of that requires guests to sign a waiver of liability for potential accidents.

The brainchild of Farmington geologist Bruce Black, Kokopelli's Cave was blasted out of a 65-million-year-old sandstone formation 280 feet above the La Plata River, but unlike the ancient cliff dwellings of the

Southwest, this cave is actually 70 feet below the surface of the cliff, accessible by a series of trails, paths, and steps. If you're willing and able to make the climb, you'll be rewarded by views of four states and several mountain ranges. And, despite its remoteness and accessibility challenges, Kokopelli's is pure luxury once you actually make it down into the cave, boasting all the comforts of home plus a cascading "waterfall" shower and a flagstone hot tub.

In lieu of being served breakfast, you'll find the refrigerator and cabinets well stocked with breakfast fixings, including fresh fruit. And

Talking Turkey about Turquoise

I spoke with Sue Carlson of Richardson's Trading Company in Gallup, one of the area's oldest and most reputable pawnbrokers, as well as with my friend and Native American artisan Jo Ann Valencia of Santa Fe, to demystify that most classic of Southwestern jewelry gemstones, turquoise. After a sprinkling of media reports on the proliferation of domestic and Asian–imported knockoffs, some buyers have become more aware of the differing quality, and in some cases, the authenticity, of Southwestern jewelry. I've learned that there are various types of "turquoise," from the real deal—gem–quality stone—right on down to the most insidious fake: plastic. It's important to work with a reputable dealer, Carlson notes, because some of the fake stuff is pretty difficult to recognize.

Because turquoise is porous, it absorbs body oils and fumes from the air, and can change color, usually becoming greener, with years of wearing. Gem–quality turquoise, which ranges in color from pale blue to bright blue, is less porous and therefore less subject to changes in color. Here's the breakdown:*

Natural turquoise: *not treated in any way.*

Stabilized turquoise: *chemically hardened with a polymer of liquid resin or plastic, but its color has not been changed.** Stabilized turquoise is frequently used in Southwestern jewelry because it resists chipping or breaking easily while it's being worked.*

Treated turquoise: *altered to produce a change in color of the natural stone, usually detectable by a shiny, unnatural color.*

Reconstituted or composite turquoise: *turquoise particles and dust, which have been combined with plastic resins and solidly compressed to resemble natural turquoise.*

As for the brown or black webbing seen on most turquoise, it's referred to as the "matrix" of a stone and is formed by mineral deposits. Its presence does not necessarily increase or diminish the quality of the stone.

*Information source: Turquoise— Gem of the Centuries, *by O. T. Branson*

**As defined by the federal Indian Arts and Crafts Sales Act of 1978.

remember, pack light, because there are no elevators! Because even getting to the cave's trailhead is complicated, guests are asked to meet their hosts at their home in Farmington to be escorted out to the site. This way you won't get lost, and you'll also get a personal rundown on the systems in the cave, so you'll know how to work them; (505) 325–7855; www.bbonline.com/nm/kokopelli/. Rates are $175 for up to two people; $210 for three to four people; with an additional $35 per individual over four persons, and may vary seasonally.

New Mexico Trivia:

A sampling of movie stars who once stayed at Gallup's historic El Rancho Hotel: John Wayne, Spencer Tracy, Katharine Hepburn, Humphrey Bogart, Gregory Peck, Barbara Stanwyck, Errol Flynn, Kirk Douglas, Rita Hayworth, and Ronald Reagan.

The *Hogback Trading Post,* on the edge of the Navajo Reservation, is *the* place to purchase authentic Navajo arts and crafts in San Juan County. Established in 1871, the Hogback is the oldest trading post—on or off the reservation—serving the Navajos. (The better-known Hubbell Trading Post at Monument Valley wasn't established until 1876.) The Hogback is now run by Tom Wheeler, the great-grandson of the trading post's founder, Joseph Wheeler. The trading post contains almost 10,000 feet of display space in two levels and specializes in fine Navajo-woven rugs. It's located 15 miles west of Farmington on U.S. Highway 64 in the community of Waterflow. The Hogback is open Monday through Saturday, 8:00 A.M.–5:00 P.M.

Another interesting trading post nearby is *Big Rock Trading Post,* also in Waterflow, 12 miles west of Farmington on Highway 64. You'll likely first notice Big Rock by seeing its sign on a large, white propane tank out front. Run by father and son Chuck and Charlie Dickens, the Big Rock serves not only as a trading post and a pawnshop (filled with authentic Native American jewelry for sale) but also as something of an Old West cowboy and Indian museum—complete with a saddle collection along with other southwestern artifacts. Big Rock is open Monday through Friday, 8:00 A.M.–5:30 P.M., and Saturday 9:00 A.M. to 5:30 P.M.; (505) 598–5184.

One of the most memorable places to visit, purely for its I-stood-on-the-spot value, is the *Four Corners Monument,* northwest of Farmington. The absolute barrenness of the area is remarkable. But you can stand on the spot—the only such spot in the United States—where you will truly be in four states at once: New Mexico, Arizona, Utah, and Colorado. It's amazing how far people will travel out of their way to visit a spot that would otherwise hold no appeal whatsoever. Still, it *is* a kick.

To get to Four Corners Monument, take U.S. Highway 64 west of Farmington until it meets with U.S. Highway 160 at Teec Nos Pos. (You're now in Arizona.) Then take U.S. Highway 160 north until it meets with Highway 597. (You're back in New Mexico.) Go left on Highway 597 to the monument. It's always open, and there's no admission charge.

On the way to Four Corners Monument from Farmington—along Highway 64, west of the largest Navajo Nation town of *Shiprock*—you'll pass within viewing distance one of the most majestic and mysterious rock formations in New Mexico: Shiprock. The 1,700-foot peak gets its name from its shape, which, at a distance, resembles a two-masted ship sailing on a sea of desert. Though Shiprock changes its appearance at different times of the day, it's said that it looks most like a ship during a midsummer sunset, occasionally appearing to shimmer and drift on an imaginary ocean. Navajos refer to the immense formation as *Tse Bi dahi*, which means "The Rock with Wings," and several of their folk myths contain references to it. (No one believes me, but I swear Shiprock switches positions across the horizon as you drive by it.)

Back to civilization, a leisurely walking tour of the Aztec Historic District in downtown Aztec offers a great change of pace. Centering on the *Aztec Museum,* more than seventy-five business and residential buildings, including shops and restaurants, are listed on the National Register of Historic Places. The museum houses a fine collection of early pioneer Americana, plus an old wooden oil drilling rig—a tribute to the lucrative oil-and-gas industry in San Juan County. The museum is at 125 North Main Avenue, (505) 334–9829. Summer hours are 9:00 A.M.–5:00 P.M. from Monday through Saturday; winter hours are 10:00 A.M.–4:00 P.M. from Monday through Saturday. There's no admission charge.

WHERE TO STAY IN NORTHWESTERN NEW MEXICO

MCKINLEY COUNTY
El Rancho Hotel,
1000 East 66 Avenue,
Gallup,
(505) 863–9311.

Holiday Inn,
2915 West Highway 66,
Gallup,
(505) 722–2201.

Best Western Inn
and Suites,
3009 West Highway 66,
Gallup,
(505) 722–2221.

CIBOLA COUNTY
Holiday Inn Express,
1496 East Santa Fe Avenue,
Grants,
(505) 285–4676.

Best Western Inn
and Suites,
1501 East Santa Fe Avenue,
Grants,
(505) 287–7901/(800)
600–5221.

Sands Motel,
112 McArthur Drive,
Grants,
(505) 287–2996/(800)
424–7679.

SAN JUAN COUNTY
Anasazi Inn,
903 West Main,
Farmington,
(505) 325–4564.

Best Western Inn & Suites,
700 Scott Avenue,
Farmington,
(505) 327–5221.

Holiday Inn of Farmington,
600 East Broadway,
Farmington,
(505) 327–9811.

Silver River Adobe Inn
Bed & Breakfast,
3151 West Main,
Farmington. (505)
325–8219/(800) 382–9251.

Stepback Inn,
103 West Aztec Avenue,
Aztec,
(505) 334–1200.

**WHERE TO EAT IN
NORTHWESTERN
NEW MEXICO**

MCKINLEY COUNTY
El Rancho,
1003 East Highway 66,
Gallup,
(505) 863–9311. Inexpensive to moderate. Fare:
Traditional New Mexican.

The Ranch Kitchen,
3001 West Highway 66,
Gallup,
(505) 722–2537. Inexpensive to moderate. Fare:
Steaks, barbecue.

The Butcher Shop,
2003 East Highway 66,
Gallup,
(505) 722–4711. Inexpensive to moderate. Fare:
Steaks, chops, chicken, etc.

Earl's Family Restaurant,
1400 East Highway 66,
Gallup,
(505) 863–4201. Inexpensive to moderate. Fare: New
Mexican and American.

CIBOLA COUNTY
El Ranchero Cafe,
613 West Highway 66,
Milan,
(505) 876–1032. Inexpensive to moderate. Fare: New
Mexican.

Mi Casita en la Frontera,
601 West Highway 66,
Milan,
(505) 285–4238. Inexpensive to moderate. Fare: New
Mexican.

Monte Carlo Restaurant,
721 West Santa Fe,
Grants,
(505) 287–9250. Inexpensive to moderate. Fare:
New Mexican.

Sirloin Stockade,
1140 East Santa Fe Avenue,
Grants,
(505) 287–2384. Inexpensive to moderate. Fare:
Steaks and seafood.

Selected Chambers of Commerce/Visitors Bureaus in Northwestern New Mexico

Aztec Chamber of Commerce
203 North Main Street
Aztec, 87410
(505) 334–9551

Farmington Convention and Visitors Bureau
203 West Main, Suite 401
Farmington, 87401
(505) 326–7602/1, (800) 448–1240
Web site: www.farmingtonnm.org

Gallup Convention & Visitors Bureau
P.O. Box 600
Gallup, 87305
(505) 863–3841, (800) 242–4282
Web site: www.gallupnm.org

Grants/Cibola County Chamber of Commerce:
P.O. Box 297
Grants, 87020
(505) 287–4802, (800) 748–2142
Web site: www.grants.org

SAN JUAN COUNTY
La Fiesta Grande
Restaurant,
1916 East Main SE,
Farmington,
(505) 397–1235.
Inexpensive to moderate.
Fare: New Mexican.

Los Hermanitos
Restaurant,
3501 East Main,
Farmington,
(505) 326–5664.
Inexpensive to moderate.
Fare: New Mexican.

Riverwalk Patio & Grille,
700 Scott Avenue,
Farmington,
(505) 327–5221.
Inexpensive to moderate.
Fare: Eclectic American.

The Spare Rib
BBQ Company,
1700 East Main Street,
Farmington,
(505) 325–4800. Inexpensive to moderate. Fare: Barbecue, etc.

Rocky Mountain Rib Co.,
525 East Broadway,
Farmington,
(505) 327–7422.
Inexpensive to moderate.
Fare: Barbeque, etc.

North Central New Mexico

North central New Mexico is a land of Indian pueblos, forested mountains, hidden hot springs, and magnificent rock formations. The region's beauty so inspired artist Georgia O'Keeffe that she made her home here. In contrast, this region also witnessed the production of the world's first atom bomb.

You'll detect a strong tradition of Hispanic culture and pride in north central New Mexico. The first Spanish colony in the territory was established here and some of the state's oldest Hispanic communities continue to thrive in this region. The Hispanic influence lives on in the old Catholic churches, the centuries-old adobe homes, and the high regard for family and quiet respect for cultural traditions.

As you set out to explore the intrigue of north central New Mexico, keep in mind that once the sun goes down—even during the summer—it's very cool.

Rio Arriba County

Although situated in one of the most economically depressed areas of the state, Rio Arriba County offers the intrepid traveler a host of adventures. As a bridge between the often stark landscape of the Four Corners region to its west and the forested, mountainous region to its east, Rio Arriba County is certainly a blending of the two.

In southern Rio Arriba County you'll find the city of Española (partly located in Santa Fe County). Lying near the site of the first Spanish settlement in New Mexico, designated San Juan de los Caballeros in 1598 by Spanish explorer Don Juan de Oñate, Española is a good place to fuel up and start exploring the county.

Just outside Española lies **Santa Clara Pueblo.** The pueblo itself, like most of New Mexico's Rio Grande–area pueblos, is similar to a small rural town and is centered on a mission church and plaza area. Santa Clara is famous for its solid-black pottery, which is prized by collectors.

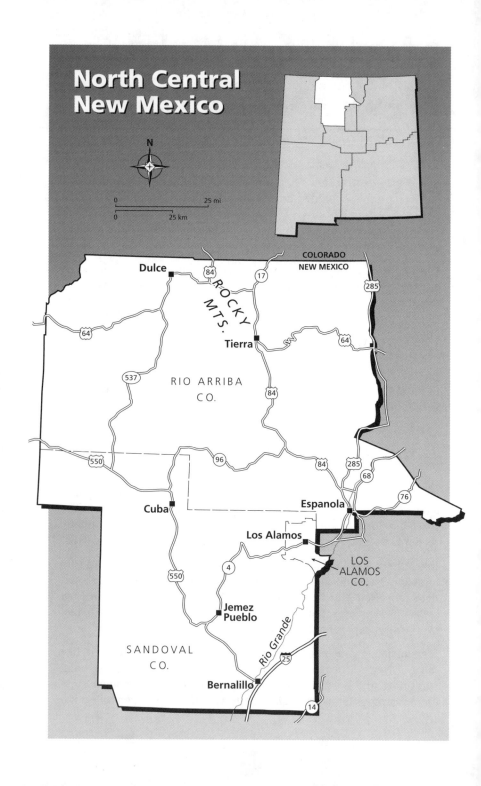

North Central
New Mexico

N

0 ——————— 25 mi
0 ——————— 25 km

COLORADO
NEW MEXICO

Dulce

84

17

285

ROCKY MTS.

64

Tierra

64

537

RIO ARRIBA
CO.

84

550

96

84

285

68

Cuba

76

Espanola

Los Alamos

LOS
ALAMOS
CO.

550

4

Jemez
Pueblo

SANDOVAL
CO.

Rio Grande

25

Bernalillo

14

NORTH CENTRAL NEW MEXICO

The neatly maintained pueblo is home to many potters and several small galleries. **Merrock Galeria** on the plaza features the work of Paul Speckled Rock. The multitalented artist channeled his creative energy into other art forms, such as painting, lithography, and sculpture, before venturing into his pueblo's traditional art form in 1983. Although a relative newcomer, Paul has amassed many awards for his works in clay.

From Española take Highway 30 south (on the west side of the Rio Grande) 1.3 miles. The well-marked pueblo entrance is on the left; (505) 753–7326.

Also on the Santa Clara Reservation but 10 miles west of the pueblo you'll find the **Puyé Cliff Dwellings,** in the Santa Clara Canyon Recreational Area. The drive into the canyon is incredibly scenic as you slowly descend among stands of evergreens into the lush, parklike canyon. Though fishing and camping are allowed, for a fee, the highlight is Puyé, which means "pueblo ruin where the rabbits assemble" in Tewa, the native Santa Clara Indian language.

As a Registered National Historic Landmark, the dwellings offer adventure to the southwestern history buff who likes a good hike. The earlier dwellings here were caves hollowed in the cliffs; later, adobe structures were built along the slopes and top of the mesa. The Anasazi Indians first settled in the Puyé area in the twelfth century and finally abandoned the area around 1580, probably because of continuing drought.

You can explore the dwellings on two different walking tours. The cliff trail begins at the visitor center and leads up semisteep trails and ladders, going past many of the ancient dwellings built into the cliffs. Stairways link the two levels of cliff dwellings to the mesa top and its large "Community House." If you prefer a less strenuous course, take the short drive to the mesa-top ruins. Here you can view the 740-room pueblo ruin and its restored ceremonial chamber. Bring a picnic to enjoy the incredible view from this vantage point.

Like exploring many ruins in New Mexico, visiting Puyé can be physically taxing—wear good nonslip shoes or sneakers. Puyé Cliff Dwellings are located off Highway 602 via Highway 30 from Española; (505) 753–7326.

FAVORITE ATTRACTIONS/EVENTS IN NORTH CENTRAL NEW MEXICO:

Spence Springs, Jemez Springs No phone

El Santuario de Chimayó, Chimayó (505) 351–4360

Puyé Cliff Dwellings, Rio Arriba County (505) 753–7326

Dixon Apple Farm, Northern Sandoval County (505) 465–2976

Bandelier National Monument, Northern Sandoval County (505) 672–0343

Cumbres & Toltec Scenic Railroad, Chama (505) 756–2151

Sandia Man Cave, near Placitas No phone

New Mexico Wine Festival, Labor Day weekend, Bernalillo (505) 867–3311

Fees are the same for guided or self-guided tours: adults, $5.00; children (ages seven to fourteen) and seniors, $4.00. Open daily during summer, 8 A.M.–7 P.M.; call ahead for hours the remainder of the year.

While northern New Mexico claims several very good wineries, **La Chiripada Winery** is particularly worth seeking out. Situated among the apple orchards in the small community of Dixon, La Chiripada's tasting room is housed in a whitewashed adobe surrounded by colorful gardens and vineyards. Besides its selection of wines with their Mimbres Indian design labels, the tasting room also sells contemporary pottery. Brothers Michael and Patrick Johnson planted their ten acres of grapes in 1977 and opened the winery on the banks of the Rio Embudo four years later. La Chiripada (meaning "A Stroke of Luck") gets half its grapes from its own vineyards and the remainder from other New Mexico growers.

La Chiripada is on Highway 75 in Dixon; (505) 579–4437. Tasting-room hours are 10:00 A.M.–5:00 P.M. Monday through Saturday and noon–5:00 P.M. Sunday. The winery also has a tasting room off the plaza in Taos that is open the same hours listed above.

Embudo Station, a historic, 1880s narrow-gauge railroad station between Santa Fe and Taos, is now a casual restaurant on the banks of the Rio Grande. Embudo Station has an outdoor area for patio dining, as well as a country smokehouse shop featuring trout, cheese, and various meats. The restaurant serves barbecued ribs and brisket, ham,

---

La Comida de Nuevo México

Simply Salsa

Why pay for expensive salsas when you can whip up a batch of your own in mere minutes at a fraction of the cost? The following recipe comes from my friend Joseph Aguirre, who wouldn't dream of ever buying the bottled stuff.

1 large can tomatoes (or one pound fresh tomatoes*)

½ onion, quartered

3 fresh jalepeno peppers, quartered (or 3 dried cayenne chiles, broken up)

2 cloves garlic, quartered

½ to 1 teaspoon salt (to taste)

Freshly ground black pepper to taste

1 tablespoon fresh cilantro (optional)

Put all ingredients in a blender and pulse until desired consistency, but not too smooth. Serve with tostadas or corn tortilla chips. Makes about 2–3 cups salsa.
*Roasting or grilling the fresh tomatoes first adds a nice smoky flavor.

El Santuario de Chimayó

turkey, trout, and catfish. Even if you're not hungry, Embudo Station is a pleasant place to enjoy an appetizer and a beer or a glass of La Chiripada wine while sitting outdoors under the huge cottonwoods. The restaurant now boasts its own microbrewery, serving up various flavored beers including green chile, red chile, and strawberry. Embudo Station also offers float trips on the Rio Grande in contrast to the white-water experience farther north near Taos. The water is much calmer on this stretch.

The restaurant and float headquarters are located on Highway 68 about 17 miles north of Española; (505) 852–4707. Summer hours are noon–9:00 P.M. Tuesday–Sunday. Early spring and late fall hours may vary, so call ahead. The restaurant closes November through March.

Just inside Rio Arriba County near its border with Santa Fe County, the village of *Chimayó* lies on the **High Road to Taos,** that romantic-sounding name for the scenic though less than direct path connecting Santa Fe to Taos. The old Spanish community of Chimayó is the most interesting stop on the High Road and boasts several "must sees."

The first place to stop is ***El Santuario de Chimayó,*** known as "Little

Lourdes" because of its reputation of miraculous healing and cures similar to those of the famous site in France. Built in 1816, the adobe chapel is widely known as the destination of an annual Holy Week pilgrimage during which thousands walk from all over New Mexico, neighboring states, and even Mexico. Nonetheless, people visit the *santuario* all year long.

The chapel's intricately carved and colorful altar spotlights a 6-foot crucifix, while scores of votive candles maintain a glow nearby. Two side rooms are attached to the chapel. The larger space is devoted to holding the various offerings made over the years, such as small statues, paintings, personal messages of thanks, and photographs. The walls of this room are also lined with the crutches of those who have been cured at Chimayó. The smaller chamber shelters the hole in the floor that contains the sacred, healing dirt (visitors are welcome to take small amounts with them).

Chimayó is accessible from Highway 285 north of Santa Fe via Highway 503 and then Highway 520. The santuario is located on the right, just as you enter the village of Chimayó on Highway 520; (505) 351–4360 (parish office). Services are still held in Santuario de Chimayó, with a 11:00 A.M. daily mass, and it's open to the public daily, from 9:00 A.M. to 4:00 P.M.

Less than ½ mile farther on Highway 520, you'll see the **Restaurante Rancho de Chimayó** on your right and the Hacienda Rancho de Chimayó (a bed-and-breakfast inn) on your left. If you want a romantic hideaway, stay at the hacienda. If you're hungry, visit the restaurant—and even if you're not hungry, go anyway to enjoy the surroundings.

The restaurant is the former home of Hermenegildo and Trinidad Jaramillo and has been open since 1965. The hundred-year-old adobe provides an intimate dining experience in several small rooms inside and a delightful openness on the terraced patios outside. During spring and summer, colorful flowers and warm temperatures make outside dining the obvious choice. Native New Mexican foods are prepared according to traditional family recipes that stress locally grown products, including the peerless Chimayó red chile. The restaurant has a full bar and carries many Mexican beers, but the house specialty is the potent Chimayó Cocktail. A waitress revealed the recipe as tequila, apple juice, triple sec, creme de cassis, and a dash of lime. The proportions are a secret, but the apple-juice ice cubes and apple-slice garnish make it a perfect before-dinner drink.

The family home of Epifanio and Adelaida Jaramillo became **Hacienda Rancho de Chimayó** in 1984, after the traditional adobe had been renovated into seven guest rooms filled with turn-of-the-century antiques. Each room has a private bath and sitting area and opens onto an enclosed courtyard. Every morning, your hosts serve a Continental breakfast featuring pastries, fruit, fresh-squeezed orange juice, and coffee or tea.

The restaurant is open daily from 11:30 A.M. to 9:00 P.M. and for breakfast on weekends from 8:30 to 10:30 A.M., with the exception of Mondays during winter, when it is closed; (505) 351–4444. The inn, whose room rates range from $69 to $105, also closes the second week of January; (505) 351–2222.

Continuing on Highway 520 to its junction with Highway 76, you'll come across **Ortega's Weaving Shop** (505–351–4215) and **Galeria Ortega** (505–351–2288). No matter what time of year you visit, these two neighboring stores are the perfect places to do your Christmas shopping. Eight generations of masterful weaving by the Ortega family

---

Solamente en Nuevo México . . . Cattle Mutilations and UFOs

*R*eports of mysterious cattle mutilations in northern New Mexico have cropped up every few years since the 1960s, most recently during 1996. The latest report came from two Chimayó ranchers who discovered the mutilated carcass of one of their bulls. As with previous slayings, the bull's heart was removed through a hole cut in its chest, and its sexual organs, intestines, and tongue also were removed. No blood was detected on the wounds, the carcass, or on the surrounding grass— and there were no tire tracks or unusual markings around the remains.

Although there has never been conclusive evidence, or consensus, regarding the purpose or the cause of the slayings, several theories exist. The FBI says the mutilations are the result of predators and scavengers; New Mexico's livestock board says they're possibly caused by secret Satanic groups, whereas others blame organ-harvesting UFOs, and still others blame chupacabras, or goat-suckers, the mythological creatures of Puerto Rican lore.

The large number of UFO-theory proponents, who say northern New Mexico ranks with Nevada's top-secret Area 51 as two of the country's UFO hot spots, believe that the cattle are taken aboard the alien crafts to be mutilated. The obvious question then becomes, "Why cattle?" UFO theorists believe the answer may lie in the bovine's blood. It's supposedly so similar to that of humans that it is regularly used in medical laboratories to create human blood plasma. It's an indication, theorists say, that the aliens may be studying the cattle to find out more about humans.

is evident in the fine wool rugs, coats, and other outerwear for sale at the weaving shop. You can even watch weavers hand-loom rugs in a room just off the sales area. In addition, the shop has a great selection of Santa Clara Pueblo pottery and books on the Southwest. It's also the place to stock up on dried Chimayó red chile.

Galeria Ortega markets contemporary New Mexican art forms. Wood carvings are featured, including a variety of *bultos,* or representations of saints crafted out of pine or cottonwood limbs. Made by *santeros,* these carvings are uniquely local in appearance. There's also a fine collection of pottery, hand-painted shirts, and handcrafted Nambé ware (bowls, platters, candleholders, etc., that are made from a secret, shiny alloy—named after Nambé Pueblo).

Ortega's Weaving Shop and Galeria Ortega are both open Monday through Saturday, 8:30 A.M.–5:00 P.M.; both are open Sunday, 11:00 A.M.–5:00 P.M. They both close on Sunday, however, from late October through early April.

The village of **Abiquiu** is known for its most famous resident, artist Georgia O'Keeffe, and for the stunning landscape that inspired her, which she referred to as the Faraway. Although O'Keeffe died in 1986 at the age of ninety-eight, for years people have been coming from all over to look at the massive adobe walls that guard her home. Now, if they plan their trip carefully, they'll actually be able to take a look inside. That's right, after years of being off-limits to the public, the **Georgia O'Keeffe Home** is finally open to visitors, though on a very limited basis. Only scheduled, guided tours are allowed, and you may even need to reserve your space months in advance.

To the extent possible, the house remains as it was left by O'Keeffe in 1984, when she moved from Abiquiu to Santa Fe prior to her death. After much speculation about the future of her home (some of which had the home slated to become a state museum), the Georgia O'Keeffe Foundation was formed to preserve not only the artist's home but her legacy as well. As foundation president Elizabeth Glassman has said, "Few places exist in America where one can see how an artist lived and worked. To experience the space created by O'Keeffe and to see the places she so often painted allow the visitor a glimpse of the artist."

O'Keeffe purchased the property—parts of which date back to the early eighteenth century—from the Catholic church in 1945. After the death of her husband, Alfred Stieglitz, in 1946, O'Keeffe spent the next three years having the house rebuilt and renovated. By 1949 the property was ready, and O'Keeffe took up full-time residence in New Mexico. Many of her best-known works were inspired by the Abiquiu house and its views, including its patio and black door, the cottonwood trees along the Chama River, and the road to Santa Fe. Once you experience the otherworldly beauty of the Abiquiu landscape, you'll see why this area enchanted O'Keeffe and others seeking artistic and spiritual awakenings.

Visitors are received on a by-appointment-only basis in small groups for tours of the property and house. Tours are suspended during the late fall through early spring. Requested donation per person is $20. To schedule a tour, call the foundation office at (505) 685–4539.

Just down the hill from O'Keeffe's home, you'll find **The Tin Moon** gallery and studio. Opened in early 1999 by artists Ans Zoutenbier Haak and Diane Haddon, The Tin Moon features contemporary folk art. Permanently on show is Haak's contemporary tin designs, which step away from traditional New Mexican tin work even though the same techniques are applied. Also, permanently on show are Haddon's paintings, drawings, and other artworks. The gallery also displays the following variety of works: jewelry, ornaments, *nicho* collages, houses built of paper mache, mirrors, boxes, candle holders, wall sconces, and lanterns. Temporary exhibitions are also housed. In addition, The Tin Moon provides a place for local as well as national and international artists.

The Tin Moon is located on Highway 84 in Abiquiu across from Bode's General Store; (505) 685–4829. It's open daily, 10:00 A.M. to 5:00 P.M., except on Wednesday when it's closed.

There's something about the awe-inspiring landscape around Abiquiu that's downright spiritual and seems to attract a global religious presence. Not only will you find the Christ in the Desert Monastery and the Presbyterian-church-owned Ghost Ranch in this area, but it's also home to the hauntingly beautiful *Dar al-Islam mosque*.

The mosque was built in the early 1980s to serve the spiritual needs of the large Muslim population of the area. The complex, which includes a 17,000-square-foot school and library complex, and a beautiful courtyard garden, is open to visitors. After visiting the mosque, continue your visit with a hike around Plaza Blanca, a beautiful white rock formation on the grounds of Dar al-Islam.

To get to Dar al–Islam, turn right on Highway 155, 6 miles north of Abiquiu. Go 2.2 miles; the entrance will be on your left. When the road makes a Y, stay left; (505) 685–4515.

Ghost Ranch Living Museum is a good place to view some of the wildlife found in northern New Mexico. The museum's residents, which include eagles, bears, and elk, were either injured or orphaned before they were brought to the facility, which is managed by the U.S. Forest Service. In addition to the wildlife exhibits, other outdoor interpretive programs include a replica of a forest ranger lookout tower complete with fire-fighting information and the "Up through the Ages" exhibit. Here, visitors can gaze through telescopes—which have been distributed along a stair-step railing—at the distant multicolored cliffs. For every step up you take, you'll be viewing a "younger" geologic period, as evidenced by the layers of fossilized sediment.

Aquatic environments are also featured. A trout-stocked stream flows throughout the wooded forest reenactment, and an indoor-outdoor beaver enclave called Beaver National Forest celebrates these masters of conservation. Because of these exhibits and many others, the museum is a great educational outing for the kids, but grown-ups also may learn a thing or two about the fragility of our natural environment.

The museum is located on U.S. Highway 84 just north of Abiquiu; (505) 685–4312. It's open daily, except for Monday; hours are 9:00 A.M.–4:00 P.M. early spring through late fall; call ahead for information on dates for winter closure. Admission is a $3.00 for adults, $1.00 for children, and free for children under 5.

Near Ghost Ranch Living Museum off of U.S. Highway 84, you'll find the Ghost Ranch Conference Center (505–685–4333), which contains two fine museums: *The Florence Hawley Ellis Museum of Anthropology* and *The Ruth Hall Museum of Paleontology.* The entire 21,000 acres that constitute what used to be the working Ghost Ranch were donated to the Presbyterian Church (U.S.A.) in 1955. (The ranch got its name from the *brujas,* or witches, that were said to haunt the canyons on the ranch.) The conference center serves as a national adult study center and as a steward of the northern New Mexico environment. The anthropology museum centers on past and present peoples who lived within a 60-mile radius of the ranch over a span of 12,000 years, whereas the paleontology museum's focus is fossils, specifically the study of *Coelophysis,* a type of dinosaur whose mass burial site was discovered here in 1947.

Hours for both museums are Tuesday through Saturday, 9:00 A.M.–noon and 1:00–5:00 P.M. The museums are closed during December. Admission for both museums is $2.00 for adults and $1.00 for children under thirteen and seniors.

Farther north, about 8 miles north of the turnoff to Abiquiu Lake on Highway 84, you'll see a sign for *Echo Amphitheater.* No, it's not New

Mexico's answer to Colorado's famed Red Rocks performance venue, but it looks as though it could be. Rather, Echo Amphitheater is a natural formation carved into a towering sandstone cliff by eons of wind and rain. Its base is accented by boulders that appear frozen in mid-tumble and by piñon trees and other evergreens. It's a great place to view some of the grandeur of the region—especially the way the light plays off the majestic sandstone cliff around sunset. Camping is allowed for a fee.

The first thing you'll notice after arriving at **Monastery of Christ in the Desert** is the quiet. Getting there is another story. The monastery lies in an isolated but dramatically beautiful canyon along the Chama River, about 27 miles north of Abiquiu, and is surrounded by miles of national forest land. Though the monastery was founded in June 1964 by three monks from New York, the present monastic community began arriving in 1974, seeking the Benedictine life of prayer, reading, studying, and manual labor. If inspiration comes with solitude, then this is the place to get it. Because the monks believe they can best continue the tradition of offering hospitality in the desert by giving their guests an opportunity to share in their way of life, limited accommodations are offered to travelers.

If you're planning an overnight stay, remember that this is not the place to bring a spouse, the kids, or even a friend. It's a place to experience alone. For overnight guests, vegetarian meals are served, and library hours are maintained. The serenity of the Chama Canyon wilderness is perfect for escaping daily stresses, meditating, hiking, and just getting back in touch with yourself.

You don't have to stay overnight to experience Christ in the Desert, though. The impressive, contemporary pueblo revival–style chapel and a gift shop are open to non-overnight visitors, whereas other buildings and the remainder of the grounds are private. The gift shop is filled with books, cards, and other items of a religious nature. (*Note:* Wearing short pants is unacceptable, and dogs are not welcome.)

The monastery is located off U.S. Highway 84, some 75 miles northwest of Santa Fe. To get there, turn left (north) about 1–2 mile past Ghost Ranch Living Museum at Forest Service Road Marker 151. Most of the 13-mile drive is not paved but is usually passable in passenger cars; however, during winter and spring a four-wheel-drive vehicle may be needed. Chapel and gift shop hours are 8:00 A.M.–5:00 P.M. daily; (505) 470–4515. Though there is no fixed fee to stay in the guest house, about $40 per person per day covers monastery expenses. For a summer or fall stay in the guest house, reservations two or three months in advance may be necessary.

New Mexico Trivia

The first Spanish colony in what is now New Mexico was established near San Juan Pueblo, north of present–day Española, in 1598.

Continuing north on U.S. Highway 84 brings you to Tierra Amarilla ("Yellow Earth"), the county seat of Rio Arriba County and the place named for the peculiar dirt found in the area. The adjacent village of Los Ojos offers visitors a glimpse at the rich wool-raising and weaving tradition of the area in the form of the *Tierra Wools* store. The shop showcases hand-spun and -dyed yarn, along with handwoven rugs, pillows, jackets, and other items. You'll usually find artisans at work in the back "loom room"—you're welcome to watch. The walls of the store are lined with thousands of multicolored skeins of yarn and rugs that set off the natural beauty of the timeworn wood planked floors. The Tierra Wools cooperative is a program of Ganados del Valle ("Livestock Growers of the Valley"), whose goal is to ensure that weaving, wool growing, and sheepherding continue as a way of life in this remote region of New Mexico.

Tierra Wools's shop is on the main street of the tiny community of Los Ojos, just west of U.S. Highway 84, north of Tierra Amarilla; (505) 588–7231. From May through October, the shop is open Monday through Saturday from 9:00 A.M. to 6:00 P.M. and Sunday from 10:30 A.M. to 4:30 P.M.; the rest of the year it's open Monday through Saturday from 10:00 A.M. to 5:00 P.M.

The neighboring community of Los Brazos welcomes travelers from all over the world with *Casa de Martinez Bed and Breakfast Inn.* Following the custom of *nuestra casa es su casa* ("our house is your house"), Clarinda Martinez de Sanchez and her husband have offered their family home to the leisurely traveler since 1988.

Although the inn is worlds away from the harshness of urban life, it's a wonderful base from which to explore Santa Fe, Taos, and the Anasazi ruins of northwestern New Mexico—all without packing up and moving each day. Gazing out of the comfortable guest rooms (each has its own bathroom) at the distant, pine-covered San Juan Mountains and enjoying Clarinda's home-cooked breakfasts are the real treats of a stay at the inn, originally built in the 1860s by Clarinda's great-grandfather. Although an addition was made to the home after the turn of the century, the thick adobe walls and vigas (ceiling beams made out of logs) are the real thing.

Casa de Martinez is located on the loop that is Los Brazos, off U.S. Highway 84 north of Los Ojos; (505) 588–7858. Daily rates range from $85 to $125, double occupancy; $20 per additional person. The inn is open from the second weekend in February to the third weekend in October, or thereabouts.

Your trek up U.S. Highway 84 ends in *Chama,* less than 10 miles from the Colorado border. Chama is a popular spot for sports enthusiasts and thus offers many choices of rustic, low-cost lodging. The area offers big-game hunting, fishing in the Chama River and nearby Heron and El Vado reservoirs, and some of the West's best and most consistent cross-country skiing in winter. The town's also a popular place for the non-sporting set because it's the New Mexican home of the *Cumbres & Toltec Scenic Railroad,* North America's longest and highest narrow-gauge steam railroad. The railroad, which connects Chama with Antonito, Colorado, is on the National Historic Register and is owned by the states of both New Mexico and Colorado.

The railroad offers one-way and round-trip excursions (to a midway point and back from either Chama or Antonito) from late spring through midfall. The train has fully enclosed and semi-enclosed cars, all of which provide for unobstructed viewing in comfort during your journey through groves of pine and aspen, striking rock formations, and other breathtaking views. Consider a late September or early October trip so as to miss the crowds and catch the aspens at their golden best. Also note that all the trips take the better part of a day (10:30 A.M.–4:30 P.M., 10:00 A.M.–5:00 P.M., etc.), and although summer is usually warm and pleasant, it's best to be prepared for cooler weather by wearing long pants and bringing a light jacket.

The 64 miles of railroad are the finest remaining example of a vast network that once connected commercial outposts in the Rocky Mountain region. Spiked down in 1880 as the San Juan Extension of the Denver & Rio Grande Railroad, the Cumbres & Toltec was built to serve the rich mining camps in the mountains.

> **New Mexico Trivia:**
>
> *Eighty-five percent of New Mexico is more than 4,000 feet in elevation.*

The Chama depot is on Terrace Street downtown; (505) 756–2151. Though tickets may be available for purchase at the depot, it's best to make reservations as far in advance as possible. The railroad has several ride options daily from late May through mid-October. Fares range from $34 to $52 for adults and $17 to $27 for children under twelve.

Heading west out of Chama on U.S. Highway 84 (it will meet U.S. Highway 64 about 15 miles west—continue on U.S. 64, otherwise you'll end up in Pagosa Springs, Colorado), you'll drive through parts of the vast *Jicarilla Apache Reservation* and into the community of Dulce, the headquarters of the Indian reservation. Unlike New Mexico's Pueblo Indians, ancestors of the Jicarilla Apache were nomadic—their lifestyle was determined by the seasons and migration of wildlife. They traveled throughout southern Colorado, northeastern New Mexico, and the panhandles of Texas and Oklahoma. The reservation was established in 1887. The word *jicarilla* in Spanish means "wicker basket," after the craft for which the Jicarillas were traditionally best known.

To learn more about the Jicarilla Apache, visit the ***Jicarilla Arts and Crafts Museum*** (505–759–3242, ext. 274), housed in a modest green building on U.S. Highway 64 (Jicarilla Boulevard) in Dulce. The museum is open daily, 8:00 A.M.–noon and 1:00–5:00 P.M.; there's no admission charge. Please note that the museum may be closed during feast days, so it's best to call ahead. The reservation will also issue permits for camping, hunting, and fishing. Call (505) 759–3242 for any

Cumbres & Toltec Scenic Railroad

information regarding the Jicarilla Apache. For thoroughly modern lodging, the Best Western Jicarilla Inn is the place to stay. It's located on U.S. Highway 64; (505) 759–3663.

Los Alamos County

A small city on the Pajarito Plateau, *Los Alamos* was once home only to a handful of ranchers and to a school for boys. But world events in the 1940s made Los Alamos forever a household name.

Los Alamos, county seat of New Mexico's smallest county of the same name, has a fascinating history because of the role it played in the top-secret Project Y (a.k.a. the Manhattan Project)—the development of the world's first atom bomb—during World War II. For historical reasons alone, Los Alamos is an interesting place to visit, but the community also happens to be set in one of New Mexico's most beautiful sites—a military requirement, along with its remoteness, to keep the scientists content during the long ordeal.

In some ways Los Alamos has the feel of a company town because Los Alamos National Laboratory, technological successor to the Manhattan Project days, is by far the community's largest employer, providing thousands of jobs. Operated by the University of California for the U.S. Department of Energy, the lab itself contains the most interesting attraction of all in Los Alamos: the *Bradbury Science Museum.*

The extensive museum chronicles the dawning of the atomic age by focusing on achievements in weapons development, alternate energy sources, and biomedical research. Additional exhibits feature the lab's ongoing work in such areas as computer technology, nuclear safeguards, and basic research exploring the nature of nuclei, atoms, and molecules. Photographs, documents, and newspaper headlines provide a timeline of significant world events covering the early 1930s to the mid-1960s.

Throughout the day, the museum's theater presents a twenty-minute film called *The City That Never Was,* which traces Los Alamos's history with actual period film footage and reenactments of notable events in the city's past. The film is a nice break from the rest of the large, info-packed museum, which can be a little overwhelming if you try to absorb everything.

The exhibits, however, are very well presented, employing lots of interactive video screens to make things a little more accessible and comfortable to nontechies. More than thirty-five hands-on exhibits invite visitor participation: You can align a laser, pinch plasma, and monitor radiation. Plan to stay at least two hours if you want a good overview of everything–and longer if you want to experience the exhibits in depth.

New Mexico Trivia

Beat generation author William Borroughs (Naked Lunch) attended the former Los Alamos Ranch School during the 1930s.

The museum is located at Fifteenth and Central in Los Alamos, in the lab's Museum Parke complex; (505) 667–4444. Memorial Day through Labor Day, it's open Tuesday through Saturday, 9:00 A.M.–5:00 P.M., and Sunday and Monday, 1:00–5 P.M. Winter hours are Saturday through Monday, 1:00–5:00 P.M., and Tuesday through Friday, 9:00 A.M.–5:00 P.M. There's no admission charge.

While the Bradbury Science Museum is high-tech and scientific, the **Los Alamos Historical Museum** is a little more low-key and personal. It traces the area's history beyond its military role, although the war years get big play here also. The small stone-and-log museum—the former infirmary and guest house of the Los Alamos Ranch School—preserves artifacts from Los Alamos's past, including a geology exhibit and household items common during the war years. It also has a well-stocked bookstore.

The Los Alamos Historical Museum is at 1921 Juniper on the grounds of the Fuller Lodge Cultural Center; (505) 662–6272. Hours are 10:00 A.M.–4:00 P.M. Monday through Saturday and 1:00–4:00 P.M. Sunday; summer hours are 9:30 A.M.–4:30 P.M. Monday through Saturday and 11:00 A.M.–5:00 P.M. Sunday. There is no admission charge.

At one time, Fuller Lodge provided the first housing for the Manhattan Project scientists, before the establishment was turned into a hotel and restaurant. Today it's the **Fuller Lodge Cultural Center,** a multipurpose community center that houses the Fuller Lodge Art Center and Gallery. The art center features the works of regional artists in its permanent collection, together with collections on loan from Los Alamos citizens, as well as traveling exhibits. Many items are for sale to the public. The art center also sponsors various classes, lectures, and shows throughout the year.

The art center is on the second floor of the Fuller Lodge Cultural Center (though it has its own entrance), at 2123 Central Avenue; (505) 662–9331. Gallery hours are 10:00 A.M.–4:00 P.M. Monday through Saturday.

Sandoval County

Although Sandoval County has led New Mexico in population growth during the past five years and is projected to continue as the fastest-growing county until the turn of the century, its growth is due to the population explosion of one city–Rio Rancho, a boomtown bedroom community of Albuquerque. Rio Rancho is, however, very atypical of the rest of the county. The remainder of Sandoval County is pleasantly rural, containing rock formations, forests, mountains, and Indian pueblos.

Southern Sandoval County would normally be considered more "central" than "north central" New Mexico, but because this book is divided by county, it'll be classified as the latter. The region, however, will be divided into southern and northern Sandoval County.

Northern Sandoval County

Beyond Cochiti Lake and nearby Cochiti Pueblo, you'll find **Dixon Apple Farm.** Visitors are welcome to the quaint orchard at the base of the Canada Valley's crimson cliffs all year, but it's the few weeks in middle to late September and early October that make this place special to those who partake in the annual fall pilgrimage, mostly Albuquerqueans, in search of Dixon's patented and prized Champagne apple. Along with the Champagne, the farm grows and sells Double Red Delicious during opening weekend; a few weeks later Dixon's other patented apple, Sparkling Burgundy, arrives, as does the popular Rome.

Off the salesroom you can watch the apples being washed, sorted, and packed. Only flawless ones make it to the salesroom; the rest are destined to become cider for those who want their apples without the crunch.

A tiny, rapidly flowing brook runs through the farm, adding even more to the valley's allure. A scattering of picnic tables is available for those wanting to linger awhile. Take a wedge of sharp cheddar to have with a crisp Champagne along the brook for your own little bit of heaven.

There's no set date when apple season begins at Dixon–fine apple growing is an art as well as a science, you know–so if you don't want to be left out, start calling (505) 465–2976 in mid- September. During season, hours are 8:00 A.M.–5:00 P.M. daily.

To get to Dixon's, take the Cochiti Lake exit off Interstate 25, about 28 miles north of Albuquerque. Go left, toward Cochiti, about 18$\frac{1}{2}$ miles (the last 2 of which are gravel) to get to the orchards.

The Jemez Mountains, particularly the **Jemez Springs** area, are a favorite with hiking, camping, and cross-country-skiing devotees. Named for the many hot springs hidden in the area, the village of Jemez Springs provides the perfect getaway weekend for weary city folks.

Let the **Jemez Mountain Inn** be your base for the weekend. The main part of the inn has been the center of activity in the area for more than a hundred years, serving as the town silver assayer's office and barbershop, among other things. The building assumed its role as the Amber Lodge in 1936 until 1989, when it was transformed into the Jemez Mountain Inn. All the rooms are different, and each has a story. There have even been claims that mobsters from the East Coast lay low here in the 1930s.

Like nearly everything else in Jemez Springs, the Jemez Mountain Inn is on the main drag (Highway 4), within walking distance of other places and attractions; (505) 829–3926. Rates range from $79 to $109, lower during winter.

The **Jemez Springs Bath House** has also been around for more than a hundred years, having originally been built by the Jemez Indians to utilize the curative waters that bubble from the ground along the Jemez River. Now owned by the town and leased out, the bath house is bare-bones and basic, qualities that add to its peculiar attraction.

Separate women's and men's wings each have four smooth, concrete tubs that are meticulously scrubbed after every use, even though they may not look like it because of the high mineral buildup over time. In addition to mineral soaks, which are said to relax muscles and heal sore joints, the bath house offers sweat wraps and massages. The bath house also has an outdoor cedar tub for those who don't like to soak alone.

The bath house now has an exercise studio and a gift shop, which features a selection of aromatherapy products and natural health and beauty supplies. Baths run from $8 to $12, and massages range from $30 to $65. The outdoor tub goes for $30 per hour. Summer hours are 9:00 A.M. to 9:00 P.M. and 10:00 A.M.–7:30 P.M. the remainder of the year. The Jemez Springs Bath House is on Highway 4 in Jemez Springs; (505) 829–3303.

If you like your soaks *au naturel,* head to the pools of **Spence Hot Springs.** The pools are the more accessible springs in the mountainous area under U.S. Forest Service jurisdiction. The forest service warns though, "Don't drink or snort the water up your nose, because some hot springs in the area may contain an amoeba called *Naegleri fowlerii,* which can cause a fatal brain infection called PAM, Primary Amoebic Meningoencephalitis." Though deaths are rare, keep your head above water just in case.

Spence Hot Springs are in the vicinity of mile markers 24 and 25 on Highway 4, 7 miles north of the Jemez Springs Bath House, on the right side of the road. You'll see a crude parking area and a sign that says NO PARKING AFTER 10 P.M. (There used to be a Spence Hot Springs sign, but apparently every time one was put up someone stole it.) Then follow the primitive path a little less than 1 mile up the hill. There are no admission charges or designated hours, but it's a good bet you won't be there after 10:00 P.M.

For a beer and burger after your soak, check out **Los Ojos Restaurant & Saloon,** across Highway 4 from the Jemez Mountain Inn (505–829–3547). It's been around since 1947. Los Ojos is HOME OF THE FAMOUS JEMEZ BURGER—ONE JELLUVA JAMBURGER, as its sign proclaims. (At the very least, the sign makes it clear how to pronounce Jemez: rhymes with "famous.") You can even play a game of pool while you wait for your jamburger.

A Glimpse of North Central New Mexico: *Impresiones de Los Ojos* . . .

*J*ust as the Catskills provide an easy weekend escape for New Yorkers, so do the Jemez Mountains for Albuquerqueans. Blessed with a beautiful, heavily forested setting, and less than an hour's drive from Albuquerque or Santa Fe, the striking red-rock Jemez Mountains and the welcoming community of Jemez Springs are the perfect destination for a spontaneous day trip.

During a recent autumn trip to Spence Hot Springs (see page 72) in "the Jemez," I was again reminded how fortunate I am to live in New Mexico. While soaking in a natural hot tub dug into the side of a mountain and gazing through towering ponderosa pines to distant rock formations, I found myself absentmindedly following a conversation between two fellow soakers, one of whom had a thick southern accent.

"I can't believe y'all got a place like this. I'm from Atlanta and I'm just amazed."

"Welcome to New Mexico," the other bather said dryly.

"I can't believe there aren't any rangers around, or that nobody gets harassed for the nudity and all."

"Look around," the other said, gesturing to the remote location reachable only by a spirited trek. "Who'd bother to police this?"

The Georgian just shook his head. "If this were Georgia, you can bet your lucky stars that clothes would not be an option. In fact," he laughed, "I'd imagine some wealthy holy-roller would buy the whole dang place and turn it into a church camp. Hell, he'd probably even charge admission."

I just smiled and turned toward a new view, thankful once again for the space and the freedom, and for the comforting los ojos, or springs, that New Mexico offers up so graciously.

For those of you who just must include something educational when you travel, don't miss the **Jemez State Monument,** 1 mile north of Jemez Springs on, what else, Highway 4; (505) 829–3530. The monument preserves the ruins of both the old village of Guisewa, built approximately 600 years ago by the ancestors of the nearby Jemez Pueblo Indians, and the mission church of San Jose de los Jemez, built by Spanish colonists in the early 1620s. The visitor center exhibits interpret the area's history from the perspective of the Jemez Indians. The monument is open daily from 8:30 A.M. to 5:00 P.M. Admission is $3.00 for adults ($2.00 in winter); children under sixteen are admitted free.

Nearby **Soda Dam** is about ¹/₂ mile farther north on Highway 4 from Jemez State Monument. The natural dam on the Jemez River does not create a lake but, rather, channels the river through a short tunnel to provide a small waterfall and pool on the other side—perfect for cooling off in the summer. (*Note:* The pool's depth is unpredictable because of rocks often deposited by the river; accordingly, never attempt to dive into the small pool.) During cooler times of the year, when the summer crowds are gone, sightseers and picnickers can walk up the trail that snakes to the top of the rock formation and provides a peek at the river on the other side. Eventually, the U.S. Forest Service plans a visitor information center at Soda Dam.

Bandelier National Monument, in northeast Sandoval County, is one of the most spectacular places to hike in New Mexico. It was designated a National Monument in 1916 to protect one of the largest concentrations of archaeological sites in the Southwest. It contains more than 70 miles of trails and 23,000 acres of designated wilderness.

The 50-square-mile monument is named for Adolph Bandelier, a Swiss-American scholar who extensively surveyed the prehistoric ruins in the region and studied the Pueblo Indians around Santa Fe in the 1880s. The most accessible feature of Bandelier National Monument is the ruins in Frijoles ("Beans") Canyon and the cliff dwellings set in the canyon walls. Most of the ruins belong to the late pre-Spanish period, although a few date back to the twelfth century.

The easiest way to experience Bandelier is first to orient yourself by stopping at the visitor center and viewing the slide program and then to walk the Main Ruins Trail, a 1-mile paved loop that takes about forty-five minutes. If you can stay a little longer, continue up the canyon to the base of the Ceremonial Cave. The cave is accessible only by climbing four steep ladders for a total of 140 feet! This ascent is not for wimps, but if you're unafraid of heights and have nonslip shoes, go for it. Once you're in the chamber, have a friend stand at one end while you stand at the other and then quietly talk into the stone walls—it's like a prehistoric intercom. Pretty cool.

Campsites are available. Backcountry hikes, including overnight trips that require a wilderness permit, are also allowed if you want to spend a significant amount of time exploring Bandelier. Because there are a lot of rules regarding exploring Bandelier's backcountry, always check with the visitor center first. Keep in mind that, as with many parts of New Mexico, brief afternoon thunderstorms are common in late summer.

The entrance to Bandelier National Monument is about 13 miles south of Los Alamos off Highway 4; (505) 672-0343. The visitor center is open daily from 8:00 A.M. to 6:00 P.M. during summer and from 8:00 A.M. to 4:30 P.M. in winter. Frijoles Canyon and other selected hiking areas are open dawn to dusk. Admission is $10.00 per car for a seven-day permit; no admission is charged for those older sixty-one or under seventeen. Camping fees are $10.00 per site per night.

> **New Mexico Trivia:**
>
> *The community of Española is known as the "low-rider capital of New Mexico" because of its preponderance of the specially equipped cars.*

Seven of New Mexico's nineteen Indian pueblos are located in Sandoval County, thereby making Sandoval the county with the most Native American communities in New Mexico. The Pueblos in Sandoval County are Cochiti, Jemez, Sandia, San Felipe, Santa Ana, Santo Domingo, and Zia.

The pueblos are each unique, with varying histories, beliefs, ceremonies, and customs. They are actually autonomous "nations" with laws of their own. Many of the pueblos are similar to small, rural towns, and most have a mission church as the most prominent architectural feature, the legacy of Spanish missionaries during the seventeenth and eighteenth centuries.

Although many pueblos welcome or even encourage tourists, it's best to remember that most have been around for centuries and do not exist for tourists. If you're interested in visiting the pueblos, it's a good idea to call ahead and request specific visitor information and policies, which vary greatly. The simplest way to get information is by calling the Indian Pueblo Cultural Center in Albuquerque (see Bernalillo County entry on page 117) at (505) 843-7270, or, if you have a specific pueblo in mind, by contacting it directly (see the list on page 193).

Southern Sandoval County

The village of **Corrales** is an old, rural community adjoining Albuquerque's North Valley along the Rio Grande. While some descendants of the area's early Hispanic settlers still farm the area, many newer residents who commute to Albuquerque enjoy the large lots for their extensive gardens, apple orchards, and horses.

Corrales, which hosts a harvest festival each October to celebrate its agricultural heritage, has several points of interest for the weekend traveler or urban dweller who wants a change of pace. At the center of the village along the main road, appropriately named Corrales Road, you'll find several distinctive shops, restaurants, and galleries.

If you plan to stay overnight, consider the **Corrales Inn Bed & Breakfast.** The U-shaped inn is built around a courtyard containing a fountain and a hot tub. Often, you'll see hummingbirds feeding in the garden. A large common room/library contains more than 2,000 volumes—many of which are regional art and travel books—as well as Western art, rugs, and collectibles to immerse visitors in the cultural diversity of New Mexico. The six guest rooms, each with its own bath and dressing area, vary in decor ranging from Southwestern to Oriental. The inn was built in 1986, so modern comforts are the rule.

To get to the Corrales Inn, go 2.7 miles north on Corrales Road from its intersection with Alameda Boulevard; then take a left at the road across from the elementary school. The inn will be on your right (58 Perea Road); (505) 897–4422. Rates range from $60 to $95.

Like Corrales, the town of Bernalillo is a bedroom community of

State Parks in North Central New Mexico (including Santa Fe County)

Coyote Creek/Morphy Lake, near Mora, (505) 387–2328

El Vado Lake, 14 miles southwest of Tierra Amarilla, (505) 588–7247

Fenton Lake, 33 miles northwest of San Ysidro (near Jemez Springs), (505) 829–3630

Heron Lake, 11 miles west of Tierra Amarilla, (505) 588–7470

Hyde Memorial, 12 miles northeast of Santa Fe, (505) 983–7175

On the web: www.emnrd.state.nm.us/nmparks/

Albuquerque with a rural flavor. Bernalillo lies along Interstate 25 north of Albuquerque and is home to one of the finest restaurants in the Albuquerque metro area—*Prairie Star.* Housed in a large adobe, the restaurant commands the most dramatic view of the Sandia Mountains at sunset, when they turn an intense watermelon red; after dark, the view is replaced by the glittering lights of Albuquerque. Prairie Star's menu is a worthy match for the view. Featuring contemporary cuisine with a southwestern flair, the restaurant serves such tempting creations as barbecued quail, lobster lasagna, pork chop with ancho balsamic sauces, and chateaubriand.

Prairie Star is 2 miles west of I–25 on Highway 44 near Bernalillo; (505) 867–3327. Dinner is served Sunday through Thursday from 5:30 to 9:30 P.M. except for Monday when it's closed, and Friday and Saturday from 5:30 to 10:00 P.M.

The annual *New Mexico Wine Festival* is held in Bernalillo on Labor Day weekend to celebrate the long wine-making tradition in New Mexico generally and in Bernalillo specifically. Spanish colonists brought grapes along with other reminders of home, and the missionaries of the period began making wine for sacramental and personal uses. Bernalillo became the center of wine production in New Mexico during the eighteenth and nineteenth centuries. The festival includes a juried art show, food booths, entertainment, and, of course, wine tastings from most of New Mexico's wineries. (See the list of wineries on page 195).

Coronado State Monument, located near Bernalillo, is popular with Albuquerque visitors because of its proximity to the city. The monument commemorates the 1540 expedition of Francisco Vásquez de Coronado in search of the riches of the legendary Seven Cities of Cibola. Coronado and his soldiers camped near the now-deserted Kuaua Pueblo, the site of the monument. The park contains a trail through the pueblo ruins, which includes a reconstructed kiva (or ceremonial chamber). The visitor center contains exhibits on the history of the Rio Grande Valley. You can even try on an armored conquistador outfit complete with headgear, just like the kind Coronado wore.

The monument is located 1 mile northwest of Bernalillo on Highway 44; (505) 867–5351. It's open daily from 8:30 A.M. to 5:00 P.M. Admission is $3.00 for those over sixteen ($2.00 during winter).

The small community of *Placitas* lies east of Bernalillo, across Interstate 25 in the foothills of the Sandia Mountains. Placitas was a popular place for communes in the late 1960s and is now a popular place for

Sandia Man Cave

pricey new homes in the rambling adobe tradition, though old adobes still exist near the community's center. An interesting site near Placitas in the beautifully lush Las Huertas Canyon is ***Sandia Man Cave,*** where artifacts of Sandia Man (prehistoric people of the area) were excavated by University of New Mexico archaeologists in the late 1930s. Though it's too dark to really see, the cave doesn't go more than about 20 feet before becoming a narrow tunnel that reaches back 300 feet. Attempting to venture far into the cave may be dangerous even with a flashlight; nevertheless, the first few feet give a good sense of what life was like for Sandia Man more than 10,000 years ago. A brief trip to the cave is a perfect urban escape from nearby Albuquerque, providing an awesome short hike to a fascinating spot. Older kids will love this!

The cave is about 4 miles southeast of Placitas on Highway 165 (3 of these miles are gravel through Cibola National Forest). You'll see a sign marking the parking area at the start of the 1/2-mile trail to the steps at the cave's entrance.

Along the Rio Grande between Albuquerque and Santa Fe, you'll find the small rural community of *Algodones,* a pastoral favorite of those who opt out of the city but need to keep their city jobs. Here you'll discover *Hacienda Vargas,* a bed-and-breakfast inn that offers guests the grace and elegance of historical New Mexico. In fact, the site itself has been both a stagecoach stop and an Indian trading post. There's even an adobe chapel nearby.

Each of the seven guest rooms and suites boasts kiva fireplaces, French doors, and private bathrooms. And the entire inn is furnished with New Mexico antiques. You'll find the tranquility you seek in the inn's courtyard and garden areas, complete with hot tub and barbecue facilities.

Rates range from $69 to $139. To get to Hacienda Vargas from Albuquerque, head north on Interstate 25. About 5 miles past the town of Bernalillo, take the Algodones exit and head left to Highway 313 (El Camino Real). Turn left and the inn is the first house on the right; (505) 867–9115 or (800) 261–0006 (out of state).

. WHERE TO STAY IN
NORTH CENTRAL
NEW MEXICO

RIO ARRIBA COUNTY
Hacienda Rancho de Chimayó,
Highway 520,
Chimayó,
(505) 351–2222.

Casa de Martinez
Bed and Breakfast Inn,
U.S. Highway 84,
north of Los Ojos,
Los Brazos,
(505) 588–7858.

The River Inn
(bed and breakfast),
north of Abiquiu off
Highway 84,
(505) 685–4203/(800)
561–6165.

Branding Iron Motel,
1511 West Main Street,
Chama,
(505) 756–2162.

Chama Trails Inn,
2362 Highway 17,
Chama,
(505) 756–2156/
(800) 289–1421.

Best Western Jicarilla Inn,
Highway 64,
Dulce,
(505) 759–3663.

LOS ALAMOS COUNTY
Adobe Pines Bed &
Breakfast,
2101 Loma Linda Drive,
Los Alamos,
(505) 662–6761.

Bandalier Inn,
132 State Road 4,
White Rock,
(505) 672–3838/
(800) 321–3923.

Hilltop House
and L.A. Suites,
400 Trinity at Central,
Los Alamos,
(505) 662–2441/
(800) 462–0936.

Los Alamos Inn,
2201 Trinity Drive,
Los Alamos,
(505) 662–7211/
(800) 279–9279.

NORTHERN SANDOVAL
COUNTY
Jemez Mountain Inn,
Highway 4,
Jemez Springs,
(505) 829–3926.

Jemez River Bed &
Breakfast Inn,
16445 Scenic Highway 4,
Jemez Springs,
(505) 829–3262/
(800) 809–3262.

SOUTHERN SANDOVAL COUNTY

Corrales Inn Bed & Breakfast, 58 Perea Road, Corrales, (505) 897–4422.

Hacienda Vargas (bed and breakfast), Highway 313, Algondones, (505) 867–9115/ (800) 732–2194.

La Hacienda Grande (bed and breakfast), 21 Baros Lane, Bernalillo, (505) 867–1887/ (800) 353–1887.

WHERE TO EAT IN NORTH CENTRAL NEW MEXICO

RIO ARRIBA COUNTY

Embudo Station, Highway 68, Embudo, (505) 852–4707. Moderate. Fare: Eclectic Southwestern.

Restaurante Rancho de Chimayó, Highway 520, Chimayó, (505) 351–4444. Moderate. Fare: Traditional New Mexican.

Anthony's on the Delta, 224 Oñate, Española, (505) 753–4511. Inexpensive to moderate. Fare: Eclectic, featuring steak, seafood, chicken, and New Mexican dishes.

El Paragua Restaurant, 603 Santa Cruz Road, Española, (505) 753–3211. Inexpensive to moderate. Fare: New Mexican.

Trade Routes Cafe, Highway 84, Abiquiu, (505) 658–4790. Inexpensive to moderate. Fare: Gourmet sandwiches, desserts.

Vera's Mexican Kitchen, Highway 17, just north of the U.S. 64/84 turnoff, Chama, (505) 756–2557. Inexpensive to moderate. Fare: Traditional New Mexican.

LOS ALAMOS COUNTY

De Colores Restaurant & Lounge, 68 Canada Circle (and 820 Trinity), Los Alamos, (505) 662–6285. Inexpensive to moderate. Fare: New Mexican and American.

Greggorio's, 13 Sherwood Drive, Los Alamos, (505) 672–9353, Inexpensive to moderate. Fare: Italian.

Selected Chambers of Commerce/Visitors Bureaus in North Central New Mexico

Chama Chamber of Commerce
P.O. Box 306, Chama, 87520
(505) 756–2306/1–800–477–0149

Española Valley Chamber of Commerce
417 Big Rock Center, Española, 87532
(505) 753–2831

Los Alamos Chamber of Commerce
P.O. Box 460, Los Alamos, 87544
(505) 662–8105
Web site: www.losalamos.com

Sandoval County Region Tourism Association
P.O. Box 40, Bernalillo, 87004
(505) 867–2341/1–800–252–0191

Hilltop House Restaurant,
400 Trinity at Central, Los
Alamos, (505)
662–2441/(800) 462–0936.
Moderate to expensive.
Fare: Upscale American.

O'Henry's,
11 Sherwood Drive,
Los Alamos,
(505) 672–9353. Inexpen-
sive to moderate. Fare:
Eclectic American.

NORTHERN SANDOVAL COUNTY

Los Ojos Restaurant &
Saloon,
Highway 4,
Jemez Springs,
(505) 829–3947. Inexpen-
sive. Fare: Hamburgers,
New Mexican fare.

SOUTHERN SANDOVAL COUNTY

Prairie Star,
2 miles west of Interstate
25 on Highway 44,
Bernalillo,
(505) 867–3327. Moderate
to expensive. Fare: Contemporary with Southwestern
flair.

Cafe de Placitas,
664 Highway 165,
Placitas,
(505) 867–1610. Moderate
to expensive. Fare: Eclectic
American.

The Range Cafe,
925 Camino del Pueblo,
Bernalillo,
(505) 867–1700. Inexpen-
sive to moderate. Fare:
Innovative and eclectic
Southwestern and tradi-
tional New Mexican.

Red River Grill,
601 West Frontage,
Algodones,
(505) 867–3021. Inexpen-
sive to moderate. Fare:
Eclectic Southwestern and
American.

Santa Fe and Taos Region

The counties that boast the art meccas of Santa Fe and Taos have more to offer the traveler than what's confined inside these cities' boundaries. But, oh what those city limits enclose! When people daydream about New Mexico, they're most likely to conjure up images of the historic districts of Santa Fe and Taos: the narrow streets, the richly textured curves of adobe walls, the quaint shops, hidden cafes, and ever-present art galleries—all, set against glorious tree-covered mountains.

But in this region, beyond the city limits, you'll discover New Mexico's highest mountain and wildest river. You'll also find Indian pueblos, first-class downhill and cross-county skiing, historic museums, a revived ghost town, and a mineral springs resort. But most of all you'll encounter spectacular scenery and awesome adventures no matter what time of year you visit.

Santa Fe County

It's a city, it's a style, it's even a cologne and a cookie (by Pepperidge Farms). It's *Santa Fe,* of course, and it's New Mexico's own. Set against the breathtaking Sangre de Cristo ("Blood of Christ") Mountains, the city of Santa Fe, aptly located in Santa Fe County, is a city of superlatives built around a historic plaza: It's the nation's oldest capital (founded in 1610), it's also the nation's highest capital, at 7,000 feet, and it boasts the nation's oldest church (San Miguel Chapel) as well as oldest public building (Palace of the Governors, now a museum).

Despite its fame—or, rather, because of it—Santa Fe presents a major dilemma when writing a book such as this. Writing only one chapter in a guidebook—albeit a selective guide—on Santa Fe is a little like being asked to explain nuclear physics in a hundred words or less. It's a little overwhelming. Add to that the rest of Santa Fe County, and it gets more than a little overwhelming. Santa Fe is certainly the most written-about city in New Mexico, and its paths have been so well beaten by visitors from all over the globe that it hardly seems anything new

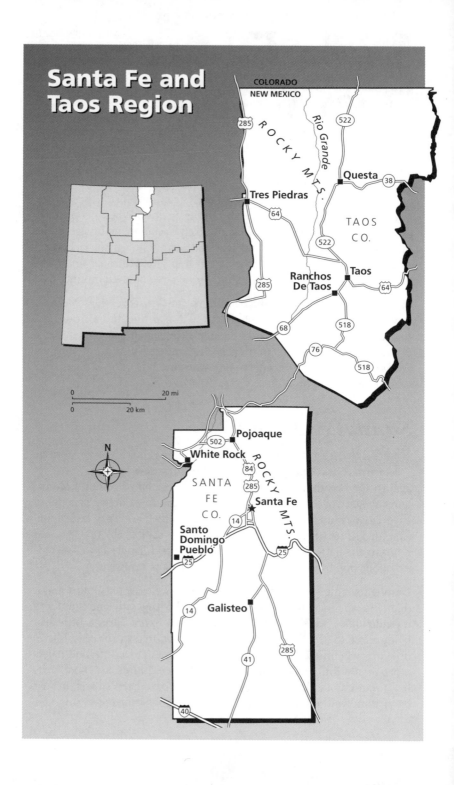

Santa Fe and Taos Region

COLORADO
NEW MEXICO

Rio Grande

ROCKY MTS.

285

522

Questa

38

Tres Piedras

64

TAOS CO.

522

285

Ranchos De Taos

Taos

64

68

518

76

518

0   20 mi
0   20 km

N

502

Pojoaque

White Rock

ROCKY MTS.

84

285

SANTA FE CO.

Santa Fe

14

Santo Domingo Pueblo

25

14

Galisteo

41

285

40

FAVORITE ATTRACTIONS/EVENTS IN SANTA FE AND TAOS

El Rancho de las Golondrinas, La Cienega (505) 471–2261

Ten Thousand Waves, Santa Fe (505) 988–1047

Shidoni Sculpture Garden and Galleries, Tesuque (505) 988–8001

Rio Grande Gorge Bridge, north of Taos
No phone

D. H. Lawrence Memorial, Taos County
No phone

Wild Rivers Recreation Area, Questa (505) 758–8851

Taos Pueblo, Taos County (505) 758–1028

Madrid, New Mexico
No phone

The Burning of Zozobra, Fiestas de Santa Fe, September, Santa Fe (505) 984–6760

Taos Talking Picture Festival, April, Taos (505) 758–3873/1–800–732–8267

could be written about "The City Different" in a travel book. Acknowledging that fact, this chapter will first advise you on experiencing the city's historic/shopping district without directing you to particular spots; it will then cover a few places outside the inner core, before moving on to concentrate on those places in Santa Fe County that are outside the city.

It's hard not to fall in love with Santa Fe. The city oozes quaintness, uniqueness, and all those other "nesses" that have made it New Mexico's most popular visitor destination for decades. If ever there was a New Mexico city perfect for exploring on foot, Santa Fe would be it. Several museums and countless galleries, shops, cafes, and historic sites are within easy walking distance from the Santa Fe Plaza. Surprises lurk around every corner. To advise visitors on what to see here is pointless and would undermine the sense of discovery that Santa Fe is all about. This is not a copout on the part of a lazy travel writer. Trust me.

If you must, go ahead and consult your conventional guidebook on the slickest galleries, the toniest restaurants, and the most chic shops. Then put it away and heed the following advice to "experience" Santa Fe's downtown by yourself or with a friend (avoid going with a group if it's your first visit).

Take off your watch and take a deep breath. Park near the plaza, if you can find a spot. Then skip the plaza (though you'll probably want to check out the jewelry sold by Native Americans under the Palace of the Governors portal). Head out on any one of the streets and wind around until you think you're a little lost. Relax. Drift around, entering whichever places appeal to you. And don't try to see everything; you'll never have time, even if you stay here for days. Duck into a cafe for a cup of coffee or a glass of wine and rest your feet awhile. Check out the museums and historic churches, if you're so inclined.

New Mexico Trivia

Santa Fe is the country's oldest capital city.

Time seems to stop when you're in Santa Fe, so above all don't hurry. Just enjoy the sensory pleasures of the city: the smell of burning piñon wafting from the chimneys, the rich textures and curves of adobe and wood, the muted colors of the city set against that intense azure sky. You'll see much more, have more fun, and be less stressed than if you felt you had to see certain places within a specified time frame. Now you're ready to venture out a bit.

To get an idea of Santa Fe's upscale appeal, take a stroll down **Canyon Road,** about 8 blocks southeast of the plaza. The most coveted address in town, this 2-mile avenue was once part of an Indian trail to the Pecos pueblos and is now synonymous with art and money, though it's remained slightly "beyond the fray" of rampant tourism so as to retain its inherent charms. You'll find many of the city's finer galleries along this narrow promenade, as well as a distinctive medley of restaurants and shops.

Even if you can't afford to purchase anything, one of the more interesting stops along Canyon Road is **Morning Star Gallery.** Though it deals in investment-quality antique American Indian art, Morning Star seems more like a museum that allows visitors to purchase the exhibits. The gallery doesn't limit itself to Indian art from New Mexico, though you'll certainly find plenty of it here. An exquisite Acoma Pueblo pot may go for as much as $4,500, and Navajo blankets from the 1800s reach into the $45,000–$50,000 range. It's incredible to see these items up close and wonder what the potter or weaver would have done with all that money.

Morning Star is located at 513 Canyon Road; (505) 982–8187. It's open Monday through Saturday, 9:00 A.M.–5:00 P.M.

Following an afternoon of gallery hopping along Canyon Road, ease into *El Farol* for a taste of the unexpected and expect to be entertained. This fine restaurant specializes in tapas (roughly translated as "appetizers"), a serving style native to Spain, where each selection is presented on its own small plate. Choose several to make a meal

from the extensive menu. They come hot or cold and run the gamut from meat and chicken to seafood and vegetarian. This is a great way to sample a variety of different foods. El Farol's bar has live entertainment every night, variously featuring jazz, blues, flamenco, and folk sounds.

El Farol is at 808 Canyon Road; (505) 983–9912. It's open daily for lunch, 11:00 A.M.–4:00 P.M., and for dinner, 6:00–10:00 P.M.; bar hours are noon–2:00 A.M.

For a quick nature escape from gallery-hopping along Canyon Road, head up the road to the **Randall Davey Audubon Center**. An information-wall outside of the center's office indicates the recent sightings of particular birds and other wildlife species on the grounds of this wildlife refuge on the eastern edge of Santa Fe. The main attraction here is El Temporal Nature Trail, which winds among the native piñon–juniper vegetation of the foothills of the Sangre de Cristo Mountains. It's a great spot for a minihike for those who may not be inclined to take advantage of the more challenging and remote hiking trails in the mountains.

To get to the center, head east on Canyon Road and continue east on Upper Canyon Road until it dead-ends at the center; (505) 983–4609. A self-pay box accepts $1.00 admission to the hiking trail. Gates are open daily, 9:00 A.M. to 5:00 P.M.

In contrast to the museums in downtown Santa Fe, the small cluster of museums off Camino Lejo in southeast Santa Fe have an open, contemporary feel. Alongside the **Wheelwright Museum of the American Indian** and the **Museum of Indian Arts and Culture** you'll find the more unusual **Museum of International Folk Art.** Set aside a few hours to soak up the eclectic exhibits of various folk arts from more than a hundred countries.

As the largest museum of its kind in the world, the facility's highlight is the Girard Collection, the lifetime collection of the famous architect Alexander Girard and his wife. The brightly colored displays reflect diverse cultures' special talents at channeling their creativity into toys, textiles, costumes, masks, and more. There are no labels in the Girard Collection wing to interfere with the aesthetics of the exhibits. There is, however, a printed guide whose entries correspond to the numbered exhibits so that you can make your excursion as "left brain" as you want.

The Folk Art Museum is at 706 Camino Lejo; (505) 827–6350. Admission is $5.00 for adults, and children under seventeen are admitted free. (*Note:* A four-day pass for all five Santa Fe museums—Museum of New Mexico system only—is available for $10.00). The museum is open Tuesday–Sunday, 10:00 A.M.–5:00 P.M.

After decades of disappointed tourists wandering the streets of Santa Fe, wondering where they could see the paintings of New Mexico's most famous artist, the long-awaited **Georgia O'Keeffe Museum** opened in Santa Fe during the summer of 1997. Dedicated to preserving and presenting the life work of one of America's most remarkable artists, the museum houses a permanent collection of O'Keeffe's art unequaled by any museum in the world. The museum features more than eighty of

O'Keeffe's works, including some of the more famous—large-scale flowers and bleached desert bones—as well as abstracts, nudes, landscapes, cityscapes, and still lifes.

As the newest member of the Museum of New Mexico system (though the O'Keeffe Museum will remain a private institution), the Georgia O'Keeffe Museum is located a few blocks from the Plaza at 217 Johnson Street; (505) 995–0785. Admission is $5.00 for adults, and children under seventeen are admitted free. (*Note:* a four-day pass for all five Santa Fe museums—Museum of New Mexico system only—is available for $10.00. Sunday admission for New Mexico residents is $1.00). The museum is open Tuesday through Sunday, 10:00 A.M. to 5:00 P.M. (until 8:00 P.M. on Friday).

When it comes to lodging, Santa Fe's outstanding choices include historic downtown hotels, quaint bed and breakfasts, and modern resorts. But the one to check out when you're interested in checking in for a while is *The Bishop's Lodge,* just five minutes north of the city in the tranquil Tesuque Valley.

In the 1800s this 1,000-acre ranch was the personal retreat of Father Jean Baptiste Lamy, who became the archbishop of Santa Fe. Father Lamy's story lives on in Willa Cather's book *Death Comes for the Archbishop,* and his chapel still stands just as he left it, as a focal point on the ranch. The historical aspect of the lodge blends well with the modern accommodations and comforts. Its guest rooms are done in classic, southwestern/Santa Fe style, many with fireplaces and balconies or terraces. As a full-service resort, the lodge allows you to opt out of going into the city for fun every day. There's much to do on the grounds of the lodge itself, and sports enthusiasts will find tennis courts, a skeet- and trap-shooting range, a swimming pool, and horses for riding. In addition, The Bishop's Lodge also boasts a first-class restaurant featuring contemporary American cuisine with just a hint of the Southwest.

The Bishop's Lodge is located off Bishop's Lodge Road; (505) 983–6377. Rates, without meals, range from $110 to $575, depending on the season and type of room or suite. A modified American Plan, which includes breakfast and dinner, is also available.

An aside is appropriate here: Avoid the city of Santa Fe during summer if you can. Though many businesses depend on this "tourist season," Santa Feans will heartily thank me if any of you heed this advice. And you, too, will be grateful after you've explored this captivating city without so many people. Avoiding Santa Fe in the summer is, however, impossible if you're a devout opera fan who's always dreamed of attending the world-famous *Santa Fe Opera;* (505) 986–5900/(800) 280–4654; www.santafeopera.org. You guessed it; the opera season runs from the end of June (with an often outrageously flamboyant Gala Opening) through August, ending with the opera's "Grande Finale Fiesta." Keep in mind, though, that it's not unheard of for tickets for specific performances to sell out months in advance. (*Note:* Inexpensive standing-room-only tickets are often surprisingly easy to come by the day of each performance; call for ticket prices and details.) And although there can be crowds in Santa Fe around the Christmas holidays as well, that's just such a magical time to be in Santa Fe that it's hard to tell someone to avoid December, too.

The community of *Tesuque,* named for nearby Tesuque Pueblo, is about 8 miles north of Santa Fe via Highway 590 (or U.S. Highway 84/285 and then Highway 591). This quiet little community has become quite pricey real estate over the years as Santa Feans and others have come to appreciate the simple tree-covered beauty of this slow-paced valley. Lately, the famous have joined the rich in discovering the appeal of Tesuque. Whether as residents or long-term visitors, the likes of Elizabeth Taylor, Candice

Solamente en Nuevo México . . .
The Burning of Zozobra

*T*he burning of Zozobra, a 40-foot effigy of Old Man Gloom, marks the beginning of La Fiesta de Santa Fe each September, the Friday after Labor Day. The event invites comparisons with New Year's Eve and Mardi Gras.

Early in the evening locals, thrill-seekers, and tourists alike stake out spots in Fort Marcy Park, a couple of blocks from Santa Fe's downtown plaza, awaiting the main event. The symbolic burning is a magical catharsis, ridding gloom and misfortune, in preparation for the weekend-long celebration.

After dusk the action heats up. Led by the traditional Firedancer, other dancers perform around the base of the intricately engineered Zozobra, who begins taunting the crowd with moaning and groaning as he arrogantly awaits his fate. (The moans are provided by an amplified human voice cleverly in sync with the puppet's mouth movements.) As the crowd claps and chants, "Burn him, burn him," Zozobra moans louder. The crowd's enthusiasm builds to a frenzied crescendo as the shouting continues. Finally, the Firedancer torches Zozobra and simultaneously sets off hundreds of colorful fireworks into the clear, dark Santa Fe sky.

Zozobra continues to moan until he's completely engulfed in flames. The crowd of thousands, now thoroughly primed, cheers and begins the trek back to the plaza for music, merrymaking, and dancing in the streets— now that all the gloom has been

Bergen, Robert Redford, Ali MacGraw, and Martina Navratilova have been spotted in town, especially at the Tesuque Village Market (see page 90).

If you're into fine art with a penchant for sculpture, **Shidoni** is the place for you. This intriguing spot is actually three spots: Shidoni Contemporary Gallery, Shidoni Bronze Gallery, and Shidoni Sculpture Garden. Shidoni (the word for a Navajo greeting to a friend) is not only a place for art lovers to visit but also an important resource for artists. Established as a foundry in 1971 by sculptor Tommy Hicks, Shidoni has evolved into an internationally known fine-art casting facility. Bronze pourings are held every Saturday from noon to 4:30 P.M., and the public is welcome to watch as 2,000-degree molten bronze is poured into the ceramic shell molds, one of several steps in the casting process.

The sculpture garden is a favorite of many visitors to Shidoni. You're immediately struck that this place is special when you pull into the parking area and are greeted by colorful shapes springing from the earth. As you gaze beyond, you'll notice that there are many more intriguing and sometimes outlandish works of art positioned among old apple trees in a spacious grassy area. A crisp sunny day is perfect for examining the garden.

Shidoni is 5 miles north of Santa Fe, just south of Tesuque on Bishop's Lodge Road; (505) 988–8001. The galleries and garden are open Monday through Saturday, 9:00 A.M.–5:00 P.M.

If you're hungry after your visit to Shidoni, grab a bite at the **Tesuque Village Market** (505–988–8848) on Highway 591 in Tesuque. This laidback restaurant, deli, and wineshop serves up great soups and sandwiches and wine by the glass; the market is also known for its selection of scrumptious desserts. It's also a great place for breakfast and a leisurely weekend brunch. Patio seating, too, is available. The market, a welcome change from some of the stuffier places in the city, is open daily, 7:00 A.M.–9:00 P.M.

While you're in the area, stop at **Camel Rock** along U.S. Highway 84/285 on Tesuque Pueblo; the site offers a great place to get your picture taken with this striking and appropriately named rock formation. The rock is fenced off, so you can't sit on its head or anything, but the fence doesn't ruin the photograph—you'll hardly notice it.

Its name may sound like a family water park, but leave the kids at home when you visit **Ten Thousand Waves,** a truly magnificent Japanese-style spa tucked into the foothills of the Sangre de Cristo Mountains, just east of Santa Fe.

From the parking lot, a series of wooden steps takes you high up through the landscape to the main entrance and into the lobby/registration area, where you'll be greeted with the soft sound of water falling in a Zen fountain. Though the spa offers herbal wraps, massages, salt glows, and aroma therapy among other treatments, the main focus is on the exquisite wooden hot tubs, with their crystal-clear, absolutely clean water. (State-of-the-art purification systems, combined with ultraviolet light, hydrogen peroxide, and ozone, assures this; and though some of the cold plunges are purified with bromine, chlorine is not used in any tub or plunge.) If a private tub is not available (which will probably be the case if you didn't make reservations, which are practically required), opt for the communal tub, which is outdoors on a large wooden deck flocked by fragrant piñon and juniper trees. A cold plunge is nearby, as is an authentic wooden sauna. Ten Thousand Waves is Santa Fe at its holistic, spiritual, sensually indulgent best. If you're not uptight about nudity (bathing suits are optional, but I've rarely seen one here) and really want to release stress, this is the place to go to let it go.

Being pampered is part of the deal: Your bathing experience includes kimonos, towels, sandals, soap, shampoo, cedar skin lotion, hair dryers, and lockers. Communal baths are $13 per person for unlimited time. TTW's private tubs vary in style—one includes a waterfall, rock deck, and steam room; others include saunas and decks—and range from $18 per person per hour to $25 per person per hour. TTW now has eight luxury guest suites, ranging from $125 to $205 per night. Call for pricing information for other services.

Ten Thousand Waves is open Wednesday through Monday, and though hours of operation vary for different tubs and seasons, it's basically open from late morning until past 10:00 P.M., later during summer; on Tuesday, it's open from late afternoon through normal closing time. You'll find this Far Eastern–Southwestern paradise 3½ miles east of Santa Fe on Artist Road (which becomes Hyde Park Road), the route to the Santa Fe Ski Area (by the way, if you haven't already guessed, this is the perfect place to wind down after a spirited day of skiing!); (505) 992–5025.

Northwest of Santa Fe you'll discover the *San Ildefonso Pueblo.* Set in the Rio Grande valley and flanked by vast stands of cottonwood, the pueblo is a beautifully maintained village laid out in the traditional manner with mission church and plaza. The Jemez Mountains in the distance complete the scene. Similar to Santa Clara Pueblo, San Ildefonso is famous for its matte black-on-black pottery, though other types are also created here. One of New Mexico's most famous Native American artists, the late Maria "Poveka" Martinez, was from San Ildefonso and revived this traditional art form. A museum on the pueblo is dedicated to her.

To get the best feel for the art and the people of New Mexico's northern pueblos all in one place, visit San Ildefonso Pueblo during the Eight Northern Indian Pueblos' Artist & Craftsman Show, held every July. Because this is a popular event, you can expect lots of people; nevertheless, if you're serious about buying Indian art or jewelry directly from Native Americans in a lovely setting, it's worth braving the crowds to attend.

Though San Ildefonso welcomes visitors Monday through Saturday from 8:00 A.M. to 4:30 P.M., you must first register with the visitor center; call ahead for specific dates of events. There's a $3.00 admission fee per carload, and camera and sketching fees also apply. San Ildefonso is 22 miles northwest of Santa Fe: 16 miles north on U.S. Highway 84/285 and then 6 miles west on Highway 502; (505) 455–3549. Winter hours are subject to change; call ahead.

Just west of the San Ildefonso Pueblo on Highway 502, you'll come across the **Cottonwood Trading Post** (505–455–7596). This tiny store exists for area pueblo residents and others who live in the vicinity. It not only buys and sell Indian-made pottery, jewelry, and weavings but is also a legitimate trading post complete with groceries and household items. Staff members are extremely knowledgeable about Native American arts because they deal directly with the artists themselves. The trading post is open 9:00 A.M.–5:30 P.M., Monday–Saturday.

South of Santa Fe, near the community of La Cienega, you'll find **El Rancho de las Golondrinas** ("The Ranch of the Swallows"). This isolated, 200-acre living-history museum is part of one of the most historic ranches in the Southwest. The ranch (of the same name) was founded in the early 1700s as a stopping place on El Camino Real, "The Royal Road" connecting Mexico City to Santa Fe. The museum has as its focus eighteenth-century life on a working Spanish colonial ranch. Every effort has been made to re-create the ranch as it was during that period: Crops are grown, orchards and vineyards are tended to, and sheep, goats, turkeys, geese, and ducks mill about. Though there's a small "traditional" indoor museum on the grounds, the joy of a visit to Las Golondrinas is walking among all the outbuildings and gardens.

Las Golondrinas really comes alive during its spring and fall festivals, especially the latter. Each October you can step back in time to all the sights and smells of an authentic fall harvest from the past. You'll witness costumed interpreters first carding, spinning, and dyeing wool and then weaving it into rugs. You can also see sugarcane becoming molasses with the help of a burro-driven press. Then there are blacksmiths and wheelwrights at work and a wonderful water-driven mill spinning among the golden poplars. And gourds, sunflowers, and red chiles lie drying in the sun, while juice is crushed from freshly picked apples (samples available). The stillness and anticipation of an autumn day in the country creep into your soul and take hold at Las Golondrinas and are well worth the trek.

El Rancho de las Golondrinas is located 15 miles south of Santa Fe. Take the exit off Interstate 25 (exit 276 coming from Santa Fe and exit 276B coming from Albuquerque) and follow the signs; (505) 471–2261. The museum is open June through September, Wednesday through Sunday, 10:00 A.M.–4:00 P.M. Admission is $4.00 for adults, $3.00 for seniors and children ages thirteen to eighteen, and $1.50 for children ages five to twelve. Spring Festival takes place the first weekend in June, and Fall Festival is held the first weekend in October. Festival hours are 9:00 A.M.–4:00 P.M. Festival admission is $5.00 for adults, $3.50 for seniors and children ages thirteen to eighteen, and $2.50 for children ages five to twelve. Call for information regarding Las Golodrinas's Wine Festival (the first weekend in July) and Civil War Weekend (May).

La Comida de Nuevo México

*H*oly Guacamole

Because avocados are native to the tropics, guacamole is not a traditional New Mexican preparation. Nevertheless, it's one of my favorite adapted Southwestern sides, so I couldn't resist sharing my favorite version.

2 large, ripe avacados, peeled and pitted

1 teaspoon red chile powder

1 tablespoon lemon juice

1 small clove garlic, minced

1 tomato, minced (optional)

1–2 green onions, minced (optional)

1 teaspoon salt

Mash avocados with a fork and mix with remaining ingredients. Serve with tostadas, or corn tortilla chips. Makes 4 servings.

Though the **Turquoise Trail** starts just outside Albuquerque in Tijeras, the bulk of it is in Santa Fe County, tracing the route of Highway 14, commonly known as North 14. The trail, designated a Scenic and Historic Area, connects the semighost towns of Golden, Madrid, and Cerrillos (among others) along this leisurely behind-the-mountain path linking Albuquerque to Santa Fe.

The trail probably got its name from Mount Chalchihuitl, near Cerrillos, which contained a vast lode of the blue-green gemstones and was the only place in New Mexico where turquoise was mined. The towns along the Turquoise Trail (sometimes known as the Ghost Town Trail) have a boom-and-bust mining legacy similar to that of towns in the southern part of the state. Mined in this area, in addition to turquoise, were coal, lead, copper, silver, and gold.

Though each of the spots along the Turquoise Trail has its own charms and history, the revived ghost town of **Madrid** (pronounced MAD-rid, unlike its namesake in Spain) is perhaps the most fun. Originally an old coal-mining town, Madrid all but died after the last mine shut down in the 1950s, when the demand for coal declined, thus leaving scores of similar, wooden company houses along this strip of North 14.

During the past twenty or so years, Madrid has been rediscovered by artistic types and former hippies drawn to its funky charm. The successful revival of this onetime ghost town was even the subject of a *60 Minutes* spot in 1982. A South American import clothing store and a New Age crystal emporium join ranks with other small shops and restaurants. The commercial establishments share Madrid with the deserted and occupied houses that dot the main drag. More so than many places in New Mexico, Madrid *evolves,* so expect to find something different each time you visit. Then, too, the weather is not the only thing that can get quite hot during the summer in Madrid—the outdoor Madrid jazz and blues concerts have become quite a popular weekend outing for folks from Albuquerque and Santa Fe.

Check out the **Mine Shaft Tavern** (505–473–0743) as a great example of a real mining-town bar. It's rustic, wooden, and dark and contains a large stone fireplace and a dart board. Hundreds of dollar bills sporting handwritten notes from visitors from all over the world are plastered on the wall above the bar. Live entertainment is also part of the Mine Shaft experience. In addition to drinks, the tavern serves up generous burgers and steaks, including buffalo steak when available, as well as sandwiches and several New Mexican dishes. The Tavern Burger is a good bet—a half-pound of ground beef laced and topped with bleu cheese:

delicious. The sign above the door says it all: WELCOME TO MADRID— MADRID HAS NO TOWN DRUNK, WE ALL TAKE TURNS.

Adjacent to the tavern you'll find the **Old Coal Mine Museum,** which contains the **Engine House Theater.** On weekends and holidays from Memorial Day through mid-October, the theater presents hilarious melodrama productions. Booing, hissing, and throwing marshmallows (available at the door for a small fee) are encouraged. Shows change each season. Call (505) 473–0743 for current show times, admission charges, and reservations.

Taos County

Taos has long been a gathering place for creative people. Its repu- tation for seducing artists and nurturing their works began before the turn of the century and continues to this day. The legacy of the Taos Society of Artists and all those who followed lives on in Taos's many fine galleries—more per capita, in fact, than in any other city in the United States. The striking Taos Pueblo and acclaimed Taos Ski Val- ley have also brought this lovely little town worldwide attention.

Though there's more to Taos County than Taos itself, the city that grew around its now-famous plaza is a good place to start. As with Santa Fe, exploring Taos's downtown museums, galleries, and shops is best done on foot. Taos is actually composed of three communities, all with Taos in their names: There's Taos the town, Ranchos de Taos, and Taos Pueblo. First, Taos proper.

The Kit Carson Historic Museums consist of three different museums that collectively bring Taos's illustrious past to life—the Kit Carson Home, Martinez Hacienda, and Ernest L. Blumenschein Home. Admis- sion to each museum is $5.00 for adults and seniors, and $2.50 for chil- dren. Discounts apply if you want to visit more than one; you can purchase the multiple ticket at any of the museums.

True to the northern New Mexico tradition of "wonderful things lie hid- den behind adobe walls," the **Kit Carson Home** lies behind a plain, storefrontlike facade. But history comes alive behind these adobe walls. Although Christopher "Kit" Carson was born in Kentucky in 1809, the legendary mountain man and scout made his home in Taos. He came to Taos in 1826 to become a trapper because the village was known as the center of the fur trade, owing to the abundance of beaver in the nearby mountain streams. In 1843, Carson bought this twelve-room adobe home as a wedding gift for his bride, Josefa Jaramillo. The home's rooms divide the museum into various exhibits. All periods of Taos's colorful history are depicted, in addition to a special display on Carson himself. Even Kit Carson's cradle is on display in the museum–and his grave is in nearby Kit Carson Park.

The Kit Carson Home is ¹/₂ block east of Taos Plaza on Kit Carson Road; (505) 758–0505. Summer hours are 8:00 A.M.–6:00 P.M. daily, and winter hours are 9:00 A.M.–5:00 P.M. daily.

For a view of Spanish colonial life in Taos, the **Martinez Hacienda** has no rivals. This fully restored compound sits defiantly on the banks of the Rio Pueblo just outside Taos as it did nearly 200 years ago. The sprawling, twenty-one-room home of Don Antonio Severino Martinez encloses two *placitas* (courtyard-type areas), has no exterior windows, and looks like a fort. In reality, it did serve as a fortress against the Apache and Comanche raids of the times.

A Glimpse of Santa Fe and Taos: *Impresiones de las Turistas . . .*

*U*nlike most cities and regions in New Mexico, Santa Fe and Taos have extensive reputations. But like most notable U.S. tourist destinations, their reputations differ among persons living in-state and those who don't. Outsiders are likely to know the two cities as prominent art centers, southwestern cultural enclaves, and mountain resorts. But for many New Mexicans, Santa Fe means state government and progressive politics, movie stars and out-of-state wealth, New Age spirituality and the metaphysical arts—and tourists. (Taos evokes pretty much the same sentiment, sans the capital-city references.) Both reputations are quite valid and well earned, but both communities take part in creating and shaping their images. Each is quite accomplished in courting tourist dollars, while at the same time expressing occasional disdain for the tourists, but the same could be said of Carmel, Cape Cod, Key West, or any other enduring vacation spot. So if you can get past the occasional resident attitude of "last one in, close the door," Santa Fe and Taos will not disappoint you with their offerings.

Even if you, as a tourist, are also sometimes annoyed by tourists, if you're going to fall in love with New Mexico, you've got to get to know Santa Fe and Taos. Only then are you allowed to sit back and muse on your jadedness toward two of New Mexico's most perfectly set communities. You'll find both—along with their tony galleries and excellent restaurants—nestled in the pricey, rolling green foothills of northern New Mexico's Sangre de Cristo Mountains.

So next time you're hiking up Santa Fe's Adalaya Mountain with your dog on a lazy Tuesday afternoon, tip your hat toward Shirley MacLaine, whose house, by the way, you'll be passing on your left.

Today the hacienda provides a glimpse back at the many components that made up the self-contained compound. A blacksmith shop, a tack room, a granary, and a weaving room have all been restored, as have living quarters with period furnishings. It's located 2 miles southeast of Taos Plaza on Highway 240; (505) 758–0505. Summer hours are 9:00 A.M.–5:00 P.M. daily, and winter hours are 10:00 A.M.–4:00 P.M. daily.

New Mexico's state flower, the yucca, is also known plurally as "Lamparas de Dios," which means "Lamps of God," due to the bright mass of white flowers that protrudes from a center stalk within the plant. Not only an attractive native plant, the yucca has also been an important resource in past decades, as its roots and palm-like leaves provided materials for making soap and baskets, respectively.

The Blumenschein Home, the third component of the Kit Carson Historic Museums, is an art museum with the feel of a traditional museum in a homelike setting. The furnishings of the Blumenschein family of artists—Ernest; his wife, Mary; and their daughter, Helen—together with their paintings and those of other prominent Taos artists take visitors back to the glory days of art and culture in Taos.

Ernest Blumenschein was the cofounder of the now-legendary Taos Society of Artists. The story of how Blumenschein ended up in Taos—and thus put Taos on the art map—is well known. Blumenschein had originally heard about Taos from a fellow artist while studying in Paris in 1895. Later, during a trip from Denver to Mexico that Blumenschein took with artist Bert Phillips, a wheel on their wagon broke north of Taos. After repairing the wheel in Taos, the artists became captivated by the valley, its inhabitants, and its brilliant light. They decided to stay and urged other artists to come to Taos as well. In 1912, Blumenschein, together with five other artists, founded the Taos Society of Artists, whose purpose was to enable its members as a group to exhibit their art in galleries throughout the country. In 1919, after spending many summers in Taos, Blumenschein and his young family moved from New York to Taos and purchased the home that was to become part of the Kit Carson Historic Museums.

The Blumenschein House is on Ledoux Street, 2 blocks west of Taos Plaza; (505) 758–0505. Summer hours are 9:00 A.M.–5:00 P.M. daily, and winter hours are 11:00 A.M.–4:00 P.M. daily.

Farther west on Ledoux Street you'll find New Mexico's second-oldest museum, *The Harwood Foundation Museum,* which was founded in 1923 and has been operated by the University of New Mexico since 1935. The art museum contains paintings, drawings, prints, sculpture, and photographs by Taos artists from 1898 to the present. The Taos Society of Artists is well represented in this permanent collection. There's also an assortment of nineteenth-century *retablos* (religious paintings on wood) that were given to the foundation by arts patron and writer Mabel Dodge Luhan. Special exhibitions of Taos artists and works from the University of New Mexico's collections are also displayed during the year.

The Harwood Foundation Museum is at 238 Ledoux Street; (505) 758–9826. Museum hours are Tuesday–Saturday 10:00 A.M. to 5:00 P.M., and Sunday, noon to 5:00 P.M. Admission is $5.00 for adults and seniors, and children under twelve are admitted free.

Like Santa Fe, Taos offers an abundance of distinctive lodging. The **Taos Inn** is the oldest hotel in town and the only one on the national and state registers of historic places. If you don't want to worry about getting around in your car, the Taos Inn is the best base from which to explore the downtown plaza area, including the shops, galleries, and cafes in the **Bent Street District,** which includes the **Governor Bent House and Museum,** across the street. The inn, restored in 1982, has uniquely outfitted each of its forty guest rooms with pueblo-style furnishings, including hand-loomed Indian bedspreads; some also have adobe kiva fireplaces.

Doc Martin's, the inn's restaurant, is named after Taos's first doctor, who lived and practiced in part of what now accommodates the inn and restaurant. It specializes in innovative fish and pasta dishes and from 1985 through 1989 was honored by the *Wine Spectator* for having one of the most outstanding restaurant wine lists in the world. The inn's Adobe Bar is a comfortable, popular gathering place for the arts crowd; local musicians often provide entertainment as well. The bar's seating area flows into the lobby so that patrons can enjoy the atmosphere there as well.

Reservations are often hard to come by, so book early. Daily room rates range from $85 to $225, depending on type of room and season. The Taos Inn is at 125 Paseo del Pueblo Norte; (505) 758–2233/(800) TAOS–INN.

Not far from the plaza, but sufficiently hidden, is a wonderful inn with a fascinating past. The **Bed & Breakfast at the Mabel Dodge Luhan House** offers guest rooms in the original home as well as in a separate addition. But as the original estate of the Taos writer, designer, and champion of the southwestern creative arts movement, it's also worth exploring on its own. The existing 200-year-old structure was expanded to its present size of twenty-two rooms in 1922 by Antonio Luhan, Mabel's husband. Spanish colonial and pueblo styles shine throughout.

Stories persist that the home is haunted by either the ghost of Mabel herself or that of a young Taos Pueblo girl. Apparitions aside, if these old adobe walls could talk, present-day visitors would gladly listen: Mabel entertained such guests as D. H. Lawrence, Willa Cather, Aldous Huxley, Georgia O'Keeffe, and Carl Jung here.

A whole different set of characters frequented the estate in the late 1960s and early 1970s, after actor Dennis Hopper purchased it when filming *Easy Rider* near Taos. Peter and Jane Fonda, Jack Nicholson, and Elizabeth Taylor were among Hopper's guests. (Some visitors would no doubt rather hear the walls talk about that period!)

The inn carries on in Mabel's tradition of hosting the creative crowd—many famous contemporary writers and artists enjoy the serenity and sense of history found here. Guests are served a breakfast buffet either in the spacious dining room or outside on the patio among the huge cottonwood, beech, and elm trees. Wine and cheese are often served in the afternoons.

Rates range from $85 to $160, with the two-bedroom gate house going for $200 for two (extra fee for additional guests). The bed and breakfast is located on Morada Street north of Kit Carson Road; (505) 751–9686.

Adjoining Taos on the south is the village of Ranchos de Taos, home of the **San Francisco de Asis Church,** built in 1850. No photographs are allowed of the mission church's interior, but you can click to your heart's desire outside. Photographers and painters have been capturing the image on film and canvas for more than a century, and, oddly enough, it's the backside that most intrigues them. The unusual cruciform shape of the church, together with the soft contours of buttresses that support the adobe walls, is impressive enough, but the added element of the changing shadows combines to make the sight truly inspiring.

The mysterious **The Shadow of the Cross** painting, by Henri Ault, is on display in the rectory hall across from the church. The mystery of the portrait—which is of Christ on the shore of the Sea of Galilee—occurs when it is viewed in the dark: After about ten minutes the portrait becomes luminescent, outlining the figure while clouds over the left shoulder of Jesus form a shadow of a cross.

The painting was completed in 1896, years before the discovery of radium. Moreover, no luminous paint has so far been developed that will not darken and oxidize within a relatively short time. Ault claimed

Santa Fe and Taos Region Trivia

New Mexico boasts the oldest road in the United States, El Camino Real (the Royal Road), which roughly follows Interstate 25 from Anthony to Santa Fe. Historically, it connected Mexico City with Santa Fe during the early days of Spanish exploration and occupation.

he didn't know why the painting changed in the dark. He even thought he was going crazy when he first went into his studio at night and discovered the luminosity.

The painting was first exhibited at the St. Louis World's Fair in 1904 and, after more than fifty years of exhibition in galleries throughout North America and Europe, is now at its permanent home. Every half-hour from 9:00 A.M. to 3:30 P.M., except from noon to 1:00 P.M., (Monday through Saturday) the church allows viewing of the spectacle by turning out the lights for visitors. There is no admission charge.

An adjacent gift shop sells religious articles, books, and cards Monday through Saturday, 9:00 A.M.–5:00 P.M. during summer; 9:00 A.M.–4:00 P.M. during winter. The plaza/parking area is lined with shops and galleries. The church is located just off Highway 68 in Ranchos de Taos; (505) 758–2754. It's open to visitors daily, except Sunday, 9:00 A.M.–4:00 P.M.

Falling somewhere between a bed-and-breakfast inn and a classic hotel is the latest incarnation of the newly renovated **San Geronimo Lodge,** a historic ten-room adobe lodge with breathtaking views of

Forest Magic Preserved with "No Trace" Ethics

*D*espite its image as a desert, New Mexico is blessed with 20 million acres of forested land, almost half of which makes up the state's five national forests. Scattered throughout its high-desert landscape, these mountainous areas are not only wildlife habitat but also green oases where human visitors can escape the summer heat and find physical, mental, and spiritual retreat among the fragrant conifers and web of life that these national treasures contain.

New Mexico forests include Gila National Forest (southwestern mountains), Cibola National Forest (central

and western mountains), Santa Fe National Forest (north central mountains), Carson National Forest (Taos and northernmost mountains), and Lincoln National Forest (southeastern mountains). In addition, within these national forests and elsewhere in the state are twenty-one protected wilderness areas, where no human activity is allowed except hiking, backpacking, and camping. To keep these backcountry areas in their wild and pristine state, it's necessary to practice no-trace ethics by remembering two basic U.S. Forest Service commandments: Make it hard for others to notice you, and leave no trace of your visit.

San Geronimo Lodge

Taos Mountain. Not only has it quickly earned a reputation as a relaxing getaway, but it has also become a popular business-retreat destination and romantic setting for weddings. The lodge originally opened in 1925 and was a gathering place for Taos's art and society crowd. In 1994, sisters Allison and Shaunessy Everett purchased the closed lodge and embarked on a painstaking process of authentically restoring the inn to its original state. The dramatic pine vigas (log ceiling beams), kiva fireplaces, and hardwood floors were all refinished by hand. Each of the guest rooms features handcrafted furniture and completely renovated private baths. All the ambiance and comforts inside notwithstanding, you won't want to stay in your room for long. Not only do you have great views of the mountains from the inn's rambling verandas and balconies, you can also enjoy the sweeping grounds that surround the lodge, which include colorful gardens, patios, an open-air hot tub, and a full-size swimming pool. The Everett sisters make fresh preserves for their guests from the cherry, apricot, apple, and pear trees that line the banks of the Acequia Madre (mother ditch) meandering through the grounds.

The lodge is located adjacent to Kit Carson National Forest at 1101 Witt Road; (505) 751–3776/(800) 894–4119. Rates range from $95 to $120, double occupancy, which include a full country-style breakfast.

Two miles north of Taos you'll find **Taos Pueblo,** New Mexico's best-known Indian pueblo. Besides its spectacular mountainside setting, Taos Pueblo gets this distinction because of its picturesque, multistory, apartmentlike architecture, which sets it apart from other pueblos. Taos Pueblo has been continuously inhabited for centuries, and the Taos Indians have lived at or near the present site for almost 1,000 years.

A walking tour is available to get a feel for the pueblo, its history, and its people. Aside from the obvious addition of tourists and the various Indian-owned shops catering to them, the pueblo looks much the way it did hundreds of years ago. The rapidly flowing, crystal-clear Rio Pueblo de Taos adds to the tranquility of the setting and is still the only source of drinking water for Taos Pueblo residents.

Though certain ceremonial dances and feast days are open to the public, here, as in most pueblos, some sacred activities are restricted to tribal members only. Therefore, if you don't want to inadvertently arrive at a closed pueblo during your visit, it's a good idea to call ahead.

Taos Pueblo is normally open to the public daily, 8:00 A.M.–5:00 P.M. during the summer and 8:30 A.M.–4:30 P.M. during winter; however, the pueblo usually closes to the public for one month during the late winter or early spring, so plan accordingly. The following fees apply: admission, $4.00 per person; still cameras, $10; movie or video cameras, $20. Taos Pueblo is 2 miles north of Taos off Highway 68; (505) 758–1028.

Taos Indian Horse Ranch, an Indian-owned venture near the pueblo, is popular with horse-loving visitors. The ranch, with 80,000 acres of riding trails, provides various rides and excursions. In winter, traditional sleigh rides are given over breathtaking terrain and come complete with Indian storytellers, music, camp fires, and marshmallow roasts.

Most of the trail guides are Taos Pueblo Indians who are master riders. The ranch features horses selected for their ability to ride responsively to the novice rider. The place has been owned and operated by Cesario Stormstar Gomez and his family for more than twenty years.

Tour prices range from $32 to $95 per person. Sleigh rides range from $17.50 to $45.00 per person (children's rate is $10). Private sleigh-ride packages are available upon request. Because all tours are by appointment only, call (505) 758–3212 or (800) 659–3210 for reservations, as well as to get directions.

Taos County's other pueblo, **Picuris Pueblo,** is not so well known to tourists and is thus more representative of most New Mexico pueblos.

Some feel it offers visitors a more authentic New Mexico Indian experience than the very visible Taos Pueblo.

Because Picuris Pueblo is located in a hidden valley, it was the last of New Mexico's pueblos to be discovered by Spanish explorers. Despite its relative isolation, Picuris is quite receptive to visitors. The **Picuris Pueblo Museum** displays pottery, beadwork, and weavings. The Hidden Valley Shop and Restaurant are also on the pueblo. Every August 10 the pueblo celebrates St. Lorenzo Feast Day, which is open to the public.

There is no fee to visit the pueblo or the museum. There are, however, modest fees for self-guided and guided tours, as well as for fishing or camping permits. In addition, there are fees for cameras and sketching. The pueblo is generally open to visitors 9:00 A.M. to 6:00 P.M. daily. To get to Picuris Pueblo, take Highway 75 east for 13 miles off Highway 68; (505) 587–2519.

The **Millicent Rogers Museum** is one of the finest and most specialized museums in the area. The private, nonprofit institution celebrates the art and culture of the Native American and Hispanic peoples of the Southwest. Built around the extensive collection of the late Millicent Rogers, the museum is a living memorial to this woman who took it upon herself to collect and preserve what she recognized as the rapidly vanishing arts of the area's people during the late 1940s and early 1950s.

In addition to a representative collection of Native American and His-

Solamente en Nuevo México . . .
The Taos Hum

*O*n a list of things the Taos Chamber of Commerce would want you to know, its community's infamous hum may not make the cut. Or, on second thought, maybe it would. The thing is, not everyone is convinced the Taos Hum even exists, and if it does, no one really knows what it is. According to the "Taos Hum Homepage" (http://www.eskimo.com/~billb/hum), the Taos Hum is a low-pitched, reverberating sound heard in many places worldwide, especially in the United States—most notably in Taos—the United Kingdom, and northern Europe.

It's usually heard only in quiet environments and is often described as sounding like a distant diesel engine. Because it has proven undetectable by microphones or VLF antennae, its source and nature remain a mystery. Taos area residents are divided on the issue, with most claiming not to have heard the hum that bears their community's name.

panic arts, the museum boasts the most important public holding of the lifework of San Ildefonso Pueblo's most famous potter, Maria Martinez, and her talented family (see Santa Fe County entry on page 83).

The museum is 4 miles north of Taos, just off Highway 522; (505) 758–2462. The museum is open daily 10:00 A.M.–5:00 P.M. except during the winter, when it's closed on Monday. Admission is $6.00 for adults, $5.00 for students and seniors, and $1.00 for children ages six to sixteen. Group rates are available.

After absorbing some of the area's culture at the Millicent Rogers Museum, head over to the **Rio Grande Gorge Bridge** for a spectacular though slightly unnerving experience. There's a parking area on each side of the bridge. From either one you can walk across the bridge—a narrow sidewalk runs alongside the highway—which spans the 1,200-foot-wide gorge. Midway across, a small lookout platform on each side allows you to peer down 600 feet into the gorge to the wild Rio Grande. Yes, there is a railing. There's a movement afoot to allow bungee-jumping from the bridge, which proponents feel would draw adventurers nationwide. However, the plan would need legislative approval, so until then, daredevils may only dream about taking the plunge.

The bridge is on U.S. Highway 64, about 11 miles west of the 64/522 junction just north of Taos. No hours, no phone, no admission fee, no rest rooms.

Small organic farms are increasingly popular as tourist attractions, as they give the opportunity to become attuned to the a local area's wisdom of using basic, natural means of enriching life. **Bluebird Herb Farm** in Taos is certainly evidence of this. Guided tours of the farm's seven display gardens (culinary, medicinal, tea, insect repellent, potpourri, birds and bees, and children's) are available, with tea and a variety of herbal and vegetable-based snacks provided after the tour. Visitors are also welcome to spend time among the gardens, sketching, taking photos, or merely relaxing. Herb and gardening talks as well as workshops on herb–related cooking, crafts, and wild plants are given on a monthly basis. Herbal body care products, teas, and farm-made cooking products are available for sale in the farm's gift shop.

The farm is located at 418A Trujillo Lane, 4 blocks from Taos Plaza, 1 1/2 blocks west of Valverde Street; (505) 751–1490; www.newmex.com/ bluebird. Call ahead for reservations for guided tours or for workshop information. The farm is open Tuesday through Friday from May through October, noon to 5:00 P.M., and selected weekends when "open houses" or workshops are held.

Just north of Taos in a remote mountain area near San Cristobal, persons with a literary bent seek out the **D. H. Lawrence Memorial,** which contains the remains of the celebrated English writer. Lawrence, whose novels include *Sons and Lovers* and *Lady Chatterley's Lover,* died in Paris in 1930, but in 1937 his widow, Frieda, brought his cremated ashes to New Mexico.

Though the Lawrences lived in northern New Mexico only eleven months, it certainly made an impact on them. Lawrence wrote: "I think New Mexico was the greatest experience from the outside world that I ever had. It certainly changed me forever. . . . What splendour!"

Visitors trek up the sloped walk, bordered by remarkably tall spruce trees, to the memorial site. The small, white building houses an altarlike stone marker that contains Lawrence's ashes. It's interesting to read the comments left by visitors in a guestbook inside the memorial, because they often express very personal opinions about Lawrence and his writing—both positive and negative. Just outside the front door is Frieda's grave site. She gave the ranch to the University of New Mexico in 1956,

D. H. Lawrence Memorial

specifying that her husband's memorial be perpetually maintained and kept open to the public.

When climbing the slope, don't look behind you until you reach the door to the memorial. Then turn and be greeted by the spectacular view: Pine and spruce forest in the foreground gives way to a vast expanse of mesa-desert-gorge beyond, north of the Taos Valley.

To experience the memorial, head north of Taos on Highway 522 for about 12 miles. A directional sign and historical marker at San Cristobal mark the turnoff. The ranch and memorial are about 7 miles off the highway at the end of a dirt road that climbs into the mountains; there is no phone (though there is a caretaker who lives near the parking area). There is no fee to visit the memorial (though most of the ranch property is off-limits to visitors), and it's open daily during daylight hours.

Fort Burgwin, an 1850s fort south of Taos that protected past residents from Apache and Comanche raids, was rescued from ruin and restored by Southern Methodist University and opened as an external campus of the school in 1974. Though the Fort Burgwin Research Center may be just school to students fortunate enough to study here, to the rest of us Fort Burgwin really comes to life during summer. From June through mid-August, Fort Burgwin hosts several public events, including evening lectures, art exhibits, and music, theater, and dance performances. Call (505) 758–8322 for performance dates and times.

The *Red River State Trout Hatchery,* near the community of Questa, is one of those rare functional places that double as tourist attractions. New Mexico is fortunate to have many hatcheries, thus ensuring a steady supply of fish to stock the state's many streams, rivers, and lakes.

Located within the Carson National Forest, the hatchery offers a delightful setting. It was originally built in 1941 and then totally reconstructed during 1985–1986. Pick up a brochure in the unstaffed visitor center to follow the self-guided tour of the hatchery facilities. You'll see huge rainbow trout at the display ponds, as well as fish in various stages of growth, from their beginning as eggs to their development into fully mature trout. The hatchery, New Mexico's largest, produces 300,000 pounds of trout annually.

Picnic tables dot the scenic 2-mile drive on Highway 515, which connects the hatchery to Highway 522, 2½ miles south of Questa; (505) 586–0222. Visitors are welcome 8:00 A.M.–5:00 P.M. daily. There's no admission charge.

After you've heard the fish story—the story of fish—at the hatchery, continue on to *Questa* and fill up on the fine fare at *El Seville Restaurant,* a local landmark for sixteen years. Though the menu is varied and extensive, the authentic New Mexican combo plates are the best bet. El Seville offers freshly prepared tortilla chips—some of the best I've had—with its New Mexican entrees. Two combo dinners, including the chips and homemade sopaipillas, can be had for under $20. Get a window table for stunning mountain views. El Seville is not fancy, but owner Virgil Martinez, Sr., knows how to consistently satisfy his loyal customers.

El Seville is at the junction of Highway 522 and Highway 38 in Questa; (505) 586–0300. It's open 7:00 A.M.–8:00 P.M. daily.

Taos County also offers an array of choices for the outdoor adventurer. From world-class skiing at Taos Ski Valley to white-water river rafting in the Rio Grande Gorge and everything in between, Taos's incredible scenery provides an inspiring setting during every season.

Taos Ski Valley is simply New Mexico's finest ski resort. Built in the European tradition and nurtured by the late Ernie Blake, the father of New Mexico skiing, Taos Ski Valley delivers an extraordinary ski experience. *Skiing* magazine says, "The secret of Taos is in the mixture. Take European style, southwestern flavor, perfect snow and exquisite mountains and stir. . . . Taos Ski Valley is a resort to fall in love with, whatever your ability." And the *London Times* says, "Without any argument the best ski resort in the world. Small, intimate and endlessly challenging, Taos simply has no equal." Enough said. Taos Ski Valley is just minutes away from Taos on Highway 150 via Highway 522; (505) 776–2291. See page 196 for ski area information.

Though there's certainly no shortage of lodging near Taos Ski Valley, the **Cottonwood Inn Bed and Breakfast** has emerged as one of the nicest places to stay en route to the ski valley. Originally built in the 1940s, the Cottonwood came into its own as the residence of the flamboyant late artist Wolfgang Pogzeba, who expanded the original structure to accommodate his visiting art patrons. Pogzeba's layout provided each of the seven guest rooms with extraordinary views and architectural touches while preserving the pueblo-revival style of the original structure. Current owners Bill and Kit Owen—an avid fly fisherman and an accomplished downhill skier, respectively—renovated the home into its current incarnation as one of the most intimate yet secluded bed-and-breakfasts in the Taos area. Each of the guest rooms is unique in style and decor and has a private bath, original art, and locally handcrafted furnishings, and most rooms have a fireplace. Several of the bathrooms have whirlpool baths, and one room even boasts a full-size spa and separate steam shower. The common areas of the inn display an impressive collection of Taos art and regional artifacts. The grounds of the inn encompass a grove of cottonwoods, thus the name, and extensive herb and colorful perennial gardens.

The Cottonwood is located just off Highway 150 (Ski Valley Road) near the junction with Highway 230; (505) 776–5826/(800) 324–7120. Rates range from $85 to $165.

Though the protected stretch of wild and scenic Rio Grande extends 48 miles, the visitor center and **Wild Rivers Recreation Area** of this region are located north of Questa. This segment of the Rio Grande was officially protected when Congress passed the Wild and Scenic Rivers Act in 1968. It's quite deserted country, but when the weather is fair, canoeists and kayakers flock here.

The 18,000-acre recreation area, close to the center of the stretch, contains six maintained hiking trails and eight campsites on the rim and in the canyon. Guided hikes and regular camp-fire presentations are offered during summer. There are picnic facilities if you just want to peer into the vast starkness of the gorge—and you might just see a soaring bald eagle.

To get to the visitor center (505–770–1600), head 3 miles north of Questa on Highway 522 and then go west on Highway 538 for 8 miles. You'll see signs. Visitor center hours are 9:00 A.M.–5:00 P.M., Memorial Day weekend through Labor Day weekend; however, the Wild Rivers Recreation Area is open year-round for camping, hiking, fishing, and sight-seeing. Various fees apply.

For the less active outdoor enthusiast—or for active ones just wanting a break and some breathtaking scenery—there's the **Enchanted Circle** drive. The Enchanted Circle is the name for the communities and countryside surrounding Wheeler Peak, New Mexico's highest spot, at 13,161 feet. The loop, which involves several highways, connects the towns of Taos, Arroyo Hondo, Questa, and Red River in Taos County with Angel Fire and Eagle Nest in Colfax County (see pages 95 and 139).

Lithia spring pump at Ojo Caliente

Although the views of many areas in the Enchanted Circle are spectacular all year, they really shine during autumn—most specifically during late September and early October, when the aspens give their all before colder weather forces them to drop their amber leaves.

The most scenic stretch involves taking U.S. Highway 64 in Taos northeast to Eagle Nest and then Highway 38 north to Red River. At a leisurely pace, the drive should take less than two hours.

Red River is an unabashedly successful tourist town charmed with a beautiful storybook setting. Like so many western resort areas (Aspen and Telluride come to mind), Red River started out as a mining town in the 1800s but was savvy enough to capitalize on its mountains and snow when the mines played out. Winter visitors enjoy the family-oriented Red River Ski Area, and year-round visitors enjoy the shopping, food, and scenery. Red River has its own funky appeal, blending a European-chalet style with a big dose of the Old West. Red River is on Highway 38, between Questa and Eagle Nest.

The tiny southeastern Taos County town of Ojo Caliente possesses a marvelous secret bubbling up from the earth. And **Ojo Caliente Mineral Springs,** one of North America's oldest health resorts, is here to take advantage of it. This is not your plush Scottsdale- or Palms Springs–type resort. Far from it. But then again, neither are the prices. The facilities and accommodations at Ojo Caliente ("Hot Spring") are rather plain and limited, but this is the place in northern New Mexico to visit if you want to relax—totally.

Separate women's and men's bath houses are equipped with pools and tubs for soaking in the natural therapeutic mineral waters that have been attracting folks to this area for probably 2,000 years, starting with the ancestors of New Mexico's Pueblo Indians. The Spanish explorer Cabeza de Vaca described his journey to Ojo Caliente this way:

> *The greatest treasure that I found these strange people to possess are some hot springs which burst out at the foot of a mountain that gives evidence of being an active volcano. So powerful are the chemicals contained in this water that the inhabitants have a belief that they were given to them by their gods. These springs I have named Ojo Caliente.*

Hotel and cabin accommodations are available, and the on-site Mineral Springs Restaurant specializes in healthful meals featuring fish, chicken, and vegetarian fare as well as New Mexican foods. But the mineral waters are the focus at the resort: iron and arsenic for soaking; iron, arsenic, lithia, and soda for drinking. (*Note:* The arsenic mineral water has only a trace of arsenic and is said to benefit persons with arthritis, rheumatism, and stomach ulcers as well as to promote relief of burns and eczema.) Various massages, herbal wraps, facials, and rubs are also available.

The resort is 1/4 mile west of the town of Ojo Caliente on Highway 285; (505) 583–2233/(800) 222–9162. Winter hours (November through February) are from 8:00 A.M. to 8:00 P.M. daily (until 9:00 P.M. on Friday and Saturday). Summer hours (March through October) are from 8:00 A.M. to 9:00 P.M. daily (until 10:00 P.M. on Friday and Saturday). Accommodations range from $85.00 to $130, which includes use of hot springs; soaks, including wraps, are variably priced. Call for details.

WHERE TO STAY IN THE SANTE FE AND TAOS REGION

SANTE FE COUNTY
The Bishop's Lodge,
Tesuque Valley,
off Bishop's Lodge Road,
Tesuque Valley,
(505) 983-6377.

Ten Thousand Waves,
Hyde Park Road,
Santa Fe,
(505) 988-1047.

La Fonda,
100 East San Francisco,
Santa Fe,
(505) 982-5511/
(800) 523-5002.

Inn at Loretto,
211 Old Santa Fe Trail,
Santa Fe,
(505) 988-5531/
(800) 727-5531.

Inn of the Anasazi,
113 Washington Avenue,
Santa Fe,
(505) 988-3030.

La Posada de Santa Fe,
330 East Palace Avenue,
Santa Fe,
(505) 986-0000.

Inn of the Turquoise
Bear (B&B),
342 East Buena Vista Street,
Santa Fe,
(505) 983-0798/
(800) 396-4104

TAOS COUNTY
Taos Inn,
125 Paseo del Pueblo Norte,
Taos,
(505) 758-2233.

Bed & Breakfast at the
Mabel Dodge Luhan Bed
and Breakfast,
Morada Street,
north of Kit Carson Road,
Taos,
(505) 751-9686.

San Geronimo Lodge,
1101 Witt Road,
Taos,
(505) 751-3776/(800)
894-4119.

New Buffalo Bed and
Breakfast,
Retreat Center,
(1 mile west of Highway
522),
Arroyo Hondo,
(505) 776-2015.

Cottonwood Inn Bed and
Breakfast,
off Highway 150 (Ski Valley
Road),
near junction with
Highway 230,
Taos Ski Valley,
(505) 776-5826/
(800) 324-7120.

WHERE TO EAT IN THE SANTE FE AND TAOS REGION

SANTE FE COUNTY
El Farol,
808 Canyon Road,
Santa Fe,
(505) 983-9912. Inexpensive to moderate. Fare: Tapas and other Spanish dishes.

Mine Shaft Tavern,
Highway 14 (Main Street),
Madrid,
(505) 473–0473.
Inexpensive. Fare: Burgers
and New Mexican.

The Pink Adobe,
406 Old Santa Fe Trail,
Santa Fe,
(505) 983–7712. Moderate
to very expensive. Fare: A
local legend serving innovative Southwestern cuisine.

SantaCafé,
231 Washington Avenue,
Santa Fe,
(505) 984–1788. Moderate
to very expensive. Fare:
Innovative blending of
Southwestern and Asian
cuisines; one of the
best restaurants in the
Southwest.

The Shed,
113 1/2 East Palace Avenue,
Santa Fe,
(505) 982–9030. Inexpensive to moderate. Fare:
Traditional New Mexican.

Gabriel's,
U.S. Highway 285 (fifteen
minutes north of Santa Fe,
2 miles north of Camel
Rock Casino),
(505) 455–7000. Moderate
to expensive. Fare: Innovative New Mexican.

Cafe Pasqual's,
121 Don Gaspar Avenue,
Santa Fe,
(505) 983–9340. Moderate
to very expensive. Fare:
Innovative New
Mexican/Southwestern;
known for its breakfasts.

Coyote Cafe,
132 West Water Street,
Santa Fe,
(505) 983–1615. Expensive
to very expensive. Fare:
Innovative,
famous Southwestern.

TAOS COUNTY
El Seville Restaurant,
at the junction of Highways
522 and 38,
Questa,
(505) 586–0300. Inexpensive to moderate. Fare:
Traditional New Mexican.

Doc Martin's,
125 Paseo del Pueblo
Norte,
Taos,
(505) 758–2233. Moderate
to expensive. Fare: Innovative Southwestern.

Apple Tree,
123 Bent Street,
Taos,
(505) 758–1900. Moderate
to expensive. Fare: Contemporary American.

Lambert's of Taos,
309 Paseo del Pueblo Sur,
Taos,
(505) 758–1009. Moderate
to expensive. Fare: Contemporary American.

Los Vaqueros
(at Sagebrush Inn),
1508 Paseo del Pueblo Sur,
Taos,
(505) 758–2254/
(800) 428–3626. Fare:
Prime rib, steaks, seafood,
New Mexican cuisine.

Selected Chambers of Commerce/Visitors Bureaus in Santa Fe and Taos New Mexico

Santa Fe Convention & Visitors Bureau
P.O. Box 909,
Santa Fe, *87501*
(505) 984–6760
Web site: www.santafe.org

Taos County Chamber of Commerce
P.O. Drawer I
Taos, 87571
(505) 758–3873/1–800–732–8267
Web site: www.taoswebb.com/nmusa/TAOS/

Central New Mexico

ompared with the other five regions in the state, central New Mexico is small in area but big on influence. Boasting the state's only true urban area (but also very rural sectors), central New Mexico combines facets of all the other regions in the state because it borders them all. That there's much to experience in this region is partly why the largest chunk of the state's population calls central New Mexico home.

Bernalillo County

ecause the Albuquerque metropolitan area contains approximately one-third of New Mexico's residents, it tends to dominate Bernalillo County. And, as the state's largest city, Albuquerque has its share of attractions to please a variety of interests.

Albuquerque was founded in 1706 by Don Francisco Cuervo y Valdes in honor of the Duke of Alburquerque, Viceroy of New Spain. The first "r" was later dropped, but Albuquerque is still known as the Duke City. The place Valdes actually designated "San Francisco de Alburquerque" is **Old Town,** just west of downtown.

In addition to its status as a historic zone of Albuquerque, anchored by the picturesque San Felipe de Neri Chapel, Old Town is home for many families whose ancestors settled the area. On the surface, the shops around Old Town's plaza seem to cater only to tourists, but the fun part of exploring Old Town is venturing off the plaza into the side streets. There you'll find an array of fun-to-explore shops, galleries, and restaurants. If your friends want to shop but you're in the mood for something noncommercial and contemplative, make arrangements to meet them in an hour at the plaza's gazebo, and then walk on over to the *Capilla de Nuestra Señora de Guadalupe* (Our Lady of Guadalupe Chapel). Despite its obvious Catholic character, this tiny chapel has a decidedly nonreligious, yet very spiritual, feel. Coupled with its beautifully landscaped courtyard, the chapel is a welcome break from the sometimes overwhelming presence of tourists. You'll

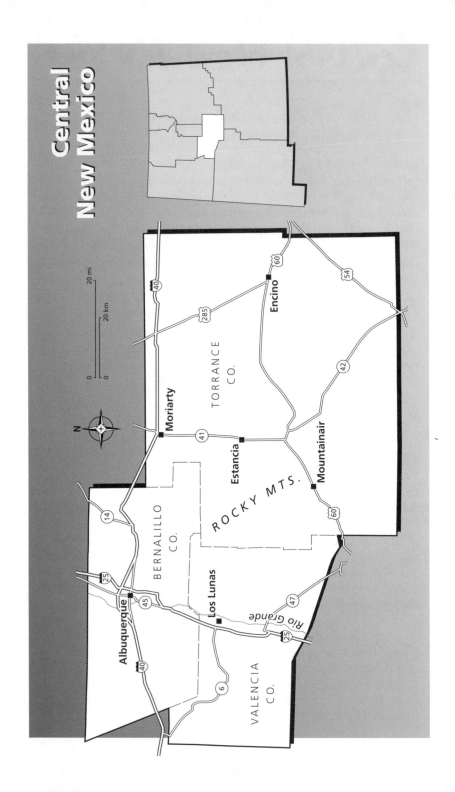

Central
New Mexico

find no pews inside, but rather two small rooms. The first contains a shrine to the chapel's namesake, complete with candles burning in brightly colored holders, but it's the second room that evokes more philosophical musings. Thought-provoking verses that are not obviously biblical are carved into wooden panels on the walls. No matter what your spiritual leanings are, it's a very welcoming place. You'll find the chapel at the end of Patio Escondido, off San Felipe Avenue. Old Town's plaza is the site of the annual Christmas Eve Luminaria Tour. Here, tens of thousands of luminarias (single candles set in a bed of sand at the bottom of small paper bags) create a golden glow on this special night at the place where Albuquerque began.

Parking is free around the plaza, if you can find a spot, but off the plaza are several parking lots that offer parking for a fee. Old Town is located near the intersection of Central Avenue and Rio Grande Boulevard. Most retail establishments are open seven days a week and maintain regular business hours whereas others stay open later. As with many destinations in New Mexico, Old Town is most crowded during "tourist season," which basically means summer. If your schedule is flexible, fall and winter (after Christmas) are the most pleasant times to visit.

New Mexico Trivia

Actress Vivian Vance of "Lucy" fame was from Albuquerque, and occasionally she would mention her then-small hometown on the I Love Lucy TV sitcom of the 1950s.

If you're interested in buying Native American Indian jewelry and crafts, there are, in addition to the shops around Old Town's plaza, two stores nearby that offer discount pricing on jewelry, pottery, kachina dolls, drums, and other authentic crafts. **Gus's Trading Company** is across the street from Old Town's plaza at 2026 Central SW (505-843-6381), and **Palms Trading Company** is also close at 1504 Lomas NW (505-247-8507).

Casas de Sueños ("Houses of Dreams"), a bed-and-breakfast inn, opened near Old Town in 1990. The inn, which has several garden areas and courtyards, is within walking distance to many Old Town and downtown attractions, such as the **New Mexico Museum of Natural History,** the **Albuquerque Museum** (which connects to the Old Town shopping district via its sculpture garden), and the **Rio Grande Zoo.** The futuristic entry building, designed by noted Albuquerque architect Bart Prince contrasts with the traditional old adobe structures that compose the inn. Accommodations range from one- and two-bedroom suites to private casitas, many with kitchens and fireplaces.

Casas de Sueños is at 310 Rio Grande SW; (505) 247–4560. Rates range from $95 to $225.

In late 1996 the **Rio Grande Botanic Garden** and the **Albuquerque Aquarium** joined the aforementioned Rio Grande Zoo(logical Park) to form the **Albuquerque Biological Park,** BioPark for short. Future plans call for the transformation of the current "Tingley Beach," a favorite urban fishing spot, into the Tingley Aquatic Park, which will then also become part of the park. When complete, the BioPark will be the first in the nation to have facilities that are physically connected and under consolidated management. The one-hundred-acre

Solamente en Nuevo México . . .
Albuqueque's Central Avenue

*I*f the Rio Grande is the lifeblood of Albuquerque, then Central Avenue is the city's soul. While the river may divide the city geographically into east and west, Central Avenue divides the city in another way. Far from its simple north-south division, the leisurely long avenue—Albuquerque's vestige of historic Route 66—also divides the city psychically. Either residents fear "Central" because their image of the area is outdated or limited, or they're quite fond of the reemerging historic strip and the urban delights it now offers.

For years after Interstate 40 started diverting travelers from the old route in the mid-1960s, much of it fell out of favor and into decay. While there remain several sections of Central that many a suburbanite might consider unsavory, the revitalizations and innovations occuring on the more prominent stretches during the past five years have been especially heartening, considering its illustrious past. For pedestrian quests in search of culinary, shopping, and entertainment adventures, you won't find a better urban venue in the state.

In addition to the renovations made to Central along its border with the University of New Mexico (University Avenue through Girard) and its passage through Downtown (Second through Eighth Streets), the Nob Hill area (Girard to east of Carlisle) has emerged as the preeminent see-and-be-seen district boasting some of the city's best restaurants and most interesting shops. And, for a tranquil change of pace, the wonderfully landscaped and architecturally significant UNM campus is just minutes away by foot.

site extends north from the zoo along more than 3 miles of the Rio Grande Bosque, which, like the Sandia Mountain foothills, is the closest thing to wilderness within the city. Planning and construction of the BioPark has been underway for years, but the wait was worth it. The clean lines and modern architecture of the botanic garden's conservatory blend well with the more traditional features of the park's other structures. From the peaceful entry complex to the Spanish-Moorish Court, the botanic garden exudes the best of southwestern garden influences.

The theme of the 45,000-square-foot aquarium complex, which includes a gift shop and restaurant, is to interpret the story of a drop of water as it enters the upper Rio Grande high in the San Juan Mountains of southern Colorado and flows through the canyons, deserts, and valleys of New Mexico, Mexico, and Texas, through the subtropical forests of the lower Rio Grande Valley, and finally into the Gulf of Mexico. A 285,000-gallon shark tank with floor-to-ceiling viewing contains various species of Gulf sharks as well as giant groupers, moray eels, manta rays, and skates, in addition to schooling fish and various invertebrates. Though there are several great aquariums in the United States (California's Monterey Bay Aquarium comes to mind), it is quite a trip to see one of this scale in the high desert of the Southwest.

Because the BioPark is evolving, please call (505) 764–6200 for up-to-date visitor information. To get to the botanic garden/aquarium complex, take Central Avenue west from Old Town about 1/2 mile to Tingley Drive. You'll see it on your right.

The *Indian Pueblo Cultural Center* near Old Town is the place to go to experience the art, history, and culture of New Mexico's nineteen pueblos (and one, Hopi Pueblo, in Arizona)—before venturing out to explore any of them. The center is owned and operated by the Pueblo Tribes of New Mexico and houses a fine museum and a restaurant that features New Mexican and Pueblo Indian dishes. The museum is divided into three main sections: the prehistoric, the historic, and the contemporary.

The center also contains gift shops and art galleries that offer authentic Indian pottery, sculpture, paintings, rugs, sand paintings, kachina dolls, and jewelry. Traditional Indian dance performances, alternated among the pueblos, are held on weekends in summer at 11:00 A.M. and 2:00 P.M.

The Indian Pueblo Cultural Center is at 2401 Twelfth Street NW, just north of Interstate 40; (505) 843–7270. Admission to the museum is $4.00 for adults, $3.00 for seniors, and $1.00 for students. Museum and gift shops are open daily from 9:00 A.M. to 5:30 P.M., and the restaurant is open daily from 7:30 A.M. to 3:30 P.M.

Like many cities' downtown areas in the past two decades, Albuquerque's downtown area is experiencing a renaissance of sorts as citizens once again take pride in their city's center. A spot worth a look during your tour of downtown is the *KiMo Theatre,* built in 1927 in the pueblo-deco style and later restored by the city. The theater hosts a wide range of performances, especially alternative and cultural performances, which are often more suitable to the ambiance of the venue. The KiMo Theatre is at 423 Central NW; (505) 848–1370.

Listed on the National Register of Historic Places, *La Posada de Albuquerque* was built in 1939 by Conrad Hilton, his first hotel in his home state. Among the hotel's claims to fame is its designation as the first air-conditioned building in Albuquerque and as the honeymoon hotel for Mr. Hilton and his bride, Zsa Zsa Gabor. La Posada, remodeled to its former glory in 1984, includes a spacious lobby bar and a first-class restaurant, Conrad's. The chic bistro, done in black and white, features Spanish fare and is known for its paella. La Posada is at 125 Second Street NW; (505) 242–9090 or (800) 777–5732. Room rates range from $69 to $275.

A great place to break for lunch downtown is *M. & J. Restaurant & Sanitary Tortilla Factory.* Located on the fringe of the downtown core, M. & J.'s offers up traditional New Mexican fare at reasonable prices. Its red chile and green chile are among the city's most flavorful and hottest—the reason the restaurant provides a pitcher of ice water at each table.

Posted on the walls above the booths are letters, cards, and even messages scrawled on napkins from satisfied diners from all over the globe. They all sing the praises of this fiery food and friendly people. You don't stay in the business for thirty years in the supercompetitive Albuquerque restaurant market unless you keep 'em coming back, something M. & J.'s owners, Bea and Jake Montoya, have always known. The wait staff keeps the complimentary homemade chips and salsa coming before and during the meal, and despite the filling nature of the cuisine, everything's heart-healthy here: The restaurant uses only cholesterol-free oil.

M. & J.'s is at 403 Second Street SW; (505) 242–4890. It's open Monday through Friday, 9:00 A.M.–4:00 P.M.

College campuses and the areas surrounding them are usually some of the most interesting places in a city, and the University of New Mexico

KiMo Theater

in Albuquerque is no different. As the largest university in the state, UNM is located along Central Avenue (old Route 66) east of downtown. A stroll around UNM's campus reveals perhaps the finest examples of pueblo revival–style architecture. These buildings were designed by New Mexico's most famous architect, the late John Gaw Meem of Santa Fe, who served as consulting architect for UNM from 1933 to 1959. Zimmermann Library, Scholes Hall, and Alumni Chapel are three of the Meem firm's most striking designs on campus and are worth a look and a few photographs. The beautifully landscaped duck-pond area in the campus's center, adjacent to Zimmermann Library, is an idyllic spot for a country picnic in the middle of the city.

Tamarind Institute, housed in a nondescript building across Central Avenue from the university, is much more than a division of UNM. It's a unique educational facility dedicated to the fine art of collaborative lithography. And it gives the best tour in Albuquerque. The good news is that the tour is free. The bad news is that it happens only once a month—the first Friday of each month at 1:30 P.M. Reservations are strongly recommended.

If you didn't know a thing about collaborative lithography before your visit to Tamarind, you'll be an expert after the two-hour tour, which includes viewing an Emmy-nominated documentary produced by the institute, a briefing by the director, and a staff-guided tour of the facility.

Tamarind began in 1960 in Los Angeles as the Tamarind Lithography Workshop. Its purpose was to rescue collaborative lithography from becoming a lost art in the United States by training a pool of master printers to work with artists. After ten years in Los Angeles, Tamarind, supported by substantial Ford Foundation grants, moved to Albuquerque in 1970 to become self-sustaining and continue the goals established in California.

If your visit doesn't coincide with a tour, you can still view some of the finished works—a small gallery at the institute displays selected lithographs. Some are available for purchase, and once you understand the lengthy collaborative lithography process, you'll understand the prices.

Tamarind Institute is at 108 Cornell Avenue SE; (505) 277–3901. Gallery hours are 9:00 A.M.–5:00 P.M. Tuesday through Friday.

The **Nob Hill District,** just east of UNM along Central Avenue near Carlisle Boulevard, re-creates that old Route 66 ambiance. This recently revived, and continually evolving, section of Albuquerque showcases antiques shops, vintage-clothing stores, other shops, theaters, and cafes, all interspersed among more practical businesses to create an eclectic mix perfect for a Saturday afternoon stroll. Among the places not to miss are Kanome, an eclectic Asian diner; Bow Wow Records; the In Crowd, a shop with trendy clothing and a fantastic postcard selection;

La Comida de Nuevo México

*C*alabacitas
(New Mexican–style squash)

Calabacitas, a New Mexican-style squash concoction, is one of my favorite local dishes.

2 cups whole kernel corn

4 tablespoons corn oil

¹/₄ teaspoon black pepper

¹/₂ chopped onion

¹/₂ cup water

2 cups chopped green chile (more or less, according to taste)

³/₄ cup grated Monterey Jack cheese

1 clove garlic, minced

1 teaspoon salt

4 medium yellow and/or zucchini squash, sliced

Combine all ingredients, except cheese, in a large saucepan. Cook at medium heat until squash is tender, approximately 20 minutes. Garnish with cheese before serving. Makes 4–6 servings.

and PeaceCraft, a nonprofit shop featuring handmade goods from Third World nations.

Although individual antiques stores abound in and around the Nob Hill District (mostly along Central and Morningside avenues), the largest selection of antiques and collector items under one roof is at *Classic Century Square.* This old department-store building houses three levels of antiques, collectibles, furniture, glassware, books, jewelry, and other items in more than 125 wall-less shops. There's an exceptionally large collection of vintage dolls in one section of the complex. You could spend a whole afternoon browsing and still not see everything.

Classic Century Square is at 4616 Central Avenue SE, just west of San Mateo Boulevard; (505) 265–3161. It's open Monday through Saturday from 10:00 A.M. to 6:00 P.M. and Sunday from noon to 5:00 P.M.

Albuquerque's rural North Valley, situated near the Rio Grande, contains some of the area's most fertile land, planted with apple orchards, alfalfa fields, extensive gardens—and grapes for wine at *Anderson Valley Vineyards.* The award-winning winery, near the vineyards, offers wine tastings and tours, in addition to a gift shop selling wine- and gourmet-related items. An outdoor patio overlooking alfalfa fields is a great spot to enjoy a picnic with friends—accompanied by a bottle of Anderson Valley wine, of course.

Anderson Valley was started in 1984 by the late Maxie Anderson and his wife. Maxie was a famous hot-air-balloon pilot who set world records with a transcontinental balloon flight (along with his son, Kris) and a transatlantic flight (with Ben Abruzzo). His family continues the winemaking tradition he began.

Tours are held hourly in summer and sporadically the rest of the year. Anderson Valley's tasting room is at 4920 Rio Grande Boulevard NW; (505) 344–7266. It's open Tuesday through Sunday, noon–5:30 P.M.

Hot-air ballooning is extremely popular in New Mexico because of the state's predictable weather and clear skies. To celebrate this colorful sport, New Mexico's largest city hosts the *Albuquerque International Balloon Fiesta* each October.

Balloonists and spectators come from all over the world to take part in the nine-day event, which draws more than 100,000 spectators. The mass ascensions on the four weekend mornings during the fiesta are worth an early rising (while it's still dark out) for the trek to Balloon Fiesta Park, located on Alameda Boulevard off Interstate 25. Up to 600 balloons take off to thousands of "oohs and ahs," while amateur and professional photographers click away at what has surpassed Pasadena's Tournament of Roses Parade as the most photographed annual event in the world.

In addition to the mass ascensions, the yearly Balloon Glow has become quite a popular event. After sunset, hundreds of inflated hot-air balloons fire up in synchronized patterns to create huge spheres of colorful, glowing light. If you make it to Albuquerque for the fiesta, don't miss the Balloon Glow. Another fun ballooning event during the fiesta is the Special Shapes Rodeo, limited to those balloons tailored a bit differently from the usual inverted teardrop configuration. You'll see Mickey Mouse, the Planter's Peanut Man, a Pepsi can, a cow jumping over a moon, and scores more of the huge floating representations of familiar items.

The fiesta begins the first weekend of each October. For more information, call (505) 821–1000/(888) 422–7277.

New Mexico is a nature lover's paradise, and Albuquerque fits right in. The *Rio Grande Nature Center* in Albuquerque's North Valley lies, as its name implies, along the Rio Grande and is a wonderful place for leisurely walks or brisk hikes. The outside part of the center consists of 270 acres of riverside forest and meadows that include stands of hundred-year-old cottonwoods, among other trees, and a three-acre pond. The *bosque,* as wooded areas are called in the Southwest, is threaded with 2 miles of trails whose unobtrusive signs identify the various forms of plant life.

The inside part of the center contains self-guided exhibits that provide insight into the natural, historical, and social implications of the Rio Grande. In the library area, there's also a glassed-in viewing room from which you can observe the wildlife at the pond without being noticed. A sign hanging here, THIS WEEK'S VISITORS, lists the species of birds and other animals that have been spotted recently.

Nature walks and children's hikes are scheduled, and you can borrow a pair of binoculars if you have a photo ID. Although the center makes for an enjoyable outing throughout the year, weekdays during fall and winter are especially tranquil. It's not—as a sign at the center's entrance prominently points out—a place to have a picnic, ride your bike or horse, run or jog, or walk your dog.

The Rio Grande Nature Center State Park is at 2901 Candelaria NW (where Candelaria dead-ends); (505) 344–7240. The visitor center is open daily 10:00 A.M.–5:00 P.M., and the grounds are open 8:00 A.M.–5:00 P.M. (And they mean it: Cars left in the parking lot after 5:00 P.M. will be locked in.) Admission is $1.00 for adults, 50 cents for children, and 25 cents for children in school groups.

The west side of Albuquerque is often referred to as the West Mesa because, well, it is a mesa. It rises out of Albuquerque's valley to form a wonderfully flat horizon (except for a few dormant volcanos, for visual interest) perfect for the setting sun to sink into. It's on the West Mesa that you'll find **Petroglyph National Monument.** At a distance, the park is a barren, unimpressive pile of rocks on a hill. But look a little closer and you'll see why the place got its name: The rocks are "decorated" with ancient Indian petroglyphs, or images carved in rock. Markers along the trails indicate and interpret the drawings. The monument is a fun place to spend a couple of hours on a sunny, brisk winter day. It may be too hot, though, because of the lack of shade, for some folks during the peak of summer.

To get to the petroglyphs, take Interstate 40 west and exit north onto Unser Boulevard. Proceed 3 miles to the park visitor center; (505) 899–0205. It's open daily 8:00 A.M.–5:00 P.M. There are no admission fees in most of the park; however, the parking fee at the Boca Negra Unit is $1.00 per car weekdays, $2.00 on weekends.

Although most of the unique places lie near the older parts of town— Old Town, downtown, the university area, the North Valley—there's much to see in the "newer" parts of Albuquerque. The Heights, specifically the Far Northeast Heights, are blessed with the Sandia Mountains, which form a lovely backdrop for the city while bordering its east side. The Spaniards named the mountains Sandia, which means "watermelon," because of the red color they turn when hit by the setting sun.

To explore the Sandias from Albuquerque, consider a hike on **La Luz Trail.** In Spanish, the name of this scenic 8-mile trail means "the light." The trail, known as the site of the La Luz Trail Run held each August, begins at the Juan Tabo recreation area and follows the western slope of the Sandias. The well-marked trail averages a 12 percent grade over the 3,700-foot rise; thus, the three- to five-hour (or more!) hike is quite a workout.

Bring along plenty of water, snacks, and matches, as well as a flashlight and bad-weather gear. It gets quite brisk at the higher elevations, even during the summer months, so dress appropriately. Because of temperature extremes, winter is not the best time to tackle La Luz. Being prepared and using common sense cannot be stressed enough, as evidenced by the media attention given to the several hikers per year who fall or become stranded. For this reason, be sure to tell someone where you are going when you hike La Luz. The ever-changing views and scenery along La Luz are amazingly beautiful. For a less strenuous hike, take the tram (see below) to the top and hike down. If you're careful to time the last leg of your descent at sunset, you'll see why the trail is called La Luz—incredible!

From Interstate 25 in north Albuquerque, exit at Tramway Boulevard and go 4 miles east to the Juan Tabo turnoff. Follow the road to the trailhead.

The foothills of the Sandias provide a wonderful vantage point from which to view the spectacular sunsets for which New Mexico is famous. And a comfortable spot for the nightly show is the new Pier 66 Restaurant. The restaurant is nestled in the foothills at the base of the **Sandia Peak Tramway,** the world's longest aerial tramway, which will whisk you to the top of 10,400-foot Sandia Peak in about fifteen minutes. At the top of the tram you'll find another restaurant, **High Finance,** which has an eagle's-eye view of Albuquerque. In addition to serving fine food, High Finance is also a great place for skiers to take a break at the top of the lifts on the other side of the mountain at Sandia Peak Ski Area.

Tram rides are popular at all times of the year, but be aware that winter temperatures can be more than thirty degrees colder at the top, which doesn't make for very comfortable sight-seeing. Still, you can always hang out at High Finance and have a cup of coffee or a glass of wine. And if you're lucky, you might see a brave hang-glider pilot take the plunge—harnessed in his glider, we hope—toward the Rio Grande valley 1 mile below.

The Tramway (505–856–7325) is at 38 Tramway Road off Tramway Boulevard. Though there's no set schedule, the tram runs about every twenty to thirty minutes from 9:00 A.M. to 8:00 P.M. daily (an hour later on Friday and Saturday). Round-trip tickets are $14 for adults and $10.00 for children and seniors. Each tram departure is announced in the adjacent restaurant, so you can wait for your "flight" in the bar if you like.

The top and the other side of the Sandias are also worth exploring. It's amazing that although most Albuquerque residents see the Sandias every day, many of them still don't realize that they can drive to the very top—**Sandia Crest,** at 10,678 feet—in less than an hour via Interstate 40 and the Sandia Crest Highway (Highway 536), which has been designated a National Scenic Byway; it's also the highest scenic drive in the Southwest. At the top, you'll find things a lot different than they were back "on the ground." Here, it's a lot cooler, which is refreshing during summer; even so, you might want to bring a sweater or light jacket.

The views from the crest are incredible. It's hard to imagine that the "small town" over the edge is bustling Albuquerque. The city becomes a distant, twinkling fairyland after sunset. From the observation deck at the summit, you can see more than 15,000 square miles of central New Mexico. You're not totally isolated, however: The **Sandia Crest House**—

A Glimpse of Central New Mexico:
Impresiones del Bosque, las Montañas, y los Volcanes

*B*y using Albuquerque merely as a gateway to New Mexico's more far-flung nature adventures, visitors often ignore what many Albuquerqueans also take for granted: its vast wonderland of hiking opportunities, literally minutes from any neighborhood in town. The three most impressive are the bosque, the foothills, and the volcanoes. And the best part is that they're free to enjoy anytime and they're usually quite deserted, despite their proximity.

The bosque, or wooded area that stretches along the Rio Grande throughout central New Mexico, has always been a beautiful place through which to hike or bike. But it's the recent arrival of the city's long-awaited new botanic center and aquarium (see page 116) that has brought the neighboring bosque new respect and visibility. Accessible from a small parking area along Central Avenue, the Rio Grande State Park allows access to the bosque via a system of trails through cottonwood groves along the river. It's a great place for morning and evening walks, especially during spring and fall, because of the activity among the native birds that nest, and migratory birds that rest, in the sanctuary of the bosque.

The foothills of the Sandia Mountains, which form Albuquerque's eastern border, provide another welcome nature escape. In addition to the celebrated La Luz Trail (see page 123), there are many other well-marked trails, such as the Piedra Lisa Trail, which begin east of Tramway Boulevard. Trail maps are available from the U.S. Forest Service by calling (505) 842–3292 or the Tijeras Ranger District at 281–3304. And as you might imagine, the sunsets are always quite spectacular from the foothills.

Albuquerque's West Mesa, with its five dormant volcanic peaks and its shrubby high-desert vegetation, provides an austere contrast to the bosque and the foothills. And, as you might also expect, the views of the Sandia and Manzano Mountains are quite spectacular and unobstructed, due to the mesa's elevation above the city.

To get to the volcanos, head west on Interstate 40 for about 9 miles, take Paseo del Volcan exit, and head north on the dirt road for a couple of miles until you find primitive parking areas and trailheads.

a combination gift shop, restaurant, and all-around base for hiking and cross-country skiing in winter—is perched at the top.

Once you've conquered the crest, check out **Tinkertown Museum** on your way back down the mountain. The museum is subtitled "Wood-Carved Miniature Village & Glass Bottle House" and is a place not to be missed. Even for people who don't think they like this sort of thing, I repeat, it's a place not to be missed!

Billed as "a collection of collections," Tinkertown explores a world gone by as well as a slightly skewed one that never existed. You'll get a month's worth of smiles after an hour of following the arrows directing you through the displays of miniature exhibits, including a general store and three-ring circus. Some displays involve mechanical action that brings the figures to life. You'll see ghost-town relics from New Mexico's Billy the Kid Country, as well as "The Wishing Buddha," accompanied by a sign that reads WISH FOR PEACE ON EARTH, NOT JUST A PIECE OF THE ACTION. The self-guided tour takes you through a structure built out of glass bottles as the sounds of old-time frontier music further remove you from time and place.

Tinkertown is the result of more than thirty years of tinkering by owner-creator-curator-artist Ross Ward. And just when you're wondering when he found the time to do all this, you'll see his motto posted on the wall: I DID ALL THIS WHILE YOU WERE WATCHING TV!

Tinkertown is 12–10 miles up Highway 536 off Highway 14; (505) 281–5233. It's open daily, 9:00 A.M.–6:00 P.M., from April to November. Admission is $2.50 for adults, $2.00 for seniors, and $1.00 for children ages four to sixteen, while children under four get a free peek at Ward's world.

One beautifully constructed and maintained bed-and-breakfast inn on the east side of the mountain perched in the Sandias is **Elaine's.** Elaine Nelson O'Neil built this lodgepole pine home for herself about fifteen years ago and turned the top two floors of it into a bed and breakfast in 1988. The common area of the no-smoking-permitted inn has a vaulted ceiling, a huge stone fireplace, and an upright piano, all with a fantastic alpine view through floor-to-ceiling windows.

Rates run from $85 to $150 per night. To get to Elaine's, take the Tijeras/Cedar Crest (Highway 14) exit and, as you drive under Interstate 40, check your odometer; then go 4.1 miles north on Highway 14. Turn left at the Turquoise Trail Campground (approximately 1 mile past Bella Vista Restaurant). Go straight on the dirt road approximately ¹/₂ mile. Turn left at the T. As you enter the gate marked "Snowline Estates," you'll see Elaine's on your right at the top of the hill. Follow the road up the hill and around the corner; (505) 281–2467.

Before going back to Albuquerque, head out east on Highway 337 near the eastern border of Bernalillo County to **Sierra Farms.** The farm is home to the goats that produce the milk that Valentin and Carmen Sanchez make into a delectable array of cheese products—traditional and specialty cheeses, cheesecake, and even a tasty chocolate-piñon-ricotta confection.

Val and Carmen moved to the tranquil Manzano Mountains (the range adjacent to the Sandias) from Albuquerque in 1976 to build a herd of dairy goats in hope of one day opening their own dairy. In 1986, Sierra Farms' Queso de Sanchez ("Sanchez's Cheese") was presented to the public in the cheese-tasting room—and the public ate it up.

In addition to sampling and sales, Sierra Farms offers self-guided and group tours on which you'll get to see those adorable kids. It's also a great place to take kids of the human variety, for there are picnic facilities and even a children's garden area during summer. And if you want to see the goats milked, by machine, plan to come out at 6:00 A.M. or P.M. Most folks choose the latter.

Sierra Farms is open for cheese sales and sampling from 10:00 A.M.–5:00 P.M., Tuesday through Sunday. Various tours and special events are regularly held; call ahead for dates, times, and fee information; (505) 281–5061. Sierra Farms is just off Highway 337, 17.2 miles south from the Tijeras/Cedar Crest exit off Interstate 40. You'll see the sign.

Back in Albuquerque, the **National Atomic Museum** stands apart from the city's more traditional museums. It is a serious but fun place to learn about the history and development of nuclear power. Though the thought of nuclear anything makes many people cringe, even devout pacifists can enjoy this fascinating display, which objectively portrays New Mexico's nuclear heritage: the development of the first atom bomb during the 1940s in Los Alamos (see Los Alamos County entry on page 60) and, subsequently, the first atomic blast at the Trinity Site (see Socorro County entry on page 1). The museum takes you through these historical developments and displays nuclear artifacts. A full range of military applications, including rockets and a B-52 bomber, is the focus of a large inside/outside exhibit.

The museum is on Kirtland Air Force Base, accessed via Wyoming Boulevard; (505) 284–3243. It's open daily 9:00 A.M.–5:00 P.M. A documentary, *10 Seconds That Shook the World,* is shown daily, usually at 10:30 A.M., 11:30 A.M., 2:00 P.M., and 3:30 P.M. A new interactive presentation entitled "Virtually Cool Tour" is shown daily at 9:30 A.M. and 12:30 P.M. Admission is $2.00 for adults and $1.00 for seniors, children, and active-duty military personnel. Note: You must stop at the guard station at the base's entrance to obtain a museum visitor's permit. Make sure to have your current car registration and proof of car insurance, or you won't be allowed on base.

In extreme western Bernalillo County near the Cibola County line, you'll find truly remote yet thoroughly modern lodging at the *Apache Canyon Ranch Bed and Breakfast Inn.* Ava and Theron Bowers converted their 3,600-square-foot home into a bed-and-breakfast in 1996 to share their home, along with the austere beauty of the landscape and endless mountain and mesa views, with their guests. Grazing cattle and wild horses are the Bowers's nearest neighbors, and in the late evening, while enjoying the cool high desert air on the patio, guests will likely be serenaded by distant coyotes. The ranch borders both Cañoncito Navajo lands and the Laguna Indian Reservation.

Ava has combined Native American, Hispanic, and her own Black culture to create a welcoming, unique decor that's built on the art and antiques from all three cultures. The largest of the inn's five guest rooms is the Sky City Suite, which includes a fireplace, a king-size bed, and a whirlpool bath. Rates range from $90 to $265. To get to Apache Canyon Ranch, head west from Albuquerque on Interstate 40 (about thirty minutes) to the Cañoncito exit; then head north for 2.9 miles; (505) 836–7220/(800) 808–8310; www.apachecanyon.com.

State Parks in Central New Mexico

Coronado State Monument, in Bernalillo (north of Albuquerque), (505) 867–5589

Manzano Mountains State Park, 13 miles northwest of Mountainair (southeast of Albuquerque), (505) 847–2820

Rio Grande Nature Center State Park, in Albuquerque, (505) 344–7240

On the web at: www.emnrd.state.nm.us/nmparks/

Valencia County

S outh of Albuquerque along Interstate 25 you'll find the rural communities of Valencia County: Belen, Los Lunas, Bosque Farms, Jarales, and Tomé. Many of the residents of this area enjoy the rural solitude of life along the Rio Grande while benefiting from the big-city advantages of Albuquerque, only a half-hour's commute to the north.

Settled by the Spanish in 1741, Belen became a major New Mexico railroad center in the 1880s. Though the railroad remains important to Belen, the heyday of passenger trains carrying travelers out west is long gone. But the *Valencia County Historical Museum* remembers. Located in the former Belen Harvey House, the small museum takes up just a part of the historic dining stop, whereas the rest of the restored mission-style building is occupied by the Belen Harvey House Civic Center.

In addition to displaying a variety of antique items donated by or on loan from area citizens, the museum pays homage to Fred Harvey and the days when his Harvey House restaurants were scattered along the railway throughout the West. Impeccable service, fine food, and the young, gracious Harvey Girls (waitresses) helped tame the wild frontier from the turn of the century until World War II, when other forms of travel took hold. One room in the museum is outfitted with furnishings typical of Harvey Girls' boarding rooms, which usually were upstairs from the dining area.

Though most of these oases of civility no longer exist, the citizens of Belen fought to save their Harvey House in the early 1980s when it faced demolition. The railroad sold the structure to the city of Belen, and residents rallied to preserve the legacy of Fred Harvey in their town.

The museum is at 104 North First Street in Belen; (505) 864–5903. Summer hours are Tuesday through Sunday from 2:00 to 4:00 P.M. (closed Monday); winter hours are Sundays from 2:00 to 4:00 P.M. and Tuesday through Thursday from 1:00 to 3:00 P.M. Hours are subject to change, so it's best to call ahead.

For a look at farm life and items from yesteryear, a visit to the *P & M Chavez Farm Museum* in nearby Jarales is a smart move. Run by Pablo and Manuela Chavez in and around their farmhouse since 1986, the museum is a wonderful mishmash of antiques and other items ranging from a late 1880s, horse-drawn hearse to a collection of 1960s Barbie dolls.

Luna Mansion

When the Chavezes were stationed in California in 1942, a fortune teller predicted that Manuela would someday have a museum of her own. The prophecy has been fulfilled in the museum, which contains artifacts collected by the Chavezes for nearly fifty years. The museum occupies several rooms in the Chavezes' house, separate from living areas, plus detached buildings, barns, and outside areas. A fine collection of antique cars—including a 1925 Studebaker, a 1959 Edsel, and a 1929 Model A Ford—and of farm implements is a highlight of the barn and outdoor exhibits. Manuela will gladly detail the background of some of the more notable displays. But don't make the mistake of asking if an item is for sale. "Nothing is for sale; this is a museum," she'll answer proudly.

From Highway 309 (Reinken Avenue) in Belen, take Highway 109 south for 3¹/₂ miles to Jarales. The museum will be on your right; (505) 864–8354. It's open Monday through Saturday from 9:00 A.M. to 5:00 P.M. and Sunday from 1:00 to 5:00 P.M. Guided tours of the museum are $5.00 for adults, $3.00 for children, and free for kids under five. Group discounts are available. Call ahead.

If venturing to Jarales on a Friday, plan a tour of the *Valencia Flour Mill.*

Not only can you see the old mill in operation, but you can also purchase freshly milled tortilla flour, whole wheat flour, wheat bran, and wheat germ.

The original mill began as the Jarales Trading Company in December 1913. The name was changed to the Jarales Roller Mill in 1919, and the mill ceased operations in the 1970s. José Cordova (grandson of the mill's founder) and his wife purchased the mill from their father's estate in 1988, and after extensive restoration the mill again began producing flour products in the summer of 1990.

The mill is located about ¹/₂ mile from the P & M Chavez Museum (see directions above), where Jarales Road joins Mill Road; (505) 864–0305. Tours are given on Fridays from 9:00 A.M. to 4:00 P.M.; additional school tours can be arranged. No admission fee is charged.

Though the Luna-Otero Mansion was once the headquarters of a livestock and land dynasty, since 1977 the stately home has been serving up appetizing entrées as the **Luna Mansion** restaurant. A National Historic Landmark, this is a restaurant with a story.

Domingo de Luna and Don Pedro Otero both came to New Mexico from Spain on land grants near the end of the seventeenth century. After nearly 200 years of amassing fortunes in land, livestock, and political influence, descendants of the two men's families were united by marriage in the late 1800s to create what is known as the Luna-Otero Dynasty.

The Luna-Otero Mansion was built by the Santa Fe Railroad in 1881 in exchange for right-of-way privileges through the Luna property (which meant the existing Luna home had to go). The southern colonial architectural design of the mansion is said to have been inspired by trips through the South by the Luna family. Though the design certainly seems out of place in New Mexico, the building material is not. You guessed it—it's constructed out of adobe.

New Mexico Trivia

"Christmas" is not only a holiday in New Mexico, but it's also the proper response to a local waiter if you want your New Mexican entree topped with both green and red chile.

Perhaps ironically, the restaurant serves up just about everything except New Mexican food—steaks, chicken, and seafood dishes dominate the menu. The closest thing to New Mexican is the Red Chile Linguini.

The Luna Mansion is at the junction of Highways 6 and 85 in Los Lunas; (505) 865–7333. Its hours are Wednesday through Sunday, 5:00–9:30 P.M.

Torrance County

Torrance County attaches to Bernalillo County's southeast side and is therefore a quick drive from Albuquerque. Many city residents enjoy a Sunday afternoon drive on the backside of the Sandia and Manzano mountains on Highway 337 (old South 14) and Highway 55. The atmosphere is decidedly rural and dotted with small towns along the route–Chilili (Bernalillo County), Tajique, Torreon, Manzano.

One particular bypass along the way is the *Tajique-Torreon Loop,* an incredibly scenic unpaved 17-mile stretch of road that indirectly connects the two towns. In Tajique, head east on Forest Road 55 (the road directing you to Fourth of July Campground off Highway 55). Unless you're in a four-wheel-drive vehicle, don't attempt to go past the Fourth of July Campground at the 7-mile mark—the road is clearly marked "primitive" at this point. The Manzano Mountain Wilderness, which is what the loop takes you through, is one of the few places in New Mexico where oak, maple, and aspen trees are interspersed with the usual mountain evergreens. It's a beautiful autumn drive. And if you're into camping or just want to have a picnic, the Fourth of July Campground (commonly known as Fourth of July Canyon) at the midway point is a great spot.

Old Catholic churches are the historic highlights of the towns along Highway 55 and attest to the rich Spanish traditional values of the villages. If you plan your visit during harvesttime, check out the area apple orchards. (*Manzano* means "apple" in Spanish, you know.) In recent years, the creative set has discovered some of the communities. You'll find artists, weavers, potters, and wood-carvers if you take the time to explore the area.

The ruins of impressive seventeenth-century mission churches and earlier pueblos are the focal points of the three units of *Salinas Pueblo Missions National Monument.* The areas included in the monument are in a basin that once held a huge lake. Because a salt marsh was left when the lake started to dry out, the Spanish explorers, upon seeing the area, named it Salinas for the salt flats. (And long before the Spanish arrived, the Indians living here used the salt as trade currency.) In the early 1600s, friars built missions at many of the pueblos in the basin. But drought, famine, and Apache raids caused both the Spaniards and the Pueblo Indians to abandon the sites by the 1670s. Over the years, the pueblos and missions were vandalized and started to collapse. It is these ruins that are now protected by the monument.

Although the ruins don't respect county lines, the monument head-quarters are conveniently located between the units in Torrance County. The visitor center is located in the community of Mountainair; (505) 847–2585. When in Mountainair, check out the historic Shaffer Hotel for lunch.

Each unit has a visitor center, picnic tables, and rest rooms, but camping is not allowed. They're all open daily 9:00 A.M.–6:00 P.M. during summer and 9:00 A.M.–5:00 P.M. during the rest of the year. There's no admission charge.

The most beautiful of the ruins are in the Quarai unit of the monument and are located on a well-marked road 1 mile west of the village of Punta de Agua on Highway 55. The 5-foot-thick red sandstone walls reach heights of 40 feet. Twenty-six miles south of Mountainair on Highway 55 you'll find the Gran Quivira unit. Though these are the most extensive of the ruins in the monument, because they are composed of gray limestone, they are not quite as attractive as those at Quarai. The ruins at the Abó unit are similar to those at Quarai in that they are made out of red sandstone. The Abó unit is 9 miles west of Mountainair on U.S. Highway 60.

> ### New Mexico Trivia
>
> *Approximately one-third of New Mexico's population of 1.7 million reside in the Albuquerque metropolitan area.*

Back in Mountainair, you'll be in for a treat at ***Rancho Bonito,*** a space dedicated to the environmental folk art created by Clem "Pop" Shaffer during the 1930s and beyond. Since his death in 1964, Pop Shaffer's family and a dedicated corps of volunteers have restored most of the buildings to their original condition. Uniquely configured and brightly painted buildings such as "The Log Cabin" adorn the ranch. Another, "The Stone House," is completely constructed of uncut rocks accented with animal shapes. On the National Register of Historic Places, Rancho Bonito is considered a classic by folk art organizations because of its humor and large scale.

There's no charge to visit Rancho Bonito, but it's shown by appointment only; (505) 847–2832.

**WHERE TO STAY IN
CENTRAL NEW MEXICO**

BERNALILLO COUNTY
La Posada de Albuquerque,
125 Second Street NW,
Albuquerque,
(505) 242–9090/
(800) 777–1901.

Apache Canyon Ranch
Bed and Breakfast Inn,
Cañoncito,
(505) 836–7220.

Casa de Sueños (bed and
breakfast),
310 Rio Grande SW,
Albuquerque,
(505) 247–4560.

Elaine's (bed and
breakfast),
Sandia Mountains,
(505) 281–2467.

Hyatt Regency
(downtown),
330 Tijeras NW,
Albuquerque,
(505) 842–1234.

Sheraton Old Town,
800 Rio Grande Boulevard
NW,
Albuquerque,
(505) 843–6300.

Rio Grande Inn,
1015 Rio Grande Boulevard
NW (Old Town area),
Albuquerque,
(505) 843–9500.

Albuquerque Marriott,
2101 Louisiana NE
(Uptown area),
Albuquerque,
(505) 881–6800.

VALENCIA COUNTY
Super 8 Motel,
428 South Main,
Belen,
(505) 864–8188.

Comfort Inn,
1711 Main Street SW,
Los Lunas,
(505) 865–5100.

Days Inn West,
1919 Main Street,
Los Lunas,
(505) 865–5995.

TORRANCE COUNTY
Days Inn,
just off Interstate 40,
Moriarty,
(505) 832–4451.

Lariat Lodge,
just off Interstate 40,
Moriarty,
(505) 832–4351.

Ponderosa Motel,
just off Interstate 40,
Moriarty,
(505) 832–4403.

Super 8 Motel,
just off Interstate 40,
Moriarty,
(505) 832–6730.

**WHERE TO EAT IN
CENTRAL NEW MEXICO**

BERNALILLO COUNTY
M. & J. Restaurant and
Sanitary Tortilla Factory,
403 Second Street SW,
Albuquerque,
(505) 242–4890.
Inexpensive. Fare:
Traditional New Mexican.

El Patio,
142 Harvard SE
(university area),
Albuquerque,
(505) 268–4245.
Inexpensive to moderate.
Fare: Traditional New
Mexican with some
heart-healthy choices.

Geezamboni's,
3851 Rio Grande NW
(North Valley),
Albuquerque,
(505) 345–3354.
Inexpensive to moderate.
Fare: Large menu,
featuring great sandwiches,
burgers, barbecue (great
patio).

Kai's Chinese Restaurant,
138 Harvard SE
(university area),
Albuquerque,
(505) 266–8388. Inexpen-
sive to moderate. Fare:
The best Chinese food
in New Mexico,
specializing in Szechwan
and Mandarin cuisines.

Kanome,
3128 Central SE
(Nob Hill area),
(505) 265–7773. Inexpensive to expensive. Fare:
Eclectic Asian-inspired
food. Innovative fare in a
stylish urban venue.

Los Cuates,
4901 Lomas Boulevard NE,
Albuquerque,
(505) 255–5079. Inexpensive to moderate. Fare:
Authentic New Mexican
(great salsa and
margaritas).

Monte Vista Fire Station,
3201 Central NE
(Nob Hill area),
Albuquerque,
(505) 255–2424. Moderate
to very expensive. Fare:
Upscale, creative New
American cuisine,
emphasizing Southwestern
ingredients.

Pattaya Thai Restaurant,
843 San Mateo SE,
(505) 255–5930,
Inexpensive to moderate.
Fare: Excellent,
traditional Thai.

Cafe Spoleto,
2813 San Mateo NE,
Albuquerque,
(505) 880–0897. Moderate
to expensive. Fare: A creative, rustic Italian grille.

Seasons,
2031 Mountain Road NW
(Old Town area),
Albuquerque,
(505) 766–5100. Moderate
to expensive. Fare: Upscale
eclectic American grille (a
way-cool rooftop patio bar).

Taj Mahal,
1430 Carlisle NE,
Albuquerque,
(505) 255–1994. Moderate
to expensive. Fare: Traditional cuisine of India.

Yanni's Mediterranean
Bar and Grill,
3109 Central NE
(Nob Hill area),
Albuquerque,
(505) 268–9250. Moderate
to expensive. Fare: Upscale
but casual Greek; some
Italian dishes.

VALENCIA COUNTY
Luna Mansion,
Junction of Highways 6/85,
Los Lunas,
(505) 865–7333. Moderate
to expensive. Fare: Innovative Southwestern.

Selected Chambers of Commerce/Visitors Bureaus in Central New Mexico

Albuquerque Convention & Visitors Bureau
P.O. Box 26866
Albuquerque, 87125–6866
(505) 243–6866/1–800–284–2282
Web site: www.abqcvb.org

Belén Chamber of Commerce
221 South Main Street,
Box 6, Belén, 87002
(505) 864–8091

Los Lunas Chamber of Commerce
P.O. Box 13
Los Lunas, 87031
(505) 865–1581

Moriarty Chamber of Commerce
P.O. Box 96
Moriarty, 87035
(505) 832–4087

Mountainair Chamber of Commerce
P.O. Box 595
Mountainair, 87036
(505) 847–2795

Teofilos,
Main near Highway 304,
Los Lunas,
(505) 865–5511. Inexpen-
sive to moderate. Fare: New
Mexican.

Henrietta's,
740 Main Street,
Los Lunas,
(505) 865–5284. Inexpen-
sive. Fare: American, New
Mexican diner.

Pete's Cafe,
105 First Street,
Belen,
(505) 864–4811. Inexpen-
sive to moderate.
Fare: New Mexican.

TORRANCE COUNTY
El Comedor de Anayas,
Old Route 66,
Moriarty,
(505) 832–0423. Inexpen-
sive to moderate. Fare: New
Mexican and American.

Rip Griffin's Restaurant,
Old Route 66,
Moriarty,
(505) 832–4421. Inexpen-
sive to moderate. Fare:
American.

Northeastern New Mexico

The scenery of New Mexico's northeastern quadrant is quite different from that most associated with the state. Grasslands upon rolling hills and plains dominate the landscape, giving it a softer quality in comparison with the state's expansive desert regions. Some of New Mexico's oldest and largest ranches share this area with modern ski resorts.

The historic Santa Fe Trail snakes through northeastern New Mexico and figures prominently in the region's geography and history. The 900-mile trail connecting Old Franklin, Missouri, to Santa Fe was the lifeline linking the New Mexico territory to the eastern United States from 1821 to the coming of the railroad to New Mexico in 1879. Not only did the trail bring much-needed goods and prosperity; it also brought a new people, language, skills, and customs—for better or worse, the Anglo had come to New Mexico.

A decisive battle of the Civil War was also fought in this region on March 28, 1862, at the summit of Glorieta Pass, between Santa Fe and Pecos. In the Battle of Glorieta Pass, Union troops defeated the Confederates, thus destroying Southern hopes for taking over New Mexico.

State Parks in Northeastern New Mexico:

Cimarron Canyon, 3 miles east of Eagle Nest, (505) 377–6271

Clayton Lake, 15 miles north of Clayton, (505) 374–8808

Conchas Lake, 34 miles northwest of Tucumcari, (505) 868–2270

Santa Rosa Lake, 7 miles north of Santa Rosa, (505) 472–3110

Storrie Lake, 6 miles north of Las Vegas, (505) 425–7278

Sugarite Canyon, 10 miles northeast of Ratón, (505) 445–5607

Ute Lake, 3 miles west of Logan, (505) 487–2284

Villanueva, 31 miles southwest of Las Vegas, (505) 421–2957

On the Web: *www.emnrd.state.nm.us/nmparks/*

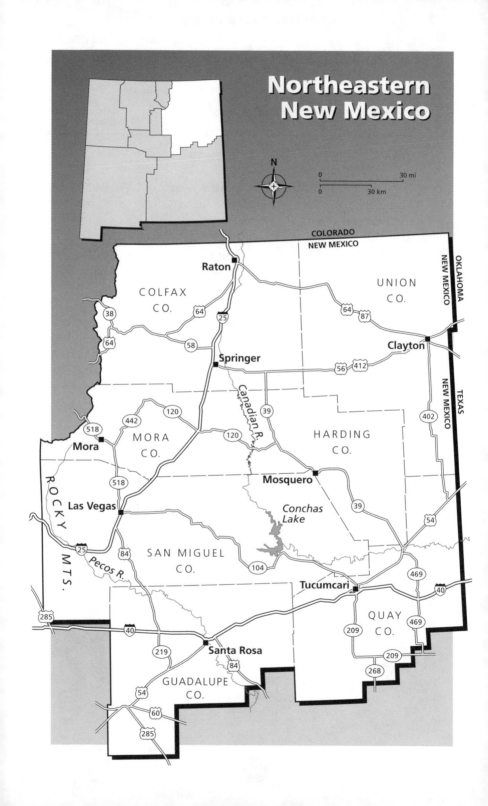

Northeastern
New Mexico

N

0   30 mi

0   30 km

COLORADO

NEW MEXICO

Raton

COLFAX CO.

UNION CO.

OKLAHOMA

NEW MEXICO

38

64

64

25

64

87

58

Springer

Clayton

56

412

NEW MEXICO

TEXAS

120

442

518

120

Canadian R.

39

HARDING CO.

402

Mora

MORA CO.

518

Mosquero

ROCKY

Las Vegas

Conchas Lake

39

54

25

84

Pecos R.

SAN MIGUEL CO.

104

Tucumcari

469

40

M T S.

285

40

219

Santa Rosa

469

QUAY CO.

209

209

84

268

GUADALUPE CO.

54

60

285

Colfax County

FAVORITE ATTRACTIONS/EVENTS IN
NORETHEASTERN NEW MEXICO:

Capulin Volcano National Monument, *Union County*
(505) 278–2201

Ft. Union National Monument, *Mora County*
(505) 425–8025

Pecos National Historical Park, *San Miguel County*
(505) 757–6032

Montezuma Castle,
United World College campus, Las Vegas
(505) 454–4200

Ratón Historic District, *Ratón*
(505) 445–3689/1–800–638–6161

St. James Hotel, *Cimarron*
(505) 376–2664

Philmont Ranch,
north of Cimarron
(505) 376–2281, ext. 46

Santa Fe Trail Heritage Days, *May, Las Vegas*
(800) 832–5947

Dinosaur Days,
April, Clayton
(505) 374–9253

The quiet community of Springer, with its tree-lined main street, Maxwell Avenue, would seem more at home in the Midwest than the plains of New Mexico. Here you'll find a slower pace, a couple of old antiques shops, and the **Santa Fe Trail Museum,** housed in the old Colfax County Courthouse, which at first glance resembles a church.

Built in 1879, when Springer sat in the county seat before Ratón took over almost twenty years later, the Santa Fe Trail Museum once served as a New Mexico reform school for boys, a public library, the town hall, and the city jail before townsfolk transformed it into a museum in 1967. It commemorates Colfax County's pioneers during the time when the Santa Fe Trail was an active route crossing the region.

The museum, which now also houses the Springer Visitors Center, is at 606 Maxwell Avenue; (505) 483–5554 (only answered during the summer). It's open Memorial Day through Labor Day, Monday–Friday, 8:00 A.M.–4:00 P.M., and Saturday, 8:00 A.M.–noon. Admission charges are $2.00 for adults, $1.50 for seniors and children.

As far as one-horse towns go, this one's got most others beat. It has its own livery stable—now known as **The Livery Stable Antiques**—which is a Springer landmark and houses a wonderful, cluttered mishmash of antiques for sale. Hidden treasures abound. Built in 1880, the stone stable is definitely from the horse-and-wagon days and is in excellent shape, considering its age and lack of restoration. Avoid this place if a little dust and dirt offend you. The Livery Stable Antiques is at the corner of Maxwell Avenue and Third Street; (505) 483–2825. Open by appointment only.

For good food and lodging in Springer, check into the historic **Brown Hotel and Cafe Bed and Breakfast** downtown. Built during 1922–24, "the Brown," as it's known to locals, features eleven guest rooms furnished with antiques. Rates range from $40 to $60; (505) 483–2269.

For the best New Mexican food in northeastern New Mexico, head over to *El Taco Cafe* at 704 Maxwell Avenue in Springer (505–483–0402). Open for breakfast, lunch, and dinner, El Taco serves all New Mexico classics, plus fajitas and steaks for dinner. The cafe recently made the "top ten" list of Mexican restaurants in *Crosswinds* magazine.

Twenty-seven miles east of Springer you'll find the grand, thirty-six-room **Dorsey Mansion.** It's pure rustic opulence in the middle of New Mexico's high plains. The log-and-stone home was built by U.S. Senator Stephen W. Dorsey of Arkansas in 1880. An addition several years later produced the castlelike structure with likenesses of the faces of Dorsey, his wife, and his brother carved in stone on the tower.

In addition to his role as a politician, Dorsey was also a railroad financier and up-and-coming cattle baron who liked to throw elaborate parties at his mansion, now listed on the National Register of Historic Places. Highlights of a tour include the black marble fireplace from Italy, the cherrywood staircase brought from Chicago, and the man-made pond with three islands, one of which once boasted a gazebo.

The mansion, currently owned by a couple from California, is protected by caretakers Ernesto and Ernestine Romero. Though it had a brief stint as a bed-and-breakfast in the late 1980s, it's now open only by appointment for tours; (505) 375–2222.

To get there, take U.S. Highway 56, proceeding 24 miles east of Springer (just past the first roadside rest area) and then going north on the dirt road for 12 miles; it's a good idea to call ahead for road conditions. There's a $3.00 per person charge for tours with a minimum charge of $5.00.

Just 7 miles south of the Colorado border the city of **Ratón** evolved along the Santa Fe Trail around three main influences: coal mining, railroading, and ranching. The days of the first two are pretty much in the past. Ratón's Spanish mission revival–style depot, built in 1903, served the city well until 1990, when Amtrak suspended its last scheduled stop (en route to Albuquerque from Chicago).

The depot is the focal point of the **Ratón Historic District,** which centers on First Street just across from the railroad tracks. Listed on the National Register of Historic Places since 1977, the district includes some seventy buildings. Businesses originally sprang up in this area in the 1880s to serve the needs of railroad workers. Today this strip is a great place to check out antiques shops and admire the diverse architecture. You can also travel back in time at the Raton Museum, which chronicles the area's history of mines, rails, and cattle through artifacts and photographs.

The **Ratón Museum** is located in the old Coors Building on First Street; (505) 445–8979. It's open Tuesday through Saturday from 9:00 a.m to 5:00 P.M., Memorial Day–Labor Day, and Wednesday through Saturday from 10 A.M. to 4:00 P.M. the rest of the year. There's no admission charge.

Just a block away, at 131 North Second Street (505–445–5528), the restored **Shuler Theatre** continues to stage theatrical productions. It opened in 1915 and was named for Dr. J. J. Shuler, Raton's mayor when the grand structure was built. The theater's exterior, described as European rococo architecture, pales in comparison with its interior, with its ornate woodwork, sky-painted ceiling, and gold-trimmed box seats. Eight Works Progress Administration (WPA) murals commissioned by the government during the Great Depression enhance the lobby and trace Ratón's history.

Solamente en Nuevo México . . .
The Santa Fe Trail

*P*erhaps nothing else impacted the civilization of northeastern New Mexico more than the celebrated Santa Fe Trail, which ends, appropriately enough, in Santa Fe on a street bearing its name. The trail is actually part of a longer, older trading route that traced the Rio Grande south into what is now northern Mexico and was used by Native American tribes.

The historic path of the trail spanned from Old Franklin, Missouri, to Santa Fe, and was officially opened as a commercial trading route by William Becknell, a trader from Missouri, in 1821. The trail connected Southwestern markets to the Mississippi and Missouri River trading systems. An early congressional document on the trail consists of an interview between Sen. Thomas Hart Benton of Missouri and Augustus Storrs, and early trader along the route. An excerpt:

Benton: "What kind of merchandise are principally carried out to the internal provinces?"

Storrs: "Cotton goods, consisting of coarse and fine cambrics . . . shawls, handkerchiefs, steam-loom shirtings . . . a few woolen goods, consisting of super blues, stroudings, pelisse cloths . . . some light articles of cutlery, silk shawls, and looking glasses . . ."

Benton: "What is received and brought back in exchange for merchandise carried out?"

Storrs: "Spanish milled dollars, a small amount of gold and silver, in bullion, beaver fur, and some mules."

Note: *The Santa Fe Trail Association, in association with New Mexico Highlands University in Las Vegas, maintains an informative Internet web site on trail history, events, and related matters. You'll find it at:* www.nmhu.edu/research/sftrail.

The theater welcomes visitors during office hours–Monday through Friday, 8:00 A.M.–5:00 P.M.—and on weekends when a show is scheduled. There's no cost for a look or a snapshot.

The *Heart's Desire Inn Bed and Breakfast* opened in 1998, replacing the Red Violet Inn, which recently closed, as the only bed and breakfast in Ratón. Located in the heart of historic downtown Ratón, the 1885 Victorian-style home is the perfect setting for a romantic getaway to northeastern New Mexico. Innkeeper Barbara Riley pampers her guests by welcoming them with fruit baskets in their rooms, providing evening hors d'oeuvres such as fresh–baked breads and cheeses, and preparing breakfasts tailored to her guests' preferences. Six theme rooms (such as the "Lodge Room," "Blue Willow Room," and "Victorian Room"), each with its own sink, are appointed with antique furnishings, as is a suite, with kitchen, private bath, and living area.

The Heart's Desire doubles as an antiques shop, with antiques and collectibles featured throughout the inn's first floor. It's open to the public Monday through Friday, 8:00 A.M. to noon, and Saturday and Sunday, 9:00 A.M. to 6:00 P.M.

The Heart's Desire Inn is located at 301 South 3rd Street; (505) 445–1000. Room rates range from $45–$90.

From Ratón, head 38 miles southwest on U.S. Highway 64 to discover the hidden Old West romance of Cimarron (roughly meaning "wild" or "unbroken" in Spanish). In fact, this *is* Marlboro Country in all its rugged, wide-open glory. Those famous cigarette ads were photographed on the CS Cattle Company ranch near Cimarron. All of Old Cimarron is ripe for exploring and centered on Santa Fe Trail (that's the name of the street here; it's also *the* trail, though it becomes Highway 21 south of town).

The *St. James Hotel* in Cimarron once bedded the famous and infamous of the Wild West. Located on the Santa Fe Trail, the St. James to this day reeks of mystery and intrigue reminiscent of its past. Built in 1873 by Henri Lambert, a former cook for Ulysses S. Grant and Abraham Lincoln, the stately, pale pink adobe hotel was once considered one of the finest in the West. Jesse James, Black Jack Ketchum, Wyatt Earp, Buffalo Bill Cody, Annie Oakley, and Zane Grey were among the hotel's early patrons. The hotel was restored and reopened in 1985 by its current owners, Ed and Pat Sitzberger.

The entire hotel, including lobby, guest rooms, and dining area, is outfitted with authentic Victorian furnishings, mounted game, and large paintings. Individual rooms are now named after some of the celebrated figures who stayed in them. Evidence of the hotel's rough-and-tumble past is apparent in the bullet holes visible in the pressed-tin ceiling of Lambert's, the hotel's restaurant (previously Lambert's Saloon and Gambling Hall). Instead of red-eye, Lambert's now serves up Continental cuisine such as Shrimp Provençale and Red Rock Filet au Dijon, among pasta, beef, chicken, and veal entrees.

Every old hotel worth its salt has a resident ghost, and legend has it that the St. James was not shortchanged—no clues, though, as to who the chandelier shaker might be. For those who get caught up in the history and aura of the St. James, the hotel occasionally hosts mystery adventure weekends called "Murder on the Santa Fe Trail." Guests become actors in a staged murder they try to solve.

The St. James is on Highway 21, just north of U.S. Highway 64 in the center of Cimarron's historic district; (505) 376–2664. Room rates range from $55 to $100.

Just down the lane, across from the St. James, you'll spot the **Old Mill Museum,** guarded by the thick rock walls of the Aztec Mill. The mill was built in 1864 by Lucien B. Maxwell, who, with his 1.7 million acres, was the single largest landowner in the Western Hemisphere of all time. Maxwell brought an engineer, a millwright, and a chief mason from back East to take on the $50,000 project. In its time, the mill could turn out 300 barrels of flour per day. Though the three-story building was converted to a museum in 1967, the stone structure itself is just as impressive as its contents, which include exhibits chronicling late nineteenth-century northern New Mexico.

The museum is open daily (except Thursday) from 9:00 A.M. to 5:00 P.M. and Sunday from 1:00 to 5:00 P.M., Memorial Day through Labor Day; otherwise during May and September, it's open only on Saturday from 9:00 A.M. to 5:00 P.M. and Sunday from 1:00 to 5:00 P.M. Admission is $2.00 for adults and $1.00 for seniors, children under twelve, and scouts in uniform (read on and you'll understand). There's no phone, but the museum's curator Buddy Morse (505–376-2913) will be glad to answer any questions.

About 5 miles south of the St. James on Highway 21 you'll find the headquarters to the vast **Philmont Ranch,** now owned by the Boy Scouts of America (BSA). Here's where the buffalo really do roam and the deer and the antelope are known to play. The jewel of the 137,493-acre ranch is **Villa Philmonte,** the Spanish Mediterranean–style mansion built as a summer home by Oklahoma oilman Waite Phillips, of Phillips 66.

Phillips gave the ranch to the BSA in 1938 "for the purpose of perpetuating faith, self-reliance, integrity, and freedom, the principles used to build this great country by the American Pioneer." And each summer since, thousands of scouts have convened at Philmont for the ultimate camping adventure.

But nonscouts, too, can enjoy Philmont. Tours of Villa Philmonte are given daily during summer. The home and most of its furnishings have been restored to their original grandeur. In addition to the living room, with its custom-built piano, the most impressive room is the trophy room, highlighted by the huge buffalo mounted above the fireplace.

The **Philmont Museum and Seton Memorial Library** (both 505–376–2281, ext. 256), just past the driveway that loops around the mansion, are also open to visitors. The museum displays exhibits of those persons who influenced this area—cowboys, Indians, miners, mountain men, and settlers. The library contains the books, art, and natural history collection of Ernest Thompson Seton, an author, artist, and naturalist and the first chief scout of the BSA. The museum and library are open daily from 8:00 A.M. to 5:30 P.M. June through August and Monday through Friday from 9 A.M. to noon and from 1:00 to 5:00 P.M. the rest of the year.

Seven miles south, in Rayado, you'll find another feature of the Philmont Ranch, the Kit Carson Museum. It's built in the adobe hacienda style and finished with 1850s period furnishings. Tours are given daily June through August; call the above number for specific schedules.

If you're no Boy Scout and the St. James is booked, consider **Casa del Gavilan** ("House of the Hawk") bed-and-breakfast for a weekend hideaway. The inn was built in the early 1900s by the eastern industrialist J. J. Nairn, who often hosted famous artists and writers in his gleaming white adobe home tucked into the foothills of the Sangre de Cristo Mountains. Only those with confirmed reservations are allowed on the premises, though, because guests' privacy is highly regarded here. Casa del Gavilan is 6 miles south of Cimarron on Highway 21; (505) 376–2246. Rates range from $75 to $105 and include evening refreshments as well as breakfast.

Heading west on U.S. Highway 64 from Cimarron, you'll come across the community of Eagle Nest—along with its attractive namesake lake—and the village of Angel Fire. Between these two towns you'll find a delightfully comfortable inn, **Monte Verde** ("Green Mountain")

Ranch Bed and Breakfast. The inn comprises most of innkeeper Sally Lebus's 1930s ranch house, which was constructed out of native granite and pine. With views of Eagle Nest Lake to the north and mountains to the east, guests enjoy total comfort at Monte Verde.

Sally is certainly no uptight innkeeper. She allows guests free run of her spacious home, including a glassed-in living area with a fireplace and a huge kitchen with a wood-burning stove. Some of the guest rooms also have fireplaces, with plenty of wood available. On cool mornings an eerie mist forms over Eagle Nest Lake, adding to the setting's magic. Sally reports that the inn has become quite popular as a setting for family reunions and weddings.

Monte Verde is located just off U.S. Highway 64 between mile markers 279 and 280; (505) 377–6928. Monte Verde is open to guests from Memorial Day weekend through October. Rates are $85 to $110.

The meadows meeting the mountains in the countryside surrounding Angel Fire give new meaning to the enchantment of New Mexico. Atop a small hill you'll find the country's first memorial dedicated to all Vietnam veterans. Originally built in 1971 by Dr. Victor Westphall in memory of his son, who was killed in the war, the memorial was expanded and taken over by the Disabled American Veterans in the early 1980s.

The small, nondenominational chapel at the *DAV Vietnam Veterans National Memorial* at Angel Fire is breathtakingly simple as it sits in harmony with the land. The tallest wing of this dovelike structure rises 64 feet, gracefully curving downward to the ground. The accompanying visitor center is just as contemporary and displays banners and poster-size photographs of wide-ranging scenes from the war.

Completed years before the celebrated memorial in Washington, D.C., the Angel Fire structure differs in the feeling it leaves within when visitors depart. There is no turbulence or divisive political statement associated with this memorial. Though powerful in the emotions it elicits, the memorial allows visitors to come away with their own reactions, rather than forcing any particular ones.

The DAV Vietnam Veterans National Memorial is just off U.S. Highway 64 at the Angel Fire turnoff; (505) 377–6900. From Memorial Day through Labor Day the visitor center is open daily 9:00 A.M.–7:00 P.M. The remainder of the year, it's open daily 9:00 A.M.–5:00 P.M. The chapel never closes, and there's no admission charge.

Union County

W hat's now a perfectly cone-shaped mountain rising from the plains was once a fiery volcano that last erupted some 10,000 years ago. What's left is known as *Capulin Volcano* and is a national monument about 30 miles east of Raton. As one of the most remote and undiscovered of the nation's national monuments, Capulin rarely gets crowded.

A road from the visitor center winds 1,000 feet up the mountain to the edge of the mouth of the volcano. From here you can hike several trails. You can see four states—New Mexico (obviously), Texas, Colorado, and Oklahoma—if you hike the Crater Rim Trail. Another trail actually leads you inside the volcano—one of the few places in the world where you can do this. (Go try this in Hawaii!) Though Capulin hasn't erupted in 10,000 years, it's considered dormant, not extinct. Scientists say volcanos 25,000 years old or less are potentially active, so no one knows if Capulin will ever erupt again. Not knowing—for certain, anyway—adds to the thrill.

To get to Capulin Volcano National Monument from Raton, take U.S. Highway 64/87 east for about 30 miles to the community of Capulin, and then head north on Highway 325 for a few miles to the monument; (505) 278–2201. The visitor center is open daily from 8:00 A.M. to 4:00 P.M. Labor Day through Memorial Day; during summer, hours are 7:30 A.M.–6:30 P.M. Admission charge is $4.00 per carload and $2.00 per person for motorcycles and bicycles.

In extreme northeastern New Mexico (mere miles from the Oklahoma and Texas borders), you'll find the thriving community of *Clayton,* Union County seat and regional trading hub–and home base for exploring several notable area attractions, including Capulin Volcano, Clayton Lake, Rabbit Ear Mountains, authentic dinosaur tracks on an ancient mud flat, and *Folsom Falls.*

Along the Dry Cimaron River, 4 miles northeast of the small community of Folsom on Highway 456, you'll find Folsom Falls, a natural spring-fed waterfall on the river, which forms a favorite fishing spot as well as a great place for a picnic. The community of Folsom boasts the Folsom Museum, which offers information on the prehistoric Folsom Man, as well as artifacts from the area's pioneer history. Folsom was named for President Grover Cleveland's bride, Frances Ruth Folsom, for whom the Baby Ruth candy bar was also named.

Back in Clayton, be sure to check out the landmark *Eklund Hotel Dining Room and Saloon* (505–374–2551), which celebrated its centennial in 1992. Specializing in Union County beef (steaks), the Old West ambiance includes a well-worn wooden bar and bullet holes in the pressed-tin ceiling.

Mora County

Fort Union National Monument is at its best when visited on a crisp, sunny autumn day. Though it's quite isolated, Fort Union is easily accessible via Interstate 25, which brings a steady stream of visitors during summer. When approaching the remains of the fort, the vision of red-brick and adobe ruins jutting up from the grassy plains is at once attractive and a little odd. Once you get to the fort site along the Santa Fe Trail, with its incredibly expansive views, you sense why this spot was chosen.

Established in 1851 by Lieutenant Colonel Edwin V. Sumner to protect the Santa Fe Trail and the New Mexico territory from Indian raids,

Ruins at Fort Union National Monument

Fort Union was the largest military depot in the Southwest. There were actually three Fort Unions, the last of whose ruins constitute the park. The fort was abandoned in 1891, after which residents from nearby communities scavenged most of its usable materials, thereby hastening its deterioration.

The visitor center provides a walking-tour map to help interpret the fort's layout. If you visit on a sunny day, follow the trail to the fort's sundial, just across from the quartermaster's quarters. It's still intact and quite accurate. The park service has done a great job preserving the frontier feeling and dignity of the fort. Interpretive audio stations at selected stops along the trail emit dialogues indicative of the situation, that is, soldier to commander, soldier to soldier. And recorded bugle calls sporadically echo across the grounds from loudspeakers hidden by the adobe walls. Fort Union is also one of the best places to see the wagon-wheel ruts of the Santa Fe Trail, those wagons last cutting through the plains more than a century ago.

To get to Fort Union, take Interstate 25 north of Las Vegas to exit 366, and then head north on Highway 161, which dead-ends at the fort after 8 miles; (505) 425–8025. A tree-shaded picnic area is available. The park is open daily 8:00 A.M.–6:00 P.M. Memorial Day through Labor Day and 8:00 A.M.–5:00 P.M. the remainder of the year. The admission price is $2.00 per person or $4.00 per carload.

Just east of the village of Cleveland, northeast of Mora, you'll come across the *Cleveland Roller Mill Museum.* Like other, earlier flour mills in the area, the Cleveland Roller Mill, built in 1901, helped satisfy the growing demands for wheat flour in the region around the turn of the century. The two-story adobe mill was the last of its kind to be built in northern New Mexico–and the last to cease operations around 1954; as such, it's the only roller mill in New Mexico of any size to have its original milling works intact. The mill's restoration began in 1979, when it was placed on the National Register of Historic Places and the New Mexico Cultural Properties Register. Providing a glimpse into the agricultural past of the area, the museum features historical and cultural exhibits focusing on the Mora Valley. On Labor Day weekend, the museum hosts Millfest, during which the operation of the mill is demonstrated. The usual food, fun, and frolic round out the event.

Museum hours are irregular throughout the summer and fall, so call ahead. However, the grounds are always open. The museum closes during winter; (505) 387–2645. Admission is $2.00.

Just outside the community of Mora, you'll encounter *La Cueva Mill,* another beautifully rustic old structure now part of Mora County's Salman Ranch. The mill was built by Vicente Romero in the 1870s, partly in response to the heavy demand for flour, owing to the establishment of Fort Union and to the steadily increasing Santa Fe Trail traffic. Though Mora County is now one of New Mexico's most economically depressed areas, during the late 1800s it was one of the most prosperous.

The old adobe and stone buildings of the mill are not accessible, for safety reasons; nevertheless, you can pull off the road for an exterior look at one of New Mexico's more impressive old water-driven mills. The cold, clear water from the *acequia* (constructed ditch) still flows around the mill, though it's now diverted from the wheel.

Though the mill has not been used for grinding wheat and generating electricity since 1949, during late summer through early fall *Salman Ranch* sets up shop at the mill to sell its produce, including vegetables, herbs, cut flowers, and, most notably, farm-fresh raspberries. You can also stock up on the ranch's prized raspberry jam. And its raspberry vinegar is perfect for dressing a salad.

The mill is located 6 miles south of Mora near the junction of Highway 518 and Highway 442. In-season produce sale hours are generally 9:00 A.M.–5:00 P.M. Tuesday through Sunday. For more information, call the ranch at (505) 387–2742.

San Miguel County

Often confused with the glitzier and much younger gambling capital of Nevada, the community of Las Vegas, New Mexico, has a charm all its own. During its railroad heyday in the 1880s, Las Vegas ("The Plains") was the largest and most exciting city in New Mexico. Today, Las Vegas has mellowed into a captivating community enhanced by a rich architectural heritage—half the state's registered historic buildings, more than 900, are located here.

To get a sense of Las Vegas's past, stop by the *City of Las Vegas Rough Riders Museum,* which is named for the heroic group of men Teddy Roosevelt organized for his acclaimed Cuban campaign during the Spanish-American War. Many of the volunteers came from New Mexico, and the Rough Riders later held a reunion in Las Vegas every year from 1899 (when the event was attended by Roosevelt while he was governor of New York) until 1967, when it was attended by only one veteran, Jesse Langdon, who died in 1975. In Las Vegas, Roosevelt even announced his candidacy for president and twice stayed at the Plaza Hotel (see page 151).

The museum began with mementos brought home by the Rough Riders and now includes a great variety of artifacts relating to Las Vegas's history

A Sampling of Movies Filmed in New Mexico*

Butch Cassidy and the Sundance Kid *(1968). Paul Newman, Robert Redford, and Katharine Ross (Taos, Chama).*

The Cheyenne Social Club *(1970). James Stewart, Henry Fonda, and Shirley Jones (Santa Fe).*

Chisum *(1970). John Wayne, Forrest Tucker and Ben Johnson (Santa Fe).*

City Slickers *(1991). Billy Crystal, Jack Palance and Daniel Stern (Ghost Ranch, Santa Fe, Abiquiu, Nambe Pueblo, Santa Clara Pueblo).*

The Cowboys *(1972). John Wayne, Bruce Dern, and Colleen Dewhurst (Chama, Galisteo, Santa Fe).*

Hang 'Em High *(1968). Clint Eastwood, Inger Stevens, and Ben Johnson (Las Cruces).*

Lonesome Dove *(1989). Robert Duvall, Tommy Lee Jones, Danny Glover, and Angelica Huston (Santa Fe, Angel Fire).*

The Milagro Beanfield War *(1988). Ruben Blades, Sonia Braga, and Daniel Stern (Truchas).*

Contact *(1997). Jodie Foster, Matthew McConaughey (Socorro County)*

My Name Is Nobody *(1973). Henry Fonda and Terence Hill (Acoma Pueblo, Mogollon).*

Silverado *(1985). Kevin Kline, Danny Glover, Kevin Costner, Rosanna Arquette, and Linda Hunt (Galisteo, Abiquiu, Santa Ana Pueblo).*

Superman *(1978). Chrisopher Reeve, Margot Kidder (in and around Gallup.)*

Wyatt Earp *(1993). Kevin Costner, Dennis Quaid, and Gene Hackman. (Santa Fe, Rancho de las Golondrinas, Chama, Las Vegas, and Zia, Tesuque and Santa Clara Pueblos).*

Young Guns *(1988). Emilio Estevez, Charlie Sheen, Lou Diamond Philips, Kiefer Sutherland, Terence Stamp, and Jack Palance (Cerrillos, Galisteo, Ojo Caliente, Rancho de las Golondrinas).*

Source: New Mexico Film Commission.

Plaza Hotel

and New Mexico's past. The museum is located at 727 Grand Avenue; (505) 454–1401, ext. 283. It's open Monday through Friday 9:00 A.M.– noon and 1:00–4:00 P.M.; from May through October, the museum is also open on Saturday, 10:00 A.M.–3:00 P.M. There's no admission charge, but donations are appreciated.

Many native New Mexicans consider Las Vegas's Old Town Plaza the most beautiful plaza in the state because of its large size, abundance of trees, and gazebo. Anchored by the historic **Plaza Hotel,** the streets around and adjacent to the plaza are dotted with shops and restaurants.

One hundred years after it originally opened, and following a $2-million renovation, the Plaza Hotel reopened in 1982 to its former Victorian grandeur. From the worn hardwood of the lobby floor to the towering twin staircases connecting the lobby to the second floor, the Plaza Hotel has an air of history and elegance. Except for the modern comforts of queen-size beds and new bathrooms, the high-ceilinged guest rooms are appointed in period antiques with wall and window treatments consistent with the Victorian era. As a welcome change from many historic hotels, the guest rooms are surprisingly well insulated and are thus quiet, each offering its own thermostat.

Byron T's, the lobby bar, is named after former Plaza Hotel owner Byron T. Mills, who's also the hotel's resident ghost. It's a comfortable place to have a drink while enjoying a street-level view of the plaza. The hotel's restaurant, the **Landmark Grill,** features New Mexican dishes as well as beef, fish, and chicken entrees, including Chicken Picatta, Filet Mignon, and Moroccan Salmon. Pasta specialties like Seafood Linguini Alfredo round out the menu.

The hotel is located at 230 on the Old Town Plaza; (505) 425–3591. Room rates range from $69 to $115.

For a more intimate overnight adventure in Las Vegas, consider a stay at the **Carriage House Bed & Breakfast.** The inn is housed in a three-story Queen Anne–style mansion built in 1893, one of the many architectural gems found throughout Las Vegas's inner core of historic districts. The inn was totally renovated in the mid-1990s and has five guest rooms, three of which have private baths. The Carriage House is located at 925 Sixth Street; (505) 454–1784. Room rates range from $59 to $79.

Head out of Las Vegas about 6 miles on Hot Springs Road (which borders the streetside corner of the Plaza Hotel) and you'll be in the small community of Montezuma at the mouth of Gallinas Canyon. The imposing **Montezuma Castle** looms on a hilltop as the focal point for Armand Hammer United World College of the American West (505–454–4200). Built in 1884 as a showpiece resort by the Santa Fe Railroad, Montezuma Castle was abandoned as a hotel during the financial depression at the turn of the century. The castle was purchased in 1981 by the late Dr. Armand Hammer—billionaire philanthropist and former chairman of Occidental Petroleum Corporation—with the intent of starting the college. The small college now has more than 200 students from more than sixty nations. Although the castle itself is not regularly open for tours, you can get a closer view by driving or walking around the campus.

Just past the castle on Hot Springs Road (Highway 65) are the **Montezuma Hot Springs,** nondescript holes that dot the banks of the Gallinas River. Located on the property of the United World College, these natural hot tubs are fed from mineral springs that bubble up from the ground. The springs are a great place to relax and enjoy the view—Montezuma Castle, the river, the rock cliffs—especially when it's a little nippy outside. A brown sign, HOT SPRINGS BATHS, marks the spot. There's no charge to enjoy the therapeutic waters, but it's a first-come, first-soak arrangement. Early morning and late night are the best times to find them vacant. You may encounter naked people milling about, so if this offends you, consider yourself warned.

About ¹/₂ mile farther on Highway 65 toward the mountains, veer left on a gravel road and you'll immediately come across **Gallinas Pond,** or City Pond, as it's also known. During most times of the year, the pond is nothing more than a small body of water bordered by shimmering, sheer cliffs on one side. But during the dead of winter, when the water has frozen and the ice skates have been brought out, the pond turns into a winter wonderland reminiscent of the Northeast and Midwest. It's one of only a few places open to the public in New Mexico where you can pond-skate.

The **Star Hill Inn,** 10 miles north of Las Vegas, is the perfect getaway for stargazers and ardent astronomy buffs alike. Several modern cabins constitute the inn, which was founded by former Dallas resident Phil Mahon. Mahon, who has led astronomy seminars at Abiquiu's Ghost Ranch (see page 63), concluded that rural New Mexico, with its clear, pitch-black nights, was the perfect place for an inn catering to the cosmically inclined.

A Glimpse of Northeastern New Mexico: *Impresiones de Las Vegas*

*W*hen I was researching the first edition of this book, a northeastern New Mexico excursion brought me to the town of Las Vegas for the first time. The city's renaissance was just getting underway, when I found myself staying at the then newly remodeled Plaza Hotel, just off the plaza. (See page 151).

I'd been looking forward to staying at the gracious old hotel, wondering if I'd have any run-ins with its resident ghost, Byron T. Mills—the former owner and namesake of the hotel's lobby bar, Byron T's. Unfortunately (or fortunately, depending on how you look at it), I did not, but the hotel's imposing presence did captivate me. There's something about staying in a grand old hotel that makes you feel a bit grander and more gracious yourself.

My visit reminded me of my job, during college, as a doorman of another historic hotel. And I remembered seeing the same relaxed feeling expressed on the faces of its guests that I myself felt at the Plaza: well-rested, hospitably attended to, and ready to head out and explore the world. Las Vegas's downtown business district has slowly come back to life with an even greater array of shops, restaurants, and galleries— but there's still the welcoming feel of a small town and a city in transition. Some may say it's no Santa Fe or Taos, but I say nor should it want to be. With its vast quanitity of Victorian homes, many on historic registers, and quiet, tree-lined streets, Las Vegas is a pleasant town to explore on foot—after a wonderful night spent in the cradling comfort of the Plaza Hotel.

The cabins are comfortably outfitted with custom-designed furnishings and individual kitchens. A library and warming house contains three telescopes that may be wheeled out onto an outside observation deck. The inn's largest telescope—6,000 millimeters in focal length—is kept in an adjoining structure with a rollback roof. When the sun is out, guests take advantage of the inn's natural surroundings—almost 200 acres of ponderosa pine forest, perfect for hiking and photography.

Moonless nights are most popular with guests because of increased visibility. Major meteor showers are also peak times for the inn. The best shows occur in the second half of the year: the Perseids in August, the Orionids in October, the Leonids in November, and the Geminids in December.

Rates range from $80 to $140, with a two-night minimum. Call (505) 425–5605 for reservations and directions.

Heading south from Las Vegas, plan a stop at **Pecos National Historical Park,** near the community of Pecos. The park boasts one of the most attractive visitor centers (Spanish hacienda–style, with impressive woodwork) and the friendliest park rangers in the state. The monument preserves the ruins of the abandoned Cicuye Pueblo. Before you start exploring, be sure to view the short film—narrated by actress Greer Garson, a former New Mexican resident—which dramatically presents the history of the pueblo site. The film will put you in the right frame of mind to better appreciate what you'll see later. It's screened every twenty minutes or so.

The park includes a walking tour, as well as a museum containing artifacts relating to the Indians, the Spanish, and the Anglo pioneers who lived at or affected the monument site. While exploring the trails that wind among the ruins, you can climb down a ladder into a restored kiva (ceremonial chamber) and see the *sipapu,* the small hole in the ground believed to connect to the spirit world in the center of the earth. To see evidence of the Spanish colonial influence, you can walk through the remains of a missionary church. The scenery is inspiring as it varies from plains, mesas, and mountains in the distance.

New Mexico Trivia

Five New Mexico counties were named for U.S. presidents: Harding, Grant, Lincoln, Roosevelt, and McKinley.

To get to the park from Las Vegas, take Interstate 25 south to the Pecos exit and proceed on Highway 63; (505) 757–6032. From Memorial Day through Labor Day, the monument is open daily 8:00 A.M.–6:00 P.M., otherwise, the park is open daily, 8:00 A.M.–5:00 P.M. The admission charge is $2.00 per person or $4.00 per carload.

Harding County

The ***Kiowa National Grasslands*** (505–374–9652) preserves thousands of acres of short prairie grasses on New Mexico's northeastern plains and stands in stark contrast to the more popular mountainous areas of the state. Though there are two regions of the preserve (the eastern section lies east of Clayton), the western section, which comprises most of northwest Harding County, is more impressive because of its proximity to the Canadian River Canyon. Highway 39 bisects the grasslands and thus serves as a convenient route for a road tour, from which you just may encounter grazing pronghorn antelope, among other wildlife.

One of the most impressive and remote areas of the federal preserve is ***Mills Canyon,*** named for a once-prosperous farmer, lawyer, and businessman named Melvin Mills, who tended thousands of fruit and nut trees in the late 1800s, before he was wiped out by the great flood of 1904. Mills's misfortune and eventual financial ruin ultimately led to his farm becoming public lands. If you've got a sturdy, high-clearance vehicle (four-wheel drive recommended, just in case) and want to explore one of the most remote, hidden river valleys in the state, then a hiking or camping trip to Mills Canyon may be just what you're looking for. After you turn off the highway, psyche yourself up for the 2-mile, 800-foot descent into the rugged Canadian River valley. In addition to the natural beauty of the area, you'll also see the ruins of the great Mills estate—including a few of the more hearty fruit trees that have barely survived decades of inattention and the unforgiving extremes of New Mexico weather.

To get to Mills Canyon, take the Wagon Mound exit off Interstate 25 north of Santa Fe/Las Vegas; head east on Highway 120 to Roy, then north on Highway 39 for 10 miles until a sign at the turnoff.

Guadalupe County

Just southeast of downtown Santa Rosa, you'll find northeastern New Mexico's most fascinating hidden jewel: Santa Rosa's city-owned ***Blue Hole,*** a true oasis. Well known in scuba-diving circles across the country as the diving mecca of the Southwest, the Blue Hole is a tiny, bell-shaped lake prized among divers for its clarity.

With a mere 60-foot diameter, (though it widens to 130 feet across the bottom), yet 81-foot depth, the Blue Hole is truly more of a hole than a lake. The crystal-clear water, which appears to glow a turquoise color with the light reflecting from the stones below, is replaced every six hours, at a rate of 3,000 gallons per minute, by a subterranean river. Often called Nature's Largest Fishbowl because of its wide variety of fish, snails, plants, and sands, the Blue Hole remains a constant sixty-four degrees.

If you're a diver, avoid the crowds by visiting during the week. If you just want to see what all the fuss is about, you'll see the most action on weekends. A dive shop rents equipment next to the Blue Hole. You'll need to buy a permit ($13 for a whole year) at the Santa Rosa Police Department or City Hall (505–472–3404) if you want to dive, and you must be certified or accompanied by a certified, insured instructor.

Quay County

The town of Tucumcari is the gateway to New Mexico from the east. But if you've driven through New Mexico along Interstate 40 from the west, chances are your curiosity has been piqued about Tucumcari because of the stark red billboards exclaiming TUCUMCARI TONIGHT—1,500 HOTEL ROOMS, along with the mileage from the sign to this model Route 66 town. The town, named after nearby Tucumcari Mountain, is proud of its abundance of lodging.

While in Tucumcari, check out the ***Tucumcari Historical Museum.*** As

Selected New Mexico Authors

N. Scott Momaday, author of House Made of Dawn

Leslie Marmon Silko, Lauguna Pueblo author of Ceremony

Tony Hillerman, author of many murder mysteries

Mark Medoff, playwright, author of Children of a Lesser God

Luci Tapahonso, Navajo poet

Oliver LaFarge, Pulitzer Prize winner for Laughing Boy

John Nichols, The Milagro Beanfield War

Robert Creeley, poet

D. H. Lawrence, author

far as New Mexico's community-based museums go, this is one of the finer ones. It contains thousands of old relics, including such large-scale ones as a nineteenth-century windmill and a 1926 fire truck. Several "reenactment" exhibits are featured, such as a 1920s hospital room, an early post office, a cowboy room complete with barbed wire and gun collections, and an old moonshine still. The museum also has a worthy collection of musical instruments.

The museum is located at 416 Adams Street; (505) 461–4201. From June 2 through September 2, it's open Monday through Saturday from 9:00 A.M. to 6:00 P.M. and Sunday from 1:00 to 6:00 P.M.; during the rest of the year, it's open Tuesday through Saturday from 9:00 A.M. to 5:00 P.M. and Sunday from 1:00 to 5:00 P.M. (though Sunday hours are subject to change during winter). Admission charges are $2.00 for adults and 50 cents for children ages six to fifteen.

About 24 miles north of Tucumcari on U.S. Highway 54, you'll come across Logan, the community nearest **Ute Lake,** New Mexico's second-largest lake, known for some of the best walleye fishing in the Southwest and as a favorite lake for houseboat owners. **Logan** is known as the "Best Little Town by a Dam Site," referring to the artificial lake. If you've

---

La Comida de Nuevo México

*B*iscochitos

(Anise-flavored shortbread cookies)

Traditionally enjoyed around the Christmas holiday, the biscochito also has the distinction of being designated New Mexico's official state cookie.

6 cups flour

¼ teaspoon salt

3 teaspoons baking powder

1 pound (2 cups) lard

1½ cups sugar

2 teaspoons anise seeds

2 eggs

¼ cup brandy

¼ cup sugar

1 tablespoon cinnamon

Sift flour with baking powder and salt. In a large mixing bowl, cream lard with sugar and anise seeds until fluffy. Beat in eggs one at a time. Mix in flour and brandy until well blended. Turn dough out on floured board and pat or roll to ¼- to ½-inch thickness. Cut into shapes. (The fleur-de-lis is traditional.) Dust with mixture of sugar and cinnamon. Bake 10 minutes at 350° F or until lightly browned. Makes approximately 5 dozen cookies.

traveled this way for simple water recreation, head over to the **Road to Ruin** bar after you've had your fun in the sun. The bar was named after a billboard the present owner saw when she was a young girl; it read WHISKEY, THE ROAD TO RUIN.

As the favorite local watering hole, the Road to Ruin serves up its share of whiskey, but beer's the drink of choice here. The old bar features a 30-foot-long, intricately carved mahogany-backed bar, the original gold-dust–backed mirror (behind the bar), and four-legged bar stools–for better balance.

The Road to Ruin is located on U.S. Highway 54 in Logan, (505) 487–2444. It's open daily from 10:00 A.M. until whenever people leave (2:00 A.M. max).

WHERE TO STAY IN NORTHEASTERN NEW MEXICO

COLFAX COUNTY
St. James Hotel,
Highway 21,
Cimarron,
(505) 376–2664.

The Brown Hotel,
Springer,
(505) 483–2269.

Monte Verde Ranch Bed and Breakfast,
just off U.S. Highway 64,
Angel Fire,
(505) 377–6928.

Casa del Gavilán,
Highway 21,
south of Cimarron,
(505) 376–2246.

Best Western Sands Motel,
300 Clayton Road,
Raton,
(505) 445–2737 or
(800) 528–1234.

UNION COUNTY
Days Inn,
1425 South First Street,
Clayton,
(505) 374–8127.

Kokopelli Lodge,
702 South First Street,
Clayton,
(505) 374–2589/
(800) 392–6691.

Holiday Motel,
Highway 87 North,
Clayton,
(505) 374–2558.

MORA COUNTY
St. Vrain Bed and Breakfast,
Intersection of Highways 518 and 434,
Mora,
(505) 387–2471.

SAN MIGUEL COUNTY
Plaza Hotel,
230 Old Town Plaza,
Las Vegas,
(505) 425–3591.

Comfort Inn,
2500 North Grand,
Las Vegas,
(505) 425–1100/
(800) 716–1103.

Inn on the Santa Fe Trail,
1133 Grand Avenue,
Las Vegas,
(505) 425–6791.

Regal Motel,
1809 North Grand Avenue,
Las Vegas,
(505) 454–1456.

HARDING COUNTY
Martha's Hotel,
downtown,
Roy,
(505) 485–2661.

Patio Bed and Breakfast,
Roy,
(505) 485–2262.

GUADALUPE COUNTY
Best Western Adobe Inn,
P.O. Box 410,
Santa Rosa,
(505) 472–3446.

Best Western Santa
Rosa Inn,
P.O. Box B,
Santa Rosa,
(505) 472–5877.

Bel-Air Motel,
Highway 60,
downtown Vaughn,
(505) 584–2241.

QUAY COUNTY
Best Western Discovery Inn,
200 East Estrella Avenue,
Tucumcari,
(505) 461–4884.

Best Western Pow Wow Inn,
801 West Tucumcari
Boulevard, Tucumcari,
(505) 461–0500/
(800) 527–6996.

Holiday Inn,
3716 East Tucumcari
Boulevard,
Tucumcari,
(505) 461–3780.

Royal Palacio Motel,
1620 East Tucumcari
Boulevard, Tucumcari,
(505) 461–1212.

**WHERE TO EAT IN
NORTHEASTERN
NEW MEXICO**

COLFAX COUNTY
The Brown Cafe,
Main Street,
Springer,
(505) 483–2269.
Inexpensive. Fare: Small-
town eclectic.

El Taco Cafe,
704 Maxwell Avenue,
(505) 483–0402. Inexpen-
sive to moderate.
Fare: New Mexican.

Stockman's Cafe,
317 Maxwell Avenue,
Springer,
(505) 483–2301.
Inexpensive to moderate.
Fare: Steaks, chicken, etc.

The Grapevine Restaurant
and Pizzeria,
120 North Second Street,
Raton,
(505) 445–0969. Inexpen-
sive to moderate. Fare:
Eclectic menu featuring
pasta, pizza, steaks, and
chicken dishes.

El Matador,
1012 South Second Street,
Raton,
(505) 445–9575. Inexpen-
sive. Fare: New Mexican.

UNION COUNTY
Eklund Hotel Dining Room
and Saloon,
15 Main Street,
Clayton,
(505) 374–2551,
Inexpensive to expensive.
Fare: American, featuring
steaks and seafood, and
New Mexican.

La Palomita Restaraunt,
1022 South First Street,
Clayton,
(505) 374–2127. Inexpen-
sive. Fare: Mexican.

Rabbit Ear Cafe,
402 North First Street,
Clayton,
(505) 374–9912.
Inexpensive. Fare: Mexican.

Santa Fe Trail Steak House,
22¹/₂ Pine Street,
Clayton,
(505) 374–8585. In
expensive. Fare: American,
featuring steaks and
chicken fried steak.

MORA COUNTY
Santa Clara Cafe,
Downtown,
Wagon Mound,
(505) 666–2011. Inexpen-
sive. Fare: Sandwiches,
burgers, roast beef, and a
great selection of home-
made pies.

El Nicho Restaurant,
Highway 518,
Mora,
(505) 387–9297. Inexpen-
sive. Fare: Traditional New
Mexican.

Hatcha's Café,
Highway 518,
Mora,
(505) 387–6034. Inexpen-
sive. Fare: Traditional New
Mexican.

Button's Deli,
intersection of Highways
518 and 434,
Mora,
(505) 387–2471. Fare:
Extensive sandwich and
salad menu, with some Italian dinner choices.

SAN MIGUEL COUNTY
The Landmark Grill,
Plaza Hotel,
230 Old Town Plaza,
Las Vegas,
(505) 425–3591. Moderate
to expensive. Fare: American and Southwestern.

El Rialto,
141 Bridge Street,
Las Vegas,
(505) 454–0037. Inexpensive to moderate. Fare: New Mexican.

Hillcrest Restaurant,
1106 Grand Avenue,
Las Vegas,
(505) 425–7211. Inexpensive to moderate. Fare: American.

HARDING COUNTY
Martha's Cafe,
downtown,
Roy,
(505) 485–2661,
Inexpensive. Fare: American.

Roy Sundries Cafe,
downtown,
Roy,
(505) 485–9939. Inexpensive. Fare: American.

Erma's Cafe,
downtown,
Mosquero,
(505) 673–2354. Inexpensive. Fare: American.

GUADALUPE COUNTY
Joseph's Restaurant
& Cantina,
865 Will Rogers Drive,
Santa Rosa,
(505) 472–3361. Inexpensive to moderate. Fare: New Mexican.

Mateo's Restaurant,
500 Coronado West,
Santa Rosa,
(505) 472–5720. Inexpensive to moderate. Fare: New Mexican.

Selected Chambers of Commerce/Visitors Bureaus in Northeastern New Mexico:

Angel Fire Chamber of Commerce
P.O. Box 547, Angel Fire, 88710
(505) 377–6353/1–800–446–8117
Web site: www.taoswebb.com/nmusa/ANGELFIRE/

Cimarron Chamber of Commerce
P.O. Box 604, Cimarron, 87714
(505) 376–2417

Clayton/Union County Chamber of Commerce
P.O. Box 476, Clayton, 88415
(505) 374–9253

Eagle Nest Chamber of Commerce
P.O. Box 322, Eagle Nest, 87718
(505) 377–2420

Las Vegas/ San Miguel County Chamber of Commerce
P.O. Box 148, Las Vegas, 87701
(505) 425–8630, (800) 832–5947

Logan Chamber of Commerce
P.O. Box 277, Logan, 88426
(505) 487–2722

Ratón Chamber of Commerce
P.O. Box 1211, Ratón, 87740
(505) 445–3689, (800) 638–6161
Web site: www.raton.com

Red River Chamber of Commerce
P.O. Box 870, Red River, 87558
(505) 754–2366/(800) 348–6444
Web site: www.redrivernewmex.com/

Santa Rosa Chamber of Commerce
486 Parker Avenue, Santa Rosa, 88418
(505) 472–3763

Springer Chamber of Commerce
P.O. Box 323, Springer, 87747
(505) 483–2998

Tucumcari/Quay County Chamber of Commerce
P.O. Drawer E, Tucumcari, 88401
(505) 461–1694

Silver Moon Restaurant,
3501 Will Rogers Drive,
Santa Rosa,
(505) 472–3162. Inexpensive to moderate. Fare:
American.

QUAY COUNTY
El Toro Cafe,
107 South First Street,
Tucumcari,
(505) 461–3328. Inexpensive to moderate. Fare:
American and
New Mexican.

La Cita Mexican
Restaurant,
812 South First Street,
Tucumcari,
(505) 461–0949. Inexpensive to moderate. Fare: New
Mexican and American.

Lena's Home Cooking,
116 East Smith Street,
Tucumcari,
(505) 461–1610. Inexpensive to moderate. Fare:
American and
New Mexican.

Southeastern New Mexico

Probably the most diverse region of the state, southeastern New Mexico can't be pigeonholed. Its varying landscape ranges from the harshness of the high desert and the glistening dunes of White Sands to the cool peaks of the Sacramento Mountains and the ever-green-laden Lincoln National Forest. Fertile river basins like the Hondo Valley produce pastoral scenes of horses grazing on green fields of oats, as well as vistas of orchards teeming with crisp, red apples. And vast areas of rich, irrigated cropland help feed the nation, thanks in part to the legendary Pecos River (as in "the law west of the Pecos").

De Baca County

De Baca County *is* Fort Sumner and Fort Sumner *is* **Billy the Kid.** Without a doubt, the Kid is New Mexico's most famous legend who actually lived. Though only twenty-one when he died, William Bonney, also known as Billy the Kid, created a legacy and a legend that just won't die. And the community of Fort Sumner is one of several locales in New Mexico where the Kid left his mark. It's also where his remains remain.

State Parks in Southeastern New Mexico:

Bottomless Lake State Park, 16 miles southeast of Roswell, (505) 624–6058

Brantley Lake State Park, 12 miles north of Carlsbad, (505) 457–2384

Living Desert State Park, in Carlsbad, (505) 887–5516

Oasis State Park, 6 miles north of Portales, (505) 356–5331

Oliver Lee Memorial State Park, 10 miles south of Alamogordo, (505) 437–8284

Sumner Lake State Park, 16 miles northwest of Fort Sumner, (505) 355–2541

Web site: *www.emnrd.state.nm.us/nmparks/*

Southeastern New Mexico

N

0   40 mi
0   40 km

268   CURRY CO.

209

84

60

Fort Sumner

84

60   Clovis

DE BACA CO.

20

267

70

285

Portales

54

LINCOLN CO.

Pecos R.

ROOSEVELT CO.

114

206

NEW MEXICO

TEXAS

Carrizozo

380

70

Roswell

70

285

13

2

CHAVES CO.

380

LEA CO.

82

Lovington

70

82

Alamogordo

Artesia

18

529

Hobbs

62

180

70

54

OTERO CO.

EDDY CO.

Carlsbad

180

176

62

285

18

NEW MEXICO

TEXAS

SOUTHEASTERN NEW MEXICO

In the *Old Fort Sumner Cemetery,* you can visit the grave of Billy the Kid. Graves are few and scattered in the small military cemetery, but the most prominent site is encaged in metal—a three-person grave, Billy's alongside those of two of his pals, Tom O'Folliard and Charlie Bowdre.

The Kid's tombstone has a history of its own. It was first stolen in 1950, and its whereabouts remained a mystery until 1976, when Joe Bowlin, owner of the Old Fort Sumner Museum adjacent to the cemetery, recovered it in Granbury, Texas. Several years later it was stolen again, but this time it was recovered within days, in California. The Kid's tombstone, now shackled in iron for protection, has an epitaph that reads THE BOY BANDIT KING/HE DIED AS HE HAD LIVED.

Each summer during the second weekend in June, Fort Sumner hosts Old Fort Days. Here a favorite event is, appropriately enough, the World's Richest Tombstone Race, wherein participants run while carrying a replica of Billy's tombstone.

To get to the cemetery (which is just behind the Old Fort Sumner Museum), head east on U.S. Highway 60/84 from Fort Sumner for 3 miles and then take a right onto Billy the Kid Road (Highway 272), proceeding for 4 miles. There's no admission charge to enter the cemetery, and it's always open.

The *Old Fort Sumner Museum* (505–355–2942), in front of the Old Fort Sumner Cemetery, contains artifacts from Fort Sumner's past. Historical paintings line the walls, and Billy the Kid newspaper clippings and photos are posted on easels throughout. If you have time on your hands, you can learn a lot about the Kid by reading the news items. Otherwise, check out the barbed-wire collection and the old Apache moccasins and articles of Indian ceremonial dress. The museum also has items that were purchased from the La Paloma Museum when it closed down in Lincoln many years ago.

Old Fort Sumner Museum is open daily from 8:00 A.M. to 6:00 P.M. during summer (roughly Memorial Day through Labor Day) and from 9:00 A.M. to 5:00 P.M. the rest of the year (although it may open late and/or close early during the winter, so consider yourself advised). Admission

---

FAVORITE ATTRACTIONS/EVENTS IN SOUTHEASTERN NEW MEXICO:

Old Fort Sumner Cemetery,
Fort Sumner
No phone

Lincoln, New Mexico
(505) 653–4025

Smokey Bear Museum,
Capitán
(505) 354–2298

Carlsbad Caverns
National Park,
Eddy County
(505) 887–6516

White Sands National
Monument, Alamogordo
(505) 479–6124

Smokey Bear Stampede,
July, Capitán
(505) 354–2748

UFO Encounter,
July, Roswell
(888) ROSWELL

Old Lincoln Days,
August, Lincoln
(505) 653–4025

---

is $3.00 for adults, $2.00 for children under fifteen, and free for those under seven. Group rates are available.

About ¼ mile down the gravel road in front of the museum, you'll find **Fort Sumner State Monument** (505–355–2573). It's here that the town gets its name, because the monument's grounds include the ruins of the old military fort. A small visitor center tells the story of Fort Sumner and showcases items excavated from the fort. Late autumn is a great time to visit, for instead of seeing other people you'll get to take a gander at the migratory birds making patterns in the blue sky above nearby Bosque Redondo, the 16 miles of wooded wetlands along the Pecos River.

Fort Sumner was created because of a horrible experiment that failed. During the Civil War, settlers in New Mexico and Arizona, feeling they were in constant danger from the non-Pueblo Indians living in the territory, built the fort as part of a new reservation on which to relocate the Mescalero Apaches and the Navajo. For five years 9,000 Indians were confined to the reservation, after having been forced to walk hundreds of miles from their homelands. Because disease and shortages of food and firewood plagued the reservation, General William T. Sherman sent the Indians home in 1868. At the monument you'll see a shrine dedicated in 1971: a small pile of rocks carried from different parts of the Navajo Nation in northwestern New Mexico and northeastern Arizona to commemorate "The Long Walk."

The fort site is also where Billy the Kid was gunned down by Lincoln County Sheriff Pat Garrett on July 14, 1881, years after the 1869 abandonment of the fort.

The monument is open daily from 8:30 A.M. to 5:00 P.M. Admission charge is $1.00, with children under seventeen admitted free.

Back in the modern-day community of Fort Sumner, you'll come across the most fun of this off-the-beaten-track area's unique spots. If you're a true lover of the legend, you might just satiate your hunger for Kid artifacts and lore at the **Billy the Kid Museum.** The privately owned facility was opened as a one-building museum in 1953 and now rambles both indoors and out through several structures.

You can spend several enjoyable hours strolling among the more than 60,000 relics—some historic, some pure kitsch—collected over the years by Ed Sweet, former owner of the museum, and his wife, Jewel. This place just plain smells old, a wonderfully sentimental scent, as if hundreds of grandmothers' houses were combined.

Kid artifacts include his guns, a jail-cell door that imprisoned the out-law, and even locks of his hair saved by a Las Cruces barber. There's also an original Billy the Kid "wanted" placard signed by territorial New Mexico governor Lew Wallace (author of the novel *Ben Hur*). In addition, you can view a fine selection of antique cars (some of which are usually parked out front, for effect), as well as fossilized dinosaur droppings.

The museum is located at 1601 East Sumner Avenue, 2 miles east of downtown; (505) 355–2380. It's open daily from 8:30 A.M. to 5:00 P.M. May 15 to October 1 and on Monday through Saturday (same hours) the remainder of the year, with the exception of Sundays, when it's open from 11:00 A.M. to 5:00 P.M., and January 1 to January 15, when it closes. Admission is $4.00 for adults, $3.50 for seniors, $2.00 for children under twelve, and free for those under six.

Lincoln County

No other town in New Mexico has preserved its past more meticulously than the community of Lincoln, nestled in the Bonito Valley. History buffs of the Southwest will want to spend the whole day in Lincoln, because the entire town is a National Historical Landmark, thus making visible commercialism absent. As Bob Hart, formerly of the Lincoln County Heritage Trust, notes, "You will find no rubber tomahawks here." Much of the one-street town constitutes the **Lincoln State Monument** and other museums.

As with many old, remote New Mexico towns, Lincoln has definitely seen its wilder days. The former county seat achieved its notoriety as the site of one of the Wild West's bloodiest events: the Lincoln County War of 1878. The war was the culmination of a dispute between opposing factions vying for political and economic control—especially of the

New Mexico Trivia

ABC newsman Sam Donaldson owns a ranch in Lincoln County.

city's lucrative mercantile business, which included nearby Fort Stanton. Billy the Kid got his infamous start during the conflict, in which he sided with one of the factions. Eventually he became a fugitive and, much later, after being captured, made his daring escape from the Lincoln County Courthouse in 1881—only to be tracked down in Fort Sumner by Sheriff Pat Garrett (see De Baca County entry). The two-story courthouse is part of the Lincoln State Monument. It's said that Billy's gun is responsible for a bullet hole visible in the wall at the foot of the stairwell.

A single ticket, available at the Lincoln County Historical Center along

U.S Highway 380, provides access to all the historical sites in town. Though everything is open daily from 8:30 A.M. to 5:00 P.M. May through September, hours and accessibility vary during other times of the year (basically 9:00 A.M.–5:00 P.M. daily, with only two of the four museums open). Tickets are $7.00 for those over fifteen, and children are admitted free. Call (505) 653–4025 for more information.

The most distinctive lodging in the area can be found at **Casa de Patrón,** a bed-and-breakfast along Lincoln's main street. The primary part of the inn was built in the mid-1800s as the home of Juan Patrón, the youngest speaker of the house in New Mexico's territorial legislature. A gracious host, Patrón entertained the likes of pre-outlaw Billy the Kid and territorial governor Lew Wallace in his home. Today, the old adobe home continues to delight persons who find themselves in this isolated part of New Mexico.

Hosts Jeremy and Cleis Jordan escaped the stress—and humidity—of Houston in the early 1980s to settle into the laid-back—and dry—landscape of Lincoln. Jeremy, an engineering consultant, and Cleis, a classical musician, occasionally treat their guests to "salon evenings" based on a particular theme, such as "An Evening in Vienna," in which an elegant dinner is combined with a concert performed by Cleis on the inn's grand piano.

For those who want to enjoy a longer stay or have a place to themselves, the Jordans offer two cabins as part of their inn: Casita Bonita and Casita Paz ("Small Pretty House" and "Small Peace House," respectively). In addition, in the mid-1990s, two new luxury guest rooms were added to the complex. The inn's grounds are the most handsome patch of green in Lincoln—a comforting contrast for the eyes.

Casa de Patrón is on U.S. Highway 380; (505) 653–4676. An ever-changing breakfast, complete with freshly ground coffee, is included in the daily rate of $74–$117.

The **Wortley Pat Garrett Hotel** is another fine place to stay in Lincoln, and it's the only public place to get a meal for miles. The original structure was built in 1874 but burned to the ground in the 1930s. The current replica was constructed some thirty years later and is open from April 28

Wortley Pat Garrett Hotel porch

through October 31. Because the hotel, formerly known as the Wortley Hotel, was briefly owned by Sheriff Pat Garrett in 1881, the current owner changed the name in 1999.

The small, comfortable rooms are simply done in period furnishings reflecting Lincoln's heyday in the late 1800s. Each of the seven rooms has an antique brass bed, fireplace, and private bath. For a great diversion on a lazy Lincoln afternoon, settle into one of the many old rockers on the porch spanning the Wortley's facade and close your eyes as the creak-creak lulls you back to Lincoln's colorful past.

The hotel's restaurant is open daily, during the season, 8:00 A.M. to 3:00 P.M. Run by renowned chef Jerrold Flores, owner of Chango's in Capitan (see page 173), the family-oriented restaurant features classic Americana comfort foods.

The Wortley is situated along U.S. Highway 380 in Lincoln; (505) 653–4300/877–WORTLEY (toll-free). Rates range from $75 to $85.

The picturesque mountain resort town of **Ruidoso,** along Highway 70 just north of the Mescalero Apache Indian Reservation, provides a beautifully polished place to kick back and relax. There's no shortage of lodging here—from luxury condos to rustic cabins and everything in between—and you'll find plenty of fine restaurants, art galleries, and interesting shops. **Ski Apache Ski Area** is also nearby and provides excellent downhill skiing.

If you're planning to spent time in Ruidoso and happen to be a horse fan, be sure to head a few miles farther east on Highway 70 to the community of **Ruidoso Downs** (known for the race track of the same name, home of the world's richest quarter-horse race) and stop by **The Hubbard Museum of the American West,** formerly known as the Museum of the Horse. This relatively new museum pays tribute to an animal the museum claims has played a dramatic role in the exploration and expansion of the cultures of the world throughout history. The museum houses the collection of Anne C. Stradling, a woman born into a wealthy East Coast family who developed a lifelong passion for horses and anything horse-related. Starting with a worn-out stirrup and bit, her collection eventually grew to more than 10,000 pieces—now housed in the handsome museum. Gracing the entrance of the museum is a work-in-progress called *Free Spirits at Noisy Water,* billed as the world's largest equine sculpture. *Free Spirits* is the creation of American sculptor Dave McGary, and when completed, it will include replicas of eight horses, representing all popular breeds, running through a meadow amid falling water.

Hours are as follows: May though Labor Day, daily, 9:00 A.M.–5:30 P.M.; and daily from 10:00 A.M. to 5:00 P.M. the remainder of the year. Admission is $6.00 for adults, $5.00 for seniors, and children under seventeen are admitted free. The museum is located 1 mile east of Ruidoso Downs racetrack, on Highway 70; (505) 378–4142/(800) 263–5929.

In the placid Hondo Valley east of Ruidoso, you'll find one of the most tranquil, unaffected spots in southern New Mexico: the tiny community of **San Patricio,** along the Rio Ruidoso. This is a place of horse ranches and apple orchards. It's also a thriving arts community—a well-hidden fact because of its low-profile location. It's neither promoted nor pretentious. San Patricio is where some of the surviving members of the Wyeth-Hurd creative dynasty continue to paint. Though the family tree has many branches of artists, some of the most celebrated members are N. C. Wyeth, Andrew Wyeth, Peter Hurd, and Henriette Wyeth.

The most imposing and beautiful brick structure in San Patricio houses the very polished Hurd–La Rinconada Gallery (505–653–4331). Built by Mike Hurd, the gallery features the art of members of the Wyeth-Hurd family, including that by Peter Hurd and Henriette Wyeth. The gallery is open Monday through Saturday, 9:00 A.M. to 5:00 P.M., and Sunday, 10:00 A.M. to 4:00 P.M., with the exception of Labor Day through Memorial Day, when the gallery is closed on Sunday.

But the most absolutely and incredibly fascinating spot to visit for any die-hard art adventurer is across the road: *Fort Meigs Galleries.* Am I gushing yet? There truly aren't enough superlatives to describe this peculiar place or the man behind it. John Meigs is one of the last true Renaissance men, and his life reads like an adventure novel: He sailed to Tahiti on the eve of Pearl Harbor's attack (and again a few years ago); he was the designer of the original "Hawaiian shirt" (collector's items now, not modern rip-offs synonymous with tackiness); and he's a veteran of both the San Francisco and the New York art scenes, as well as an international jet-setter extraordinaire. He was encouraged to come to New Mexico almost four decades ago by the late Peter Hurd to assist in painting murals.

A close friend of Georgia O'Keeffe and the Wyeth-Hurd clan, Meigs collected their art as well as art and assorted artifacts the world over. Now it's all for sale in his rambling home/galleries located on this prime patch of pastoral San Patricio. Meigs even goes so far as to say, "Everything's for sale, even me. Just make an offer."

You'll find antique architectural fixtures and Samoan tapestries sharing space with the likes of a soldier's trunk (dated discharge papers lining the inside) from George Washington's army. But the art takes center stage in the many Mexican-tiled and whitewashed rooms of the galleries—filled with the works of both famous and obscure talents.

Call ahead to make sure John will be there when you arrive (he has others staffing the galleries when he's away, though), and set aside a few hours to savor the art and the accompanying stories. *(Note:* John recently donated his estate to a nondenominational order of Benedictine monks, which will eventually convert it into a retreat and counseling center during the next several years. In the meantime, John continues to operate the galleries.)

Fort Meigs Galleries are in San Patricio just off (south) of U.S. Highway 70. Take the gravel road to the left around the old church and the polo field (yes, the polo field) and follow the signs; (505) 653–4320. It's generally open daily 9:00 A.M.–5:00 P.M., but call ahead.

Farther east on U.S. Highway 70 you'll come across the tiny town of Tinnie. The focus here is the *Tinnie Silver Dollar*—restaurant, bar, old-time mercantile, and gallery. The red-roofed adobe structure with its wooden bell tower dominates the landscape and provides a wonderful time-travel experience inside.

Alternately a private residence, mercantile company, and post office dating from 1882, the building became a restaurant in 1959 and was later reconditioned to become the polished gem of southeastern New Mexico. The Silver Dollar's authentic Brunswick bar in its lounge and the hand-beveled glass, fine art, and exquisite antiques galore provide a visual feast for diners. Especially notable is the Victorian Room, which hosts special one-sitting dinners featuring a custom predetermined menu. Selections from the regular menu include a full range of steaks and seafood, most notably Tinnie's Choice-Cut Ribeye and Pasta Diablo (shrimp sautéed with tomatoes, basil pesto, crushed red pepper, and white wine, served atop green chile fettucini).

During summer the Silver Dollar hosts jazz festivals and serves drinks on its long veranda. The colorful and carefully landscaped backyard that slopes toward the Rio Hondo adds to this establishment's charm—and its appeal as a site for weddings.

In addition to the high-society glamour of territorial New Mexico it provides for its ordinary customers, the Silver Dollar is patronized by some of New Mexico's most powerful economic and political players who like to keep a low public profile. In fact, ABC newsman San Donaldson owns a ranch nearby.

Adjacent to the restaurant and bar you'll find a mercantile/gallery that sells everything from flour to Arabian horses, including a selection of locally made gifts. The manager explains that the store stocks things for the community residents, not tourists, adding, "If we don't have it, you don't need it."

The Silver Dollar is on U.S. Highway 70 near the intersection of Highway 368; (505) 653–4425. It is open daily from 11:00 A.M. to 11:00 P.M.

The favorite son of the village of **Capitan** wasn't even human. He was none other than Smokey Bear. (No one knows where that pesky middle name "the" came from, but for the record it's *not* Smokey *the* Bear.) Yes, it's a fact, the national symbol of forest-fire prevention really did exist, and he lived right here in the Capitan Mountains. And the now-legendary story of Smokey's life is amazingly accurate.

In May 1950, a fire crew rescued a badly singed black bear cub that had been clinging to a charred pine tree after devastating man-caused fires destroyed much of the Lincoln National Forest near Capitan. After recuperating at a veterinary hospital in Santa Fe, Smokey was flown to the National Zoo in Washington, D.C., where he "spoke out" for forest-fire prevention until his death in 1976. He was buried in Capitan in the **Smokey Bear Historical State Park** (505–354–2748), which also has a fine visitors center filled with Smokey memorabilia. But his legacy and his message live on. According to the U.S. Forest Service, the Smokey Bear fire-prevention campaign is the longest-running public-service-announcement campaign in the history of The Ad Council.

Adjacent to the park you'll find the **Smokey Bear Museum,** which documents Smokey's story. The museum contains several scrapbooks filled with photographs and news clippings on Smokey's life and times. The fact that a museum would even make scrapbooks accessible to visitors is odd, but the effect is very personal, down-home, and nostalgic—a detail that adds to the sentimental feeling of this small log museum.

An exhibit of Smokey Bear toys, books, and comics from the 1950s and 1960s shows how popular culture was used to convey an important message to the youth of the era.

The museum is on Highway 380 in downtown Capitan; (505) 354–2298. It's open Monday–Saturday from 9:00 A.M. to 4:00 P.M. and on Sunday, 11:00 A.M.–4:00 P.M. There's no admission charge.

For an international flavor deep in the heart of Lincoln County, check out **Chango's Restaurant and Art Gallery.** Opened in 1982 by chef-artist Jerrold Flores, Chango's is a favorite of area innkeepers and consistently receives excellent reviews. Though it may seem out of place in the small community of Capitan, the food is definitely uptown in both presentation and flavor. Entree selections change weekly on Jerrold's whim but also in reflecting the cuisines of different countries. Recent selections have included scallops in a white chocolate, Chardonnay, and fresh herb sauce, Mediterranean-style chicken, and pork tenderloin in essence of orange and chipotle sauce.

The gallery part of Chango's, which is primarily the restaurant walls, features contemporary art and antiques, collectibles, and primitive art. Like the food, the art changes regularly. As an avid art collector, Jerrold often highlights items from his personal holdings. Recent exhibits include masks from East India, Mexico, and Guatemala; Japanese kimonos; and Imperial Chinese items.

Chango's is at the corner of First Street and Lincoln Avenue; (505) 354–4213. It's open Wednesday through Saturday from 5:00 to 9:00 P.M.

Farther north in Lincoln County you'll find the remains of New Mexico's most raucous mining town in the ghost town of **White Oaks.** One version of White Oaks's birth in the 1870s says that the discoverer of the North Homestake mine sold it to a friend for $40, a pony, and a bottle of whiskey. He probably lived to regret that decision when the mine eventually produced $500,000 in gold.

Along came other mines with names like Rip Van Winkle, Large Hopes, Little Hell, and Smuggler, and the boomtown was under way with a population that swelled to 4,000. The town became a hangout for cattle rustlers and outlaws, including Billy the Kid. Saloons, gambling houses, and "houses of another sort" took hold as White Oaks entrepreneurs thought of quick ways to wheedle away the day's take from area miners.

White Oaks faded when a planned railroad link with El Paso went instead to the New Mexico town of Capitan. The gold played out at about the same time.

A simple historical marker, a cemetery, and many abandoned buildings are all that's left of old White Oaks. A few hardy folks have rediscovered the town, elevating its status to semighost town. An impressive building is Hoyle's Castle, a brick Victorian mansion that looms over the town from its hilltop site. A retired schoolteacher from Carrizozo lives in the structure, which resembles a classic haunted house out of an old movie. It's not open to visitors.

White Oaks does have a bar and a museum. They're one and the same housed in the old post office, a tiny wooden shack near the center of town. It's not only an interesting place in which to look at relics from the mining days but also a fun, though eerie, place in which to grab a beer and play a game of pool in the back room.

White Oaks is 9 miles off of U.S. Highway 54 on Highway 349, 11 miles northeast of Carrizozo.

Otero County

Driving into Otero County from the north along U.S. Highway 54, observant motorists and spider fanciers should be on the lookout for the brave tarantulas that cross the highway on warm summer days. I'm sure highway department TARANTULA CROSSING signs wouldn't last out here, as less-than-honest souvenir seekers would pick them off as fast as they could be placed. Tarantulas aside, Otero County offers weekend adventurers several special spots. Though much of the county is off-limits (White Sands Missile Range, Fort Bliss Military Reservation, and the Mescalero Apache Indian Reservation), the parts that are accessible make up for it.

The missile range isn't the only place that's privy to the soft, snow-white gypsum dunes just southwest of the city of Alamogordo. Adjacent to the range is the ***White Sands National Monument***—part of the largest gypsum dune field in the world—whose majesty you're welcome to explore.

White Oaks Bar and Museum

This extremely stark park is the perfect place for uninhibited barefoot frolicking. It's also the place for people who are afraid of the water: lots of beach, no ocean. Pack plastic sleds and snowboards to slide down the up-to-60-foot-tall sand dunes. During the height of summer, the sand tends to get quite hot, but you wouldn't want to visit then anyway—tourists, you know. Plan a late autumn visit—or, better yet, camp out during a full moon (allowed at a backcountry campsite only; registration required). At night, the reflection of moonlight from the sand provides an unearthly adventure you won't soon forget—it's bright enough to read by!

A visitor center and museum explains how the dunes were formed and contains an exhibit on those species of plants and wildlife hardy enough to thrive in such a harsh environment. Still, it's the Dunes Drive, an 8-mile scenic loop, that forms the highlight of a visit to White Sands. The "sands" are almost like a living entity. Gusting winds cause them to shift, which makes keeping the roads clear a full-time chore. Occasionally, the Dunes Drive is closed because of missile-range testing, so call ahead.

White Sands National Monument is 15 miles southwest of Alamogordo, just off U.S. Highway 70/82; (505) 479–6124. It's open daily, with hours as follows: in summer (Memorial Day through mid-August), visitors center 8:00 A.M.–7:00 P.M. and Dunes Drive 7:00 A.M.–10:00 P.M.; in winter, visitors center 8:00 A.M.–4:30 P.M. and Dunes Drive 7:00 A.M. to sunset. There's a $3.00 fee per person for the Dunes Drive.

Just north of Alamogordo you'll find **Eagle Ranch Pistachio Groves,** producer of "Heart of the Desert" pistachio nuts. Though the bulk of domestic pistachio farming occurs in the fertile San Joaquin Valley in California, a new agricultural industry has emerged in this southern New Mexico town after a little research showed that climate and elevation were nearly perfect in Alamogordo for growing the fickle nut.

Never dyed red to appeal to consumers or cover blemishes, Eagle Ranch's off-white and green nuts are available only by mail or at the ranch store. The outlet recently introduced red chile pistachios for die-hard New Mexican chileheads who need an extra kick to everything they eat.

Marianne Schweers, who owns the groves with her husband, George, shares an interesting bit of pistachio lore: When the Shah of Iran was overthrown in 1979, not only was the world oil market affected but the Middle Eastern country's other principal export also suffered when its markets were cut off. Yes, until that time Iran was the world's premier pistachio supplier. The situation was a big boost to U.S. pistachio production, and the timing couldn't have been better for fledgling Eagle

Ranch. Marianne sums up the situation by saying, "The Ayatollah was the best friend that [U.S.] pistachio growers ever had."

Though visitors are always welcome to look at the groves, guided tours are available only to groups of ten or more. The Eagle Ranch store, which also sells other southwestern food and gift items, is located 4 miles north of Alamogordo on U.S. Highway 54/70; (505) 434–0035/(800) 432–0999. The store is open daily 9:00 A.M.–6:00 P.M.

In Alamogordo ("Fat Cottonwood"), you'll find the **Space Center** nestled in the foothills of the Sacramento Mountains. This shimmering, massive gold cube of a building houses four levels of museumlike exhibits in the International Space Hall of Fame (annual induction ceremony held the last Saturday in September).

You start on the top floor and work your way down ramps through exhibits like the "There's Space in New Mexico" room, which combines traditional New Mexico ambiance—adobe walls, pine-planked floor, vigas (ceiling beams)—with the state's cutting-edge research and contributions to the nation's space program. You can also step inside the interactive "Space Station 2001" exhibit for an astronaut's view of space travel in the future, as well as examine a Skylab space suit and even Soviet space food.

For those who want to take a load off, the Space Center is also home to an Omnimax theater with a 2,700-square-foot screen, as well as to a high-tech planetarium system. Outside, on the grounds of the Space Center, you'll find the John P. Stapp Air and Space Park, which is filled with actual space hardware and rocket equipment. This is also a good place to get a broad view of White Sands in the distance.

To get to the Space Center, turn east on Indian Wells Road off U.S. Highway 54/70/82 in Alamogordo and follow the signs; (505) 437–2840. It's open daily 9:00 A.M.–6:00 P.M. Memorial Day through Labor Day; otherwise, 9:00 A.M.–5:00 P.M. Hall of Fame admission charges are $2.50 for adults, $2.25 for seniors and military personnel, and $2.00 for children ages six to twelve; theater admission charges are $5.50 for adults, $4.50 for young adults, and $3.50 for children; and kids

New Mexico Trivia

Ham, the first chimpanzee in outer space, and Minnie, the longest-surviving "astrochimp," are both buried at the International Space Hall of Fame in Alamogordo.

under six are admitted to both attractions free. There are also special combination rates and family, senior citizen, and active-duty military rates. (*Note:* Admission for all attendees is free to the Hall of Fame on the day of the annual induction ceremony; see above.)

New Mexico Trivia

Alan Hale, co-discoverer of the much-celebrated Hale-Bopp comet, lives and watches the sky near Cloudcroft in the Sacramento Mountains of Otero County in southeastern New Mexico.

Highway 82, from Alamogordo to the village of **Cloudcroft,** is one of southern New Mexico's most beautiful drives. In just 16 miles you'll climb nearly 5,000 feet, passing through all the climatic zones from the Sonoran Desert region of Mexico to the Hudson Bay region of Canada. As the road winds through the forested Sacramento Mountains, you'll come across many scenic overlooks, as well as roadside stands selling apples, cider, and various other forms of produce. New Mexico's only highway tunnel is also on this route.

Once you experience the breathtaking setting of Cloudcroft high in the Sacramentos, you'll understand why getting here is worth the effort. The small town is a year-round playground where you can beat the heat in summer and marvel at the turning of the aspens in fall. And Cloudcroft's magical winters bring snow skiing at Ski Cloudcroft (see appendix, page 197), the southernmost ski area in the United States, and ice skating at Sewell Skate Pond, one of only a few outdoor places in the state where you can pursue this sport.

Cloudcroft is also home to **The Lodge,** a romantic mountain getaway. This place has a history. Built as a railroad resort in 1899, the inn was reconstructed after the original lodge burned in 1909. Famous guests include Judy Garland and Clark Gable, and Conrad Hilton, founder of the hotel chain that bears his name, owned the place in the 1930s.

The Lodge's European-style architecture, with its four-story copper tower, adds to a mood of romantic seclusion in a chalet high in the Alps. Inside, Victorian ambiance takes over in the high-ceilinged guest rooms outfitted with antique furnishings and down comforters. Select a stay when your weary bones need a rest and you couldn't care less about roaming the byways for further adventure.

Because it's usually chilly at this altitude (9,200 feet), expect a cozy fire in the lobby fireplace any time of year. Just off the lobby is Rebecca's, the lodge's dining room, named after the ghost who is said to roam the inn's halls; Rebecca, the story goes, was a flirtatious, redheaded chambermaid who in the 1930s was killed by a jealous lover.

The Lodge is just off Highway 82 in Cloudcroft; (505) 682–2566/(800) 395–6343. Room rates range from $75 to $299, depending on the particular room and season.

The **National Solar Observatory at Sacramento Peak** (505–434–7000) in the village of Sunspot offers visitors a chance to see why and how astronomers study the sun from their vantage point at 9,200 feet in the Sacramento Mountains. The observatory is open to the public between dawn and dusk for self-guided tours. Weekend-afternoon guided tours, beginning at 2:00 P.M. May through October, begin with a slide-show presentation about the observatory and the sun and a walk around the observatory, including a visit to the Vacuum Tower Telescope, the largest at the site. The observatory has a gift shop, which is generally open weekends, May through October. Even if you're not into astronomy, the drive through, and the setting in, the Lincoln National Forest are quite awe inspiring. In addition to the million-dollar views of the Tularosa Basin (including White Sands National Monument), you'll find plenty of hiking trails and remote picnic spots.

From Cloudcroft, take Highway 130 East to its junction with Highway 6563 (a designated scenic byway). Follow Highway 6563 to its end, about 15 miles, to Sunspot. Guided tours are $2.00 for adults and $1.00 for seniors and children; self-guided tours are free.

By planning ahead, you may combine your visit to the solar observatory

A Glimpse of Southeastern New Mexico: *Impresiones de las Cavernas Magníficas . . .*

*W*ithout knowing it, I became an explorer of New Mexico more than twenty years ago during an out-of-state family vacation with my dad, mom, and older sister. I'd known little about Carlsbad Caverns, but the thought of any escape from the unbearable heat and humidity of another South Texas August was enough to get me excited.

Though our trip included running barefoot through the endless soft dunes of White Sands National Monument, escaping into the forests and mountains of Cloudcroft, and watching the horses run at Ruidoso Downs, it was the caverns that had begun to cast their spell on my nine-year-old imagination. My energy level increased on the final hours of the drive, and all I could do was fantasize about the darkness, the coolness, and the otherworldly, eerie silence that awaited me.

After parking, gathering gear, and trekking toward the entrance, we saw the mouth-shaped, giant cave entrance loom before us. As the opening swallowed us up on our descent, the air became cooler, and, now glad that my mom had made me bring along my blue windbreaker, I smiled as I blocked voices and other sounds from my mind. Confident I would not get lost, I broke away from the slow pace of my family and sped around a blind bend in the trail. I had begun chasing my first New Mexico adventure, and I was hooked.

with a tour of neighboring **Apache Point Observatory** (505–437–6822), which offers tours only by advance reservation. Unlike the former, the latter is oriented toward nighttime astronomical observation.

Chaves County

The city of **Roswell** is one of those near-perfect all-American cities. Cited by national publications as one of the ten best small cities in the country, Roswell has also been included in the list of "Ten Peaceable Places to Retire" compiled by *Money* magazine. (Though lately the media cannot get enough coverage of Roswell as the "UFO capital of the world." See page 181.) As the largest city in southeastern New Mexico, Roswell has its share of interesting sites and cultural diversions as well as the century-old New Mexico Military Institute. But the most impressive spot to visit is the **Roswell Art Center and Museum.** With twelve galleries in the grand adobe structure, the center focuses on art, history, and science.

Known for its excellent paintings of the Southwest, the center has the finest single collection of art in southeastern New Mexico. Featured New Mexico artists include Georgia O'Keeffe, Ernest Blumenschein, Henriette Wyeth, Andrew Dasburg, and Fremont Ellis. The museum's nationally acclaimed Hurd Collection is the most extensive collection of Roswell-native Peter Hurd's works.

A special wing of the center displays the actual engines and rocket assemblies developed by Dr. Robert H. Goddard, who worked in Roswell from 1930 to 1942. The Goddard Wing also has a replica of the early space scientist's laboratory, where he built the world's first liquid-fuel rockets. In addition, the Robert Goddard Planetarium on site presents various programs, for which fees are generally $2.00–$5.00 per person.

New Mexico Trivia

Actress Demi Moore was born in Roswell.

The museum is located at 100 West Eleventh Street; (505) 624–6744. It's open Monday through Saturday from 9:00 A.M. to 5:00 P.M. and Sunday and holidays from 1:00 to 5:00 P.M. There's no admission charge.

People take UFO sightings seriously in Roswell—people like Walter Haut, president of the **International UFO Museum & Research Center** (505–625–9495). He has reason to believe. In 1947 Haut made national headlines when, as a public relations officer from the former Roswell Army Air Field, he announced the recovery of a crashed flying saucer at a nearby ranch. The increasingly known museum features interesting displays and published accounts of reported UFO sightings from all over the world.

Though the army later denied that extraterrestrial matter was found from what is often known as "The Roswell Incident," claiming the debris came from a downed weather balloon, Haut remains convinced that aliens have visited earth. He wants museum visitors to decide for themselves, however. Volunteers staff the nonprofit museum to answer questions and help interpret displays. The museum, located at 114 North Main (Highway 70), now has a popular gift shop and is open daily from 10:00 A.M. to 5:00 P.M. There's no admission charge.

In the wake of Roswell's increased notoriety as a mecca for those who believe in UFOs—especially after the release of the 1996 sci-fi block-buster film *Independence Day* and the acclaimed 1997 film *Contact,* plus an appearance by Roswell's mayor on *The Late Show with David Letterman*—the community now hosts the annual **Roswell UFO Encounter,** a festival held during, appropriately, the July Fourth weekend. The event includes talks by well-known conspiracy theorists and other *ufo*logists, a fireworks display, a nighttime golf tournament (complete with glow-in-the-dark balls), an alien costume contest, and a UFO Crash and Burn Expo, a nonmotorized vehicle competition. For information on the event—as well as for information regarding guided tours of the alleged crash site, complete with an area rancher as the unlikely guide—call the Roswell Chamber of Commerce at (800) 295–7611.

Other notable museums in Roswell include the **Gen. Douglas L. McBride Museum** (505–622–6250), a U.S. military history museum located at the New Mexico Military Institute, and the **Historical Center for Southeastern New Mexico,** formerly the Chaves County Historical Museum, at 200 North Lea (505–622–8333).

Eddy County

ddy County should probably be called Cave County. In addition to containing the world-famous Carlsbad Cavern, the county has untold numbers of other caves, most of them patiently waiting to be discovered by some daring young spelunker. And if the name changed to Cave County, the county seat would undoubtedly be **Carlsbad Caverns National Park,** probably the single most-visited spot in New Mexico and certainly one of the best known.

Despite its name, the park is located not in Carlsbad but, rather, 26 miles southwest of the city. Actually, it's closer to Whites City, named after Jim White, who discovered this underground fantasyland in 1901. Because you'll be underground in a constant-temperature (read: quite cool) environment during most of your visit, pleasant weather is not a major factor for enjoyment. Therefore, it's a good idea to avoid the crowds of summer, when the above-ground temperatures can soar.

From May through October the park offers visitors the fun of viewing mass bat flights. After dusk, almost a million Mexican freetail bats swirl out of the cave's entrance for their nightly escapades and insect-feeding frenzies. The bat flight is preceded by informative—and humorous—talks by rangers about the tiny winged mammals. Though it's true that these same bats are in the cave during the day, don't worry: The caverns are enormous, and you won't even notice the slumbering bats.

Though the park is decidedly remote, access is no problem. Of course, after making the significant trek to the park, you'll undoubtedly want to view the famed stalactites and stalagmites decorating the grand chambers of Carlsbad Cavern, but as a true adventurer you'll also be drawn to its other less accessible caves, such as Slaughter Canyon Cave, Spider Cave, Lower Cave, and Hall of the White Giants.

These alternative caves preserve some of the thrill cavers experience when exploring a new find. The guided-lantern tours (limited to groups) take you through the undeveloped caves in all their eerie, dark splendor. You'll need to bring along a flashlight, water, and nonslip shoes. (*Note:* Don't attempt this type of cave adventure unless you're in reasonably good physical shape.)

In a remote section of the park is the world's largest cave: **Lechuguilla Cave,** whose magnitude was discovered only in 1986. It's designated a "wild" cave and open just to experienced cavers in organized expeditions (park permit required). Neither does the National Park Service plan to develop Lechuguilla; it, along with several other wild caves, may be designated the world's first cave wilderness.

The park entrance is located just west of Whites City on Highway 7; (505) 785–2232/(800) 967–CAVE. Though Carlsbad Cavern is open daily with continuous self-guided tours, other caving experiences are limited and often require reservations. Fees vary widely, from $6.00 for adults for the normal self-guided tour to $20 for select guided tours. Hours for self-guided tours are 8:30 A.M.–3:30 P.M. Memorial Day–mid-August; otherwise, hours are 8:30 A.M.–2:00 P.M.

Closer to the city of Carlsbad you'll find **Living Desert State Park.** This unique park atop the Ocotillo Hills combines botanical gardens and a zoo in a natural setting. It concentrates on plants and animals indigenous to the Chihuahuan Desert. You'll see mountain lions, bobcats, buffalo, antelope, and the endangered Mexican wolf, as well as an excellent collection of exotic cacti and succulents from around the world. The views of Carlsbad and the Pecos River valley from parts of the trail are spectacular.

The park is located just off Highway 285 on Skyline Drive in the northwest edge of Carlsbad; (505) 887–5516. It's open daily from 8:00 A.M. to 8:00 P.M. (last tour at 6:30 P.M.) Memorial Day through Labor Day and from 9:00 A.M. to 5:00 P.M. (last tour at 3:30 P.M.) the rest of the year. Admission is $4.00 for adults and $2.00 for children, with children under six admitted free.

The small southeastern community of *Artesia* often gets short-changed due to its convenient location halfway between the larger and more well-known cities of Roswell and Carlsbad. It's here, however, where you'll find authentic small-town hospitality and a leisurely pace. If you're passing through and looking for good eats, check out the classic *La Fonda Restaurant* at 201 West Main (505–746–9377).

Following in the path of unusual locations of public buildings—Artesia boasts the first underground elementary school, built as a bomb

Solamente en Nuevo México . . . The Goodnight-Loving Trail

*N*ineteenth-century cattle trails were just about as important to the settlement of the American West as were the celebrated commerce trails like the Santa Fe Trail and the Oregon Trail. The Chisolm Trail may have more name recognition as a cattle trail, but it was the trail with the soothing name that made its mark on southeastern New Mexico.

The Goodnight-Loving Trail adventure began because two particularly ambitious ranchers, like many southern ranchers, had experienced problems selling "recovered" cattle (those that had scattered during the Civil War) in war-ravaged markets. In 1886, Charles

Goodnight and Oliver Loving set out from the northwest-Texas frontier to blaze a trail that would allow them to seek out more lucrative markets to the west. The Goodnight-Loving Trail led for hundreds of miles, looping up into New Mexico near present-day Carlsbad and Roswell, and ended in Fort Sumner, where Goodnight and Loving separated. Loving continued north to Colorado and Goodnight returned to Texas for another herd of cattle.

That lucrative first trip started a new industry in New Mexico. Cattle ranching and beef processing continue the legacy of the Goodnight-Loving Trail in eastern New Mexico to this day.

shelter—is the town's first bed-and-breakfast inn. The **Heritage Inn Bed & Breakfast** is at once one of the most likely places for a small town inn—in the oldest building on Main Street, built in 1905—yet also in one of the most unlikely: It's perched above a Radio Shack! But you won't even be aware of the steady business of a retail chain store below as you enjoy the well-insulated country Victorian atmosphere of the inn, with its old 8-foot-high windows, gleaming hardwood floors, and Colonial American furnishings and decor. In addition to eight guest rooms, each with a queen-size bed and its own bathroom, the inn provides a parlor/lounge for its guests, complete with TV/VCR and a small library. Though the building may be old, the inn is not. The space was completely renovated in the mid-1990s, so you can expect the conveniences of a modern hotel: remote-control TVs, telephones, and modem hookups in every room, with fax services available.

You'll find the inn at 209 West Main; (505) 748–2552. Rates range from $50 to $65.

Lea County

The Llano Estacado, or "Staked Plains," makes up a large part of the landscape of New Mexico's southeasternmost county, one of the last major land areas in the continental United States to be settled. Homesteading and open-range ranching were a way of life on this often-harsh land during the early part of this century. For the most part, working cowboys have given way to rodeo cowboys in these parts. In fact, Lea County has produced more professional rodeo champions than any other county in the United States, starting with Henry Clay McGonagill in 1901. He was the first professional rodeo cowboy. In 1978, the county's heritage was honored with the founding of the **Lea County Cowboy Hall of Fame and Western Heritage Center** in the county's largest city, Hobbs.

The result of the dream of Dale "Tuffy" Cooper, the Hall of Fame captures the essence of the early days and the pioneers of Lea County. It honors county residents who have distinguished themselves in rodeo, as ranch cowboys, or as pioneer or present-day women on ranches. In contrast to many museums, the chronologically displayed exhibits are glimpses of history depicting entire scenes rather than just labeled artifacts. Complete portrayals of a pioneer bedroom and kitchen look as though someone might return any minute. Memorabilia of all inductees are also displayed in the Hall of Fame.

The Hall of Fame is on the campus of New Mexico Junior College, 5317

La Comida de Nuevo México

*C*lassic Gold Margarita

This comida is actually a bebida (drink) and is the perfect accompaniment or prelude to a traditional New Mexican meal.

1 oz. any premium gold tequila

¹/₂ oz. Cointreau (or triple sec, a less expensive orange liqueur)

1 oz. fresh-squeezed lime juice

¹/₄ oz. fresh-squeezed lemon juice

margarita or kosher salt (coarser than table salt)

1 wedge lime and/or 1 wedge lemon

Make a slice in a lime wedge and run the edge around the rim of a glass (in order to dampen the edge). Dip dampened glass edge in salt. Fill a large cup with ice and add remaining ingredients. Shake gently. Pour ice and drink into the salt-rimmed glass for your margarita "on the rocks"; for a margarita "neat," strain out the ice. ¡Salud! Makes 1 Margarita.

Lovington Highway, in Hobbs; (505) 392–5518. It's open Monday through Friday, 8:00 A.M.–5:00 P.M., and Saturday, 1:00–5:00 P.M. There's no admission charge.

Other notable museums in the area include the ***Confederate Air Force Museum*** (505–392–5342) at the ***Lea County Airport*** on Highway 180 in Hobbs and the Lea County Museum (505–396–5311) at 102 South Love in the town of Lovington (northeast of Hobbs via Highway 18). This local-history museum, situated in a former landmark hotel, built in 1918, displays exhibits of pioneer families.

Roosevelt County

N orth of the city of Portales—the home of Eastern New Mexico University—you'll come across one of the most significant archaeological sites in North America: Blackwater Draw. And the ***Blackwater Draw Museum*** is on hand to help interpret exactly why this spot is so important. (The Blackwater Draw site is actually a little northwest of the museum, but visit the museum first.)

On this site in 1932, A. W. Anderson of nearby Clovis discovered the oldest evidence of human existence in the New World—11,000 years ago. Spear points, bones, and fossilized remains of woolly mammoth, saber-toothed tiger, camel, and bison have been recovered from the sprawling maze of canyons. At one time Blackwater Draw was a large pond used as a watering hole for animals and, subsequently, as an ambush site for the early human inhabitants. The pond dried up 7,000 years ago, eventually forcing the hunter-gatherers to move on.

Though the museum displays some of what has been discovered at the site, archaeological excavations continue. Over the years, the digs have been funded by the likes of the Carnegie Institute, the National Geographic Society, and the Smithsonian Institution.

The museum is located 7 miles northeast of Portales on U.S. Highway 70; (505) 562–2202. From Memorial Day through Labor Day, the museum is open Monday through Saturday from 10:00 A.M. to 5:00 P.M. and Sunday from noon to 5:00 P.M.; during other times of the year, hours remain the same except that the museum is closed on Monday. The site's hours are the same during summer; however, it's closed November through February and is open only on weekends (museum hours) during the spring and fall seasons, when it will also close during inclement weather. Admission is $2.00 for adults, $1.00 for seniors and children (ages six to fifteen), and free for children under six. A single ticket allows visits to both museum and site. (*Note:* On the fourth Sunday of each month, a "free" day is held, on which no admission fees are charged.)

What with the huge *scientific* brain trust in New Mexico (Sandia and Los Alamos National Laboratories, White Sands Missile Range, Intel), it's only fitting that the genre of science fiction would earn a place of respect here as well—and it did, with the opening and dedication of the **Jack Williamson Science Fiction Library** in 1982 on the campus of Eastern New Mexico University in **Portales.** Combine that with all the renewed attention focused on "the Roswell incident" of 1947 (see International UFO Museum, page 180), and you'd imagine the public interest in this little-known specialty library is bound to increase.

Begun in 1967, when Dr. Williamson—noted pioneer science-fiction writer, teacher, student, and benefactor—first donated his personal collection of materials, the library has grown to house one of the top science-fiction collections in the world, now including more than 13,000 volumes. Among the collection are the manuscripts and papers of noted authors Edmond Hamilton and Leigh Brackett, thousands of issues of science-fiction "pulps," dating back to the early 1900s, and an original copy of Gene Roddenberry's pilot script for the

Star Trek television series. Among authors designedly collected are Isaac Asimov, Edgar Rice Burroughs, Harlan Ellison, Robert Heinlein, Robert Silverberg, Spider Robinson, Ursula LeGuin, and Gordon Dickson. And the best part is, most of the books can be borrowed, with the exception of autographed or fragile editions.

The library is open Monday through Friday, 8:00 A.M.–5:00 P.M., and Sunday, 1:00–5:00 P.M., (505) 562–2636.

Curry County

lovis, the largest city in Curry County and trade center for nearby Cannon Air Force Base, holds a place in rock-and-roll history with its **Norman Petty Recording Studios.** The old studio is now a shrine to Buddy Holly, the pioneering rock-and-roller who propelled such hits as "That'll Be the Day" and "Peggy Sue" to the top of the charts in the 1950s–hits that were recorded right here at the then state-of-the-art studio.

The studio was founded by the late producer-arranger-musician Norman Petty, who died in 1984, and his wife, Vi, who later cleaned and restored the studio to its former glory and personally led tours through the place before her death in 1992. She'd point out the drink machine where Holly would buy Cokes, Holly's microphone and Fender guitar amplifier, the room where Holly and other studio guests stayed, all its furniture intact. Besides Holly, the studio drew other musicians from West Texas and New Mexico, most notably Roy Orbison.

Kenneth Broad, an area minister and executor of the Pettys' estate, feels it's important to keep the restored studio open as a shrine for Holly's fans. Broad and other locals would like to open the studio for regular tours as well as turn it into a working recording studio again. In the meantime, however, the little gray building on Seventh Street in downtown Clovis is officially open only during the four-day Clovis Music Festival held each July as an annual tribute to Petty and local musicians. During other times, anyone wanting to see the place must call in advance (505–356–6422) to make sure someone's there to show them around. There's no admission fee, but donations are accepted.

Like many sizable towns across America, Clovis has a historic theater on its Main Street, 411 Main to be precise. A tall, rather ordinary facade, with that familiar vertical neon spelling out "Lyceum" in an Art Deco typeface, belies the grand interior of the town's **Old Lyceum Theatre.** Built during

1919–20 as a theater that would be used for both live performances and films, the Lyceum's huge screen was tailor-made to reflect the glory of early Hollywood, including Tom Mix cowboy movies and those starring Shirley Temple. The vision of the theater's founder, Eugene F. Hardwick, was to create the best performing stage west of Kansas City. Many folks at the time believe he succeeded.

The Lyceum closed in 1974, and later a group of locals formed to "Save the Lyceum!" and ended up purchasing it for $40,000. A nonprofit group then began restoring and, eventually, operating the theater. At present, the Lyceum presents a full season of play productions September through June. Guided tours are available upon request, (505) 763–6085.

WHERE TO STAY IN SOUTHEASTERN NEW MEXICO

DE BACA COUNTY
Coronado Motel,
309 West Sumner,
Fort Sumner,
(505) 355–2466.

Oasis Motel,
1704 East Sumner,
Fort Sumner,
(505) 355–7414.

Fisherman's Hideaway,
Sumner Lake
(call for directions),
Fort Sumner,
(505) 355–2629.

LINCOLN COUNTY
Casa de Patrón,
U.S. Highway 380,
Lincoln,
(505) 653–4676.

Wortley Pat Garrett Hotel,
U.S. Highway 380,
Lincoln,
(505) 653–4300.
(877) WORTLEY (toll-free)

Best Western Swiss
Chalet Inn,
1451 Mecham Drive,
Ruidoso,
(505) 258–3333/
(800) 477–9477.

Forest Home Cabins,
436 Main Road,
Ruidoso,
(505) 257–4488.

Holiday Inn Express,
400 West Highway 70,
Ruidoso,
(505) 257–3736.

Shadow Mountain Lodge,
107 Main Road,
Ruidoso,
(505) 257–4886/
(800) 441–4331.

OTERO COUNTY
The Lodge,
just off Highway 82,
Cloudcroft,
(505) 682–2566.

Inn of the Mountain Gods
(resort),
Mescalero Apache
Reservation,
(505) 257–5141/
(800) 545–6040.

Satellite Inn,
2224 North White
Sands Boulevard,
Alamogordo,
(505) 437–8454/
(800) 221–7690.

White Sands Inn,
1020 South White
Sands Boulevard,
Alamogordo,
(505) 434–4200/
(800) 255–5061.

CHAVES COUNTY
Best Western
El Rancho Palacio,
2205 North Main Street,
Roswell,
(505) 622-2721.

Best Western Sally
Port Inn and Suites,
2000 North Main Street,
Roswell,
(505) 622–6430.

Days Inn,
1310 North Main Street,
Roswell NM,
(505) 623–4021/(800)
DAYSINN.

Roswell Inn,
1815 North Main Street,
Roswell,
(505) 623–4920 or
(800) 323–0913.

EDDY COUNTY
Heritage Inn Bed
& Breakfast,
209 West Main,
Artesia,
(505) 748–2552/
(800) 594–7392.

Best Western Pecos Inn,
2209 West Main,
Artesia,
(505) 748–3324/
(800) 676–7481.

Best Western Stevens Inn,
1829 South Canal Street,
Carlsbad,
(505) 887–2851/
(800) 730–2851.

Carlsbad Super 8,
3817 National Parks
Highway,
Carlsbad,
(505) 887–8888.

Holiday Inn,
601 South Canal Street,
Carlsbad,
(505) 885–8500/
(800) HOLIDAY.

Best Western Cavern Inn,
17 Carlsbad Caverns
Highway,
Whites City,
(505) 785–2291/
(800) CAVERNS.

LEA COUNTY
Innkeepers of New Mexico,
309 North Marland
Boulevard,
Hobbs,
(505) 397–7171.

Ramada Inn,
501 North Marland,
Hobbs,
(505) 397–3251.

Sands Motel,
1300 East Broadway,
Hobbs,
(505) 393–4442.

ROOSEVELT COUNTY
Morning Star Inn
(bed and breakfast),
620 West Second,
Portales,
(505) 356–2994.

Classic American
Economy Inn,
1613 West Second,
Portales,
(505) 356–6669.

Super 8 Motel,
1805 West Second,
Portales,
(505) 356–8518.

CURRY COUNTY
Best Western La Vista Inn,
1516 Mabry Drive,
Clovis,
(505) 762–3808/
(800) 528–1234.

Clovis Inn,
2912 Mabry Drive,
Clovis,
(505) 762–5600/
(800) 535–3440.

Holiday Inn,
2700 Mabry Drive,
Clovis,
(505) 762–4491.

**WHERE TO EAT IN
SOUTHEASTERN
NEW MEXICO**

DE BACA COUNTY
Fred's Restaurant
& Lounge,
1408 East Sumner,
Fort Sumner,
(505) 355–7500.
Inexpensive.
Fare: American.

Sprout's Cafe,
1701 East Sumner,
Fort Sumner,
(505) 355–7278.
Inexpensive to moderate.
Fare: American.

Fisherman's Hideaway,
Sumner Lake (call for
directions),
Fort Sumner,
(505) 355–2629.
Inexpensive to moderate.
Fare: American.

Sadie's Mexican
Restaurant,
Highway 60 West,
Fort Sumner,
(505) 355–7820.
Inexpensive to moderate.
Fare: New Mexican.

LINCOLN COUNTY
Chango's Restaurant
and Art Gallery,
First Street and Lincoln
Avenue,
(505) 354–4213. Moderate
to expensive. Fare: Innovative New American.

Tinnie Silver Dollar,
U.S. Highway 70,
Tinnie,
(505) 653–4425. Moderate
to expensive. Fare: American and Southwestern.

Smokey Bear Restaurant,
downtown,
Capitan,
(505) 354–2253. Inexpen-
sive. Fare: American.

OTERO COUNTY
Angelina's,
415 White Sands Boulevard,
Alamogordo,
(505) 434–1166. Inexpen-
sive to moderate.
Fare: Italian.

Cattleman's Steakhouse,
2904 North White Sands
Boulevard,
Alamogordo,
(505) 434–5252. Inexpen-
sive to moderate. Fare:
Steaks, chicken, etc.

Ernesto's Mexican
Restaurant,
1459 U.S. Highway 70 West,
Alamogordo,
(505) 434–8714. Inexpen-
sive to moderate.
Fare: New Mexican.

La Luz Restaurant,
#2 Main Street,
La Luz. Inexpensive to
moderate. Fare: Eclectic
American.

CHAVES COUNTY
The Cattle Baron,
1113 North Main Street,
Roswell,
(505) 622–2465. Inexpen-
sive to moderate. Fare:
Steaks, seafood, etc.

Selected Chambers of Commerce/Visitors Bureaus in Southeastern New Mexico:

Alamogordo Chamber of Commerce
P.O. Box 518, Alamogordo, 88310
(505) 437–6120, (800) 826–0294
Web site: www.totacc.com/alamo/

Artesia Chamber of Commerce
P.O. Box 99, Artesia, 88211
(505) 746–2744

Capitán Chamber of Commerce
P.O. Box 268, Capitán, 88316
(505) 354–2273
Web site: www.juge.com/ed/capitan.htm

Carlsbad Convention & Visitors Bureau
P.O. Box 910, Carlsbad, 88220
(505) 887–6516
Web site: www.caverns.com/~chamber/

Cloudcroft Chamber of Commerce
P.O. Box 1290, Cloudcroft, 88317
(505) 682–2733

Clovis/Curry County Chamber of Commerce
215 North Main Street, Clovis, 88101
(505) 763–3435

De Baca County Chamber of Commerce
P.O. Box 28, Fort Sumner, 88119
(505) 355–2462

Hobbs Chamber of Commerce
400 North Marland, Hobbs, 88240
(505) 397–3202, (800) 658–6291

Portales/Roosevelt County Chamber of Commerce
7th & Abilene, Portales, 88130
(505) 356–8541, (800) 635–8036

Roswell Convention & Visitors Bureau
912 North Main Street, Roswell, NM 88201
(505) 624–6860, (888) ROSWELL
Web site: www.roswell.org/

Ruidoso Valley Chamber of Commerce
P.O. Box 698, Ruidoso, 88345
(505) 257–7395, (800) 253–2255
Web site: www.ruidoso.net/

The Claim Restaurant & Saloon,
1310 North Main Street,
Roswell,
(505) 623–6042. Inexpensive to moderate. Fare: Steaks, etc.

El Toro Bravo Restaurant,
102 South Main Street,
Roswell,
(505) 622–9280. Inexpensive to moderate. Fare: New Mexican cuisine.

Nuthin' Fancy,
2103 North Main Street,
Roswell,
(505) 623–4098. Inexpensive to moderate. Fare: Homemade comfort food including meat loaf, chicken, and wonderful vegetables.

Pasta Cafe,
4501 North Main Street,
Roswell,
(505) 624–1111. Inexpensive to moderate. Fare: Authentic Italian entrees and New York–style hand-thrown pizza.

EDDY COUNTY
La Fonda Restaurant,
201 West Main,
Artesia,
(505) 746–9377. Inexpensive to moderate. Fare: New Mexican.

The Flume Restaurant,
1829 South Canal Street,
Carlsbad,
(505) 887–2851/(800) 730–2851. Moderate to expensive. Fare: Prime rib, steaks, etc.

Sirloin Stockade,
710 North Canal Street,
Carlsbad,
(505) 887–7211. Inexpensive to moderate. Fare: Steaks, etc.

Lucy's Mexicali Restaurant,
701 South Canal Street,
Carlsbad,
(505) 887–7714. Inexpensive to moderate. Fare: New Mexican, steaks, etc.

China Lantern,
3400 National Parks Highway,
Carlsbad,
(505) 885–3450. Inexpensive to moderate.
Fare: Chinese.

LEA COUNTY
The Cattle Baron,
1930 North Grimes,
Hobbs,
(505) 393–2800. Inexpensive to moderate. Fare: Steaks, seafood, etc.

La Fiesta Restaurant,
604 East Broadway,
Hobbs,
(505) 397–1235. Inexpensive to moderate.
Fare: New Mexican.

Saturday's,
312 North Bender,
Hobbs,
(505) 342–3651. Inexpensive to moderate.
Fare: American.

ROOSEVELT COUNTY
The Cattle Baron,
1600 South Avenue,
Portales,
(505) 356–5587. Inexpensive to moderate. Fare: Steaks, seafood, etc.

Hank's Bar-B-Q,
600 East Second,
Portales,
(505) 356–8242. Inexpensive. Fare: Barbecue.

Juanito's,
813 South Avenue C Place,
Portales,
(505) 359–1860. Inexpensive to moderate. Fare: New Mexican.

CURRY COUNTY
Juanito's,
1608 Mabry Drive,
Clovis,
(505) 762–7822. Inexpensive. Fare: New Mexican.

Poor Boy's Steakhouse,
2115 North Prince,
Clovis,
(505) 763–5222. Inexpensive to moderate. Fare: Steaks, etc.

The China Star,
1221 North Main,
Clovis,
(505) 762–8489. Inexpensive to moderate.
Fare: Chinese.

Appendixes

New Mexico Indian Pueblos
(Keyed to county where most of the reservation is located)

Bernalillo County
Isleta Pueblo
P.O. Box 1270
Isleta, NM 87022
(505) 869–3111

Cibola County
Acoma Pueblo
P.O. Box 309
Acomita, NM 87034
(505) 470–4967

Laguna Pueblo
P.O. Box 194
Laguna, NM 87026
(505) 552–6654

McKinley County
Zuni Pueblo
P.O. Box 339
Zuni, NM 87327
(505) 782–4481

Rio Arriba County
San Juan Pueblo
P.O. Box 1099
San Juan, NM 87566
(505) 852–4400

Santa Clara Pueblo
P.O. Box 580
Española, NM 87532
(505) 753–7326

Sandoval County
Cochiti Pueblo
P.O. Box 70
Cochiti, NM 87041
(505) 465–2245

Jemez Pueblo
P.O. Box 100
Jemez, NM 87024
(505) 834–7359

Sandia Pueblo
P.O. Box 6008
Bernalillo, NM 87004
(505) 867–3317

San Felipe Pueblo
P.O. Box 4339
San Felipe, NM 87001
(505) 867–3381

Santa Ana Pueblo
2 Dove Road
Bernalillo, NM 87004
(505) 867–3301

Santo Domingo Pueblo
P.O. Box 99
Santo Domingo, NM 87052
(505) 465–2214

Zia Pueblo
Pueblo of Zia
Administration Building
135 Capital Square Drive
Zia Pueblo, NM 87053
(505) 867–3304

Santa Fe County
Nambé Pueblo
Route 1, Box 117–BB
Santa Fe, NM 87501
(505) 455–7692

Pojoaque Pueblo
Route 11, Box 71
Santa Fe, NM 87501
(505) 455–2278

San Ildefonso Pueblo
Route 5, Box 315–A
Santa Fe, NM 87501
(505) 455–2273

Tesuque Pueblo
Route 11, Box 1
Santa Fe, NM 87501
(505) 983–2667

Taos County
Picuris Pueblo
P.O. Box 127
Penasco, NM 87553
(505) 587–2519

Taos Pueblo
P.O. Box 1846
Taos Pueblo, NM 87571
(505) 758–1028

Non-Pueblo Indian Tribes in New Mexico

(Keyed to the county where most of the reservation is located)

Navajo Nation
Tourism Department
P.O. Box 663
Window Rock, AZ 86515
(520) 871–6436
http://www.atiin.com/navajoland
(San Juan and McKinley counties
in New Mexico but also in northeast Arizona and southeast Utah)

Alamo Chapter (*Navajo*)
Alamo Route
Magdalena, NM 87825
(505) 854–2267
(Socorro County)

Cañoncito Chapter (Navajo)
P.O. Box 398
Laguna, NM 87026
(505) 836–4221
(Bernalillo County)

Ramah Chapter (Navajo)
P.O. Box 308
Ramah, NM 87321
(505) 775–3319
(Cibola County)

Jicarilla Apache Tribe
P.O. Box 507
Dulce, NM 87528
(505) 759–3242
(Rio Arriba County)

Mescalero Apache Tribe
P.O. Box 176
Mescalero, NM 88340
(505) 671–4494
(Otero County)

New Mexico Wineries

Alamosa Cellars
P.O. Box 690
Elephant Butte, NM 87935
(505) 744–5319

Anderson Valley Vineyards
4920 Rio Grand Boulevard NW
Albuquerque, NM 87107
(505) 344–7266

Balagna Winery
(San Ysidro Vineyards)
223 Rio Bravo Drive
Los Alamos, NM 87544
(505) 672–3678

Binns Winery
3910 West Picacho
Las Cruces, NM 88005
(505) 526–6738

Black Mesa Winery
P.O. Box 432
Velarde, NM 87582
(800) 852–MESA

Blue Teal Tasting Room
Calle de Guadalupe
Mesilla, NM 88046
(505) 524–0390

Gruet Winery
8400 Pan American Freeway NE
Albuquerque, NM 87113
(505) 344–4453

Domaine Cheurlin Winery
(Méthode Champenoise)
P.O. Box 506
Truth or Consequences, NM
87905
(505) 744–5418

La Chiripada Winery
P.O. Box 192
Dixon, NM 87527
(505) 579–4437

La Viña Winery
P.O. Box 440
Chamberino, NM 88027
(505) 882–7362

Las Nutrias Winery
P.O. Box 1156
Corrales, NM 87048
(505) 897–7863

Mademoiselle de Santa Fe Winery
3910 West Picacho
Las Cruces, NM 88005
(505) 524–0481

Madison Vineyards and Winery
Star Route 490
Ribera, NM 87560
(505) 421–8028

Mountain Vista Vineyards
1325 Foothill Road SW
Albuquerque, NM 87105
(505) 877–4345

Ponderosa Valley Vineyards
and Winery
3171 Highway 290
Ponderosa, NM 87044
(505) 834–7487

St. Clair Winery
P.O. Box 1180
Deming, NM 88031
(505) 546–9324

Sandia Shadows Winery
11704 Coronado NE
Albuquerque, NM 87122
(505) 298–8826

Santa Fe Vineyards
P.O. Box 216A
Española, NM 87505
(505) 753–8100

Tularosa Vineyards
Star Route 2, Box 5011
Tularosa, NM 88352
(505) 585–2260

New Mexico Ski Areas

As part of the southern reaches of the Rocky Mountains, New Mexico's mountain ranges are home to many downhill and cross-country ski areas. During ski season, which is roughly late November or early December to mid-March or early April, most ski areas are open 9:00 a.m.–4:00 p.m. For New Mexico road conditions, call 827–5213 or (800) 432–4269 (out of state); and for detailed or updated information on the downhill ski areas listed below, or for information on cross-country ski areas, please call Ski New Mexico at (505) 982–5300; http://www.skinewmexico.com.

Angel Fire (Angel Fire, NM)
(800) 633–7463
Accommodations:
(800) 633–7463
Number of runs: 69
Adult all-day lift ticket: $39*

Red River (Red River, NM)
(505) 754–2223
Accommodations:
(800) 331–7669
Number of runs: 58
Adult all-day lift ticket: $37*

Sandia Peak (Albuquerque, NM)
(505) 242–9133
Accommodations:
(800) 473–1000
Number of runs: 25
Adult all-day lift ticket: $34*

Santa Fe (Santa Fe, NM)
(505) 982–4429
Accommodations:
(800) 776–7669
Number of runs: 43
Adult all-day lift ticket: $40*

Sipapu (northern New Mexico)
(505) 587–2240
Accommodations:
(800) 587–2240
Number of runs: 20
Adult all-day lift ticket: $29*

Ski Apache (Ruidoso, NM)
(505) 336–4356
Accommodations:
(800) 253–2255
Number of runs: 55
Adult all-day lift ticket: $40*

Ski Cloudcroft (Cloudcroft, NM)
(800) 333–7542
Accommodations:
(505) 682–2733
Number of runs: 21
Adult all-day lift ticket: $25*

Taos Ski Valley (Taos, NM)
(505) 776–2291
Accommodations:

(800) 776–1111
Number of runs: 72
Adult all-day lift ticket: $42*

Note: Lift fees are included for comparison purposes only; they are subject to change from season to season. Fees for half-day lift tickets and those for children and seniors are lower.

General Index

INDEXES

INDEXES

Art Galleries

Bed and Breakfasts

Inns

Museums

About the Author

Todd Staats is a New Mexico–based writer, permaculture garden designer, and holistic astrologer. His previous positions include staff writer and managing editor of the *New Mexico Business Journal* as well as managing editor of *Albuquerque Monthly* and *New Mexico Monthly* magazines.

Todd recently completed his master's degree in English and creative writing at the University of New Mexico in Albuquerque, where he's currently at work on several projects. For links to many of New Mexico's unique locales and to provide direct feedback about this edition of *New Mexico: Off the Beaten Path*®, Todd invites you to visit his Internet Web site at www.toddstaats.com.